Mail Order Nurse
TO THE ARCTIC

By Sue Lium

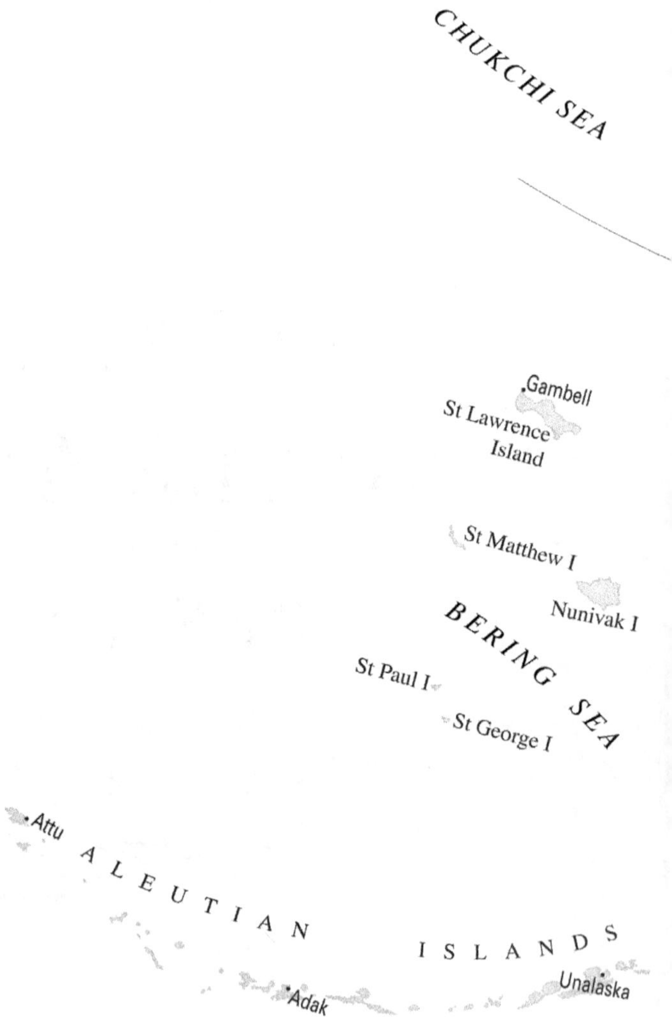

CHUKCHI SEA
Gambell
St Lawrence Island
St Matthew I
Nunivak I
BERING SEA
St Paul I
St George I
Attu
ALEUTIAN
ISLANDS
Adak
Unalaska

Map of Alaska

Cirque Press

Published by
Cirque Press

Sandra Kleven — Michael Burwell
Editors and Publishers
3157 Bettles Bay Loop
Anchorage, AK 99515

cirquejournal@gmail.com
www.cirquejournal.com

Cover Photograph: Author at Point Barrow (author's collection)
Author Photograph: Steve Lium
Graphic Design and Illustrations: Dale Champlin

Disclaimer:
Most of the names of the people who appear in this book
have been changed to protect their privacy.

ISBN 9798890345592

This book is dedicated to
~

*The people of Kotzebue and Barrow who showed me
another way of living, and to members
of the Burn Thompson Memorial Writers' Group
who taught me how to write.*

Table of Contents

Alaska by Plane

Chapter 1

Introduction

~

It was only my second time flying in a small plane in Arctic Alaska. In an instant, it looked like it would be my last. For one brief terrifying moment, my short twenty-four years of life flashed in front of me. I was flying into a monstrous cliff and sudden death.

I was a new nurse, recently hired by United States Public Health Service (USPHS) to work in their fifty-three bed hospital in Kotzebue, Alaska, thirty miles above the Arctic Circle. An hour earlier, on a day off from hospital duty, I was asked to fly to Cape Lisburne, 160 miles north, to pick up a young man from a remote White Alice radar site. He had been suffering increasing anxiety, but now was leaning more towards psychosis and was threatening to walk out. Since their location was on the shore of the Chukchi Sea surrounded by high cliffs with the only reasonable way out by plane or boat, his crew mates were alarmed for his safety and called the hospital for help. The doctor on duty felt it was in everyone's best interest to remove the young man from the remote setting to his home down south for some psychiatric care. Although his crew reported he was stable at the time, the doctor did not want him in the plane alone with the pilot. I was recruited to accompany him into the hospital. I was a little nervous as my psychiatric training was minimal, but more than anything, I hoped he wouldn't become agitated or combative as I wasn't sure I could restrain a grown man, especially in a small plane.

My first ride in one of those small planes a month earlier had been over a continuous expanse of white snow with nothing breaking the monotony. We had been flying over land to an Interior Alaska village. This looked different. Stretched out below in the miles of white landscape were traces of grey shadows lining elevated, white jagged ridges running in no logical pattern. And everywhere there were dark lines zigzagging through the white mass looking like pieces of a jigsaw puzzle that had been laid out in proper order, ready to be pushed together for the picture to be complete. Except there was no picture, just blinding white with black outlines separating the expanse into uneven patterns.

"Breakup," the pilot said. "People anxious to launch boats to hunt ugruk soon."

That's when I realized we were not flying over land, but endless miles of ice. Those jigsaw pieces were actually ice pans. The black outlines were cold, deep sea water that became larger as we flew farther out from the towering cliffs. To a girl from the prairies, it was terrifying.

Sea ice is not smooth. It is rough and jagged with ridges formed from pressure during its formation. It was the beginning of spring breakup. The ice was thinning and melting. Large chunks were cracking and breaking apart in jagged patterns. The flows I saw off to our left were slowly drifting further apart. The cliffs I was seeing off to the right were not rising up from land, but out of the sea.

Nowhere did I see a place where a plane could land. What would we do if there was a problem? Planes, especially little ones like this, often had problems. You heard about it all the time down south. Small planes have landed in fields and in ball parks. They have even landed on highways. On my first Arctic flight in a small plane, if we went down, at least it would be on solid ground where we could be found and rescued. Even I could see those ice pans were not large enough to land a plane on, and since they were breaking up, probably not strong enough to hold a plane. We would sink into the sea, never to be found. The only other alternative was closer to land but I had seen no break in those cliffs for the last ten minutes. No flat land anywhere.

"No place to land?" I asked squeamishly.

"Will be when we get there." the pilot said.

"How much longer is that?" I asked.

"Maybe ten minutes," he said. We had been flying for close to twenty minutes. And we would have to fly back too. That was a lot of time to worry. I tried to concentrate on the patterns made by the breaking ice pans but mostly my eyes were searching for one area large enough for a plane to land on. I wasn't finding one and my anxiety level was slowly increasing when the pilot hollered above the racket of the engine.

"OK we're here, hold on!" he shouted making an abrupt right-hand turn. We had not been flying very high and my focus had been on the ice below. As I looked up, the plane finished the turn and was flying straight into the cliffs towering so very close to us. I wondered if they would find my body plastered against those cliffs or if it would fall into the ocean below. Maybe it would land on one of those ice pans that would keep me above the deep dark sea until rescuers arrived. It would help my parents with closure to have a body.

Without question in a few more seconds, we would hit those cliffs. The pilot started to drop altitude but it was apparent we would hit the cliffs long before we reached ground level. What was I thinking, I hadn't seen any level ground the whole trip. My mouth opened as I felt a scream welling up in my throat, but before I could voice it, or squeeze out a prayer, the plane, seconds before the impending impact, made another very sharp right turn and dropped down to solid ground. Not ice or snow or water, but gravel long enough for the tires to set down and coast to a stop. And as we did, we taxied past the cliffs and into a huge flat open gap with a radar installation in the middle. The ocean was still beside us on our right, and I could see how narrow the runway was between the cliffs and the sea. My knees had turned to jelly and my heart was pounding in my chest. I was feeling a little shaky too. The pilot turned to me. I'm sure my eyes were as big as saucers and my face drained of color. He grinned and said:

"See? No problem."

"You could have warned me," I said. "I thought I was going to die."

"Yah," he chuckled. "That's generally people's reaction first time landing here. Runway is parallel to the ocean and it's a real tricky sharp turn to approach it. You did real good. I was ready for a scream."

While our passenger was being brought to the plane on a snow machine, I used the time to calm myself and get my pulse and blood pressure back down to normal. The patient appeared to be in better shape than I. If he was feeling anxious, I was sure I could match what he was feeling, and then some. It would be another half hour of high anxiety for me on our way back worrying about falling into the sea in the middle of winter. Worrying about the patient would take a back seat. If he showed one sign of agitation beginning, I had no doubt I would holler him into subdued submission. I had my own anxiety to deal with. A small plane flying over an ocean was not the place to have a nervous breakdown, not for him or me.

We both made it back to Kotzebue. He left on an Alaska Airlines jet the next morning, back to where he had come from. I slept soundly that night, thankful to be alive and wondering again what I had got myself into.

Kotzebue by Air

Chapter 2

The Dream

Four months earlier, in January 1969, I had arrived in Alaska on a large modern Alaska Airlines jet. Now, on a sunny, crisp, cold day in Anchorage, Alaska, I was soaring into a clear blue sky on another jet, carrying me north to Kotzebue, a small Eskimo village thirty miles above the Arctic Circle. I would not see this city again for many months. I was flying to a place beyond the borders of my small world of experience.

I was twenty-four years old, a registered nurse having graduated just fifteen months earlier from the Misericordia Hospital School of Nursing in Edmonton, Alberta. My chosen career was taking me to another country, and another way of life. After spending a year working at my training hospital, I was looking forward to a new job, new friends and new experiences.

I was both excited and nervous. Sitting in a window seat with my face pressed against the glass, we flew for miles over snow-capped mountain tops and bleak white terrain with no signs of civilization below us. Then, just in front of the wing, a cluster of buildings appeared off in the distance in the middle of a flat white landscape that stretched endlessly in every direction. At the edge of this village of 1,700 people, I could see a long runway which, from the air, seemed to be the focal point of the town. Although the town was situated on the shores of Kotzebue Sound, that body of water would not be apparent until spring when the ice melted to expose a whole new landscape.

As the plane dropped lower, the town appeared to grow larger, but still seemed insignificant compared to the empty landscape surrounding this tiny piece of human existence. It was frightening seeing the enormity of the land and how small the town looked in relation to it. On reflection, that runway became a reassuring visual. There was, in fact, a way out if I ever needed to escape. This place would be my home for the next two years, and I would soon learn that mother nature would be the force in control.

In 1965, I was accepted into the Misericordia Hospital School of Nursing in Edmonton, Alberta and began my training that fall. At the time tuberculosis was still a large public health threat. During my three years of schooling, I spent two months working on a male ward at the Charles Camsell Tuberculosis Sanitarium for Native patients from northern Alberta, the Yukon and the Northwest Territories.

I decided I wanted to see and experience the culture and environment of the far north for myself. Since Inuvik, the only hospital in the Canadian western Arctic, wanted nurses with experience, I turned my sights west and applied to the United States Public Health Service (USPHS) in Alaska. They ran two hospitals in the Arctic. Kotzebue had a 53-bed hospital; Barrow had 10 beds. I applied to Kotzebue as I felt there would be more staff and more support for a new nurse in the larger hospital. My request for information, my application for a position with Public Health Service and supplying the subsequent paper work required for the job was all done by mail. It was a long process made even longer by a mail strike in Canada, but finally I was hired. I was heading north. I became a "mail order" nurse to the Arctic. Even getting there would be a new experience as I had never before flown in a jet.

My first flight took me to Seattle, Washington. The second leg of my trip got me as far as Anchorage, the largest city in Alaska. My excitement was mounting. I kept peering out the small window of the jet looking for something other than white clouds or mountain tops. This was my first look at Alaska, a place that held mystery and adventure. Would I make it here? Had my training prepared me enough to work in a remote setting with perhaps limited facilities? It was a new country, a new place, a new job and would definitely be a very new way of life. Would it be all I had hoped for? Would I fit in? Would I be happy here?

Finally, the plane began its long slow descent into Anchorage. As it broke through the cloud cover, I marveled at the beauty spread out before me. A city nestled in a winter wonderland. Although I grew up with the Rocky Mountains in my sights, the largest bodies of water in Alberta were lakes. Anchorage was nestled between high mountains and Cook Inlet, a large body of water that connects Anchorage to the Pacific Ocean. Snow covered peaks sparkled in the sunlight as we slipped through the clouds and landed. I was to spend a day here being oriented to the Public Health Service policies. I was also hoping to learn more about my final destination.

I was met at the Anchorage airport by Diane, the nurse recruiter for Public Health Service. She told me Anchorage was a large sea port city shipping in supplies to be distributed throughout the state. Air transportation was also critical to moving goods and people into rural areas. As we came into sight of the medical center, she was quick to fill me in on some facts around the history of the facility.

"The Alaska Native Medical Center hospital began as a tuberculosis sanitarium but has now been converted to a medical center for the Native population of northern Alaska," she told me. One of those areas was the Kotzebue service unit where I would be working.

Alaska Native Medical Center, 1969

I spent the next day in orientation with Diane which focused on facts about Alaska, Public Health Service and the Kotzebue service unit. I learned that Public Health Service, which began in the 1700's for American seamen, took over health care for Native people in the United States from the Bureau of Indian Affairs in 1955.

"Our Alaska Natives, the Indians, Eskimos and Aleuts suffered huge death tolls in the early twentieth century from infectious diseases," Diane told me. "Smallpox, measles, influenza and tuberculosis were the most devastating. A hospital was established in Kotzebue in 1939, but don't worry," she said, "the new hospital you will be working in was built in 1961 and is very modern, as are your quarters." Later I learned many of the first medical professionals in rural Alaska were missionaries. They, along with the influx of American whalers from the eastern states, were the first to cause disruption in centuries old ways of life of the Arctic Native people, all in the name of God.

"Wait a minute," I said, as the facts she was spilling out began to register in my brain. "Indians, Eskimos and who?"

"Aleuts," she said.

"I have never heard of them. Who are they?" I asked. "Aren't all Native people either Indian or Eskimo?"

"Well," she said. "that's better than some who come here know, but Alaska also has Aleut people who live along the Aleutian chain west of here." She took me to a wall map telling me who the Native people of Alaska were and where they lived. I was amazed to see such a variation spread throughout the state. Diane continued, "There are three major Native groups in Alaska with many sub-groups within the main populations: (1) The Indian groups which cover the Athabaskan's of the Interior, and the Tlingit, Haida and Tsimshian of Southeast Alaska; (2) the Aleut, who live along the string of volcanic islands referred to as the 'Ring of Fire' called the Aleutians that jut to the west of Alaska's mainland; and (3) the Eskimo, who are by far the largest group of Natives in Alaska.

"The term Eskimo," Diane went on to explain, "is associated with the Indigenous or Native people of the circumpolar regions of various countries." Although the word Eskimo was used while I lived in the North and has very positive connotations for me, in my writing I have, as much as possible, substituted the term Inupiaq for Eskimo, a more precise qualifier preferred by Native people. In the Canadian north the term Eskimo now has negative connotations and the word Inuit is used. This is not true for Alaska. The term First Nations is used in Canada in reference to the Indian populations. In Alaska, Native people wish to be identified by their specific cultural groups. Here there are three distinct Eskimo groups:

    (a) the Siberian Yup'ik of St. Lawrence Island,

    (b) the Yup'ik along the Western Bering Sea coast, and

    (c) the Inupiaq of the northern Arctic coast.

However, even when specific terms are used for each group in Alaska, it is often accompanied by the word Eskimo as a qualifier, i.e., Inupiaq Eskimo vs. Yup'ik Eskimo.

For me, the wonderful people of the Arctic I lived and worked with will forever be Eskimos and I use the term with love and respect.

"Kotzebue," Diane told me, "started as a trading place. Today the town has a population composed of both southern coastal Yup'ik and northern Inupiaq people of the Arctic coast." I would later learn from reading Alaska history that ancestors of present-day northern Alaska Natives are believed to have migrated from Asia 14,000 to 16,000 years ago across the Bering Land Bridge, a corridor of land connecting Asia with North America after the last Ice Age. People migrated into northern Alaska gradually, traveling both East along the Northern coast of the American continent and South along the Bering Sea coast.

Chapter 3

Into the Arctic

~

The next morning after a hearty breakfast complete with fresh fruit, some which would be the last I would experience for a long time, Diane and I said our goodbyes and I was whisked to the airport in another of the hospital vans. The driver wished me good luck as I was handed my two suitcases, but when I got to the ticket counter, I was informed Kotzebue was experiencing blizzard conditions and all flights had been cancelled for the day. In a panic, I picked up my bags and ran from the airport building in time to see the hospital van pulling away from the curb.

Being young and spry and afraid to be left alone at a strange airport in an American city with only Canadian money in my pocket, I dropped my bags, bolted off the curb and began banging on the back of the van as people looked on in amusement. Fortunately, the driver heard me and stopped. He had a good laugh as he drove me back to the Medical Center.

"Should have stayed a while," he chided. "Lots of good Alaskan men there. Maybe they were grounded too. Maybe take you to coffee, tell you about the real Alaska." And he laughed again when he saw the look on my face. I was in no mood to meet new men, especially of the Bush kind. I was driven back to the hospital.

The next day the airport run was successful and the plane made it to my destination. Flying, I would soon learn is the most common way in and out of the bush. In 1969 the two airlines serving Kotzebue, and the other large towns, weather permitting, were Alaska and Wien Airlines. I was told they were the main form of transportation. Bush pilots carried people and goods to smaller villages in smaller planes. There were no roads in our area. Planes were the lifeline to our part of the Arctic. Diane had mentioned that a supply ship called the *North Star* delivered supplies once a year in the fall to all the coastal towns as far north as Barrow.

As low and as close as my plane came to the village of Kotzebue before its tires touched a well-plowed runway, I could not see any roads, only a mix of different shaped buildings rising out of virgin whiteness. On disembarking, I followed the other passengers into the terminal. The airport complex was nothing like big city airports I had passed through on my way north. I arrived to a miniature layout of airport necessities, one ticket counter, a space set aside for baggage on the floor, not a carousel, and a half dozen seats. As small as it was, it was busy with those greeting new arrivals and scurrying to pick up luggage. I felt out of place as my attire, the latest in winter wear from the Sears department store, did not match the norm in outerwear of the townspeople. Men wore handsome fur parkas; women were in bright colored full length corduroy coats outlined with pretty rickrack and fur ruffs on attached hoods. Before I had time to get my bearings, I was approached by a man and woman with big smiles, hearty handshakes and wearing coats and boots closer in style to mine. They introduced themselves as Miss Byrd, the director of nurses and Mr. Gains, the hospital administrator.

"Finally you made it," exclaimed Miss Byrd with a sigh of relief. She was bundled from head to foot in a large bulky full-length coat, wearing a hand knit hat covering her head with only a small opening swath around her eyes, nose and mouth. She was holding matching knit gloves in her hand and wore large, bulky boots that looked as if they could easily carry her through any amount of snow to anywhere she needed to go. While Mr. Gaines hunted for my luggage, Miss Byrd continued to fill me in on the most recent weather catastrophe to hit the town.

"We've had a very bad blizzard the last two days," she exclaimed. "Nothing is moving in town. Folks here know when to stay inside. One or two of our nursing staff from town had to spend the night at the hospital. Just too dangerous to be out in such weather. We don't want to lose anyone going home in a storm," she said. "Even going from the hospital to the nurses' quarters can be a challenge sometimes."

This was certainly not the kind of problem a director would face in a big city hospital but according to Miss Byrd it had been happening more than usual this winter.

"People could get lost in a white out and freeze to death," she said.

I wondered what other things she worried about with her nurses. She seemed committed to her staff with a huge sense of responsibility for them.

As I was trying to picture what that kind of blizzard looked or felt like, Mr. Gaines arrived with my luggage. With both my bags claimed and one director on each side of me, I was whisked out of the busy airport building. I noticed that even at ground level, there still did not appear to be any roads in the immediate expanse of white.

My next surprise was our mode of transportation. I was not being transported by car, truck or van. Others were climbing onto large snow machines pulling sleds that carried their luggage and whisked them away over mounds of snow. My ride was a square shaped red tracmaster equipped with metal tracks used to carry people over ice and snow in places where wheeled vehicles could not maneuver. I had ridden in one many years ago as a summer tourist, lumbering up the Athabasca Glacier at the Columbia Ice Fields between Banff and Jasper, Alberta. I assumed this one would be safe as all it appeared to have to tackle were some hard packed snowdrifts. If a tracmaster could tackle a glacier, I felt quite safe and sure it would get us over the fairly level landscape to our destination.

"It takes a while to recover from such severe storms," said Mr. Gaines. "The roads are impassible by wheeled vehicles and the snowplows haven't been able to clear the streets yet, (which explained why I could not see them). This 'cat' will have to do," he said latching onto my arm and leading me briskly to its door. They both appeared relieved when I remained calm. I suspect they were afraid this city girl might make a dash for the plane still sitting on the runway. What they didn't hear was the voice in my head saying, "Oh Lord, what have I gotten into?" But there was no going back now.

It was not an easy road to my new job. A very long Canadian mail strike in the middle of my application process, along with waiting for a United States work visa added a few months delay to my departure. One would think being a professional and having a job with a United States government agency would speed the immigration process, but that was not the case. Evidently there was a quota system. I did not know what my number was for that year but when I finally arrived for my interview with the American consulate in Calgary, one of the things I had to do was swear I wasn't a prostitute, nor had any intentions of becoming one after immigrating to the good old U.S. of A. I was greatly offended by that question.

With a scowl on my face, I did so promise, and as soon as the official stamp and signature were attached to my application, I let the agent know what I thought of their vetting process, and let the door slam behind me on the way out. By this time, it was mid December 1968. I would spend Christmas with my family, New Year's with friends, then head off to Alaska in early January.

My parents, on the other hand, who had been so supportive in my quest to become a nurse, were less enthusiastic about me heading off into the hinterland of another country. They tried to be optimistic but frequently dropped questions or comments that were aimed at making sure I had given thought to what I might be getting into.

"I don't suppose the stores will carry the latest fashions way up there, and they probably won't have television." This from my mother who knew the things I enjoyed.

"What if your patients don't speak English? How will you communicate? You'd better pack lots of books to read during the long dark winter months." That from my dad who knew I could survive anywhere if I had a good book to read.

The information brochures Public Health Service sent me about Kotzebue said there was a grocery store in town, but my mother suggested there would only be basics and teased me about things I would miss, like green olives. I loved green olives. So when the trunk was almost full, I pulled out a couple of sweaters and a pair of soft woolly pajamas, wrapped them around a few jars of green olives and nestled them down into the four corners of the trunk before sending it on its way. Finally, I was ready, and beyond excited for my new job and new experiences.

Chapter 4

My New Home

~

And so, I had finally arrived at my new home in the Arctic. It had been a long journey but my dream was coming true. I couldn't see much out the small round windows of the tracmaster as we slowly lumbered over white cloaked roads. It was the middle of winter and the sun barely rose above the horizon in January. What I could see was nothing remotely like any town I had known. There did not seem to be much order in the layout of the buildings set back a fair distance from the road. Most of them were the size of small boxes, some square, some rectangular, some L shaped and most with what appeared to be long enclosed entryways jutting towards the road we were traveling along. The size of the homes in Kotzebue seemed

Kotzebue Houses

to be no larger than a living room/ dining room in a medium sized house from my neighborhood back home. And some were just living room size. There was not much color to the dwellings, just bare wood slapped together and covered with tarpaper to protect people from the elements. Later I heard that people also lived in some of the small Quonset huts and metal containers I saw hidden away from the main thoroughfares. Thoughts of those being someone's home saddened me.

It was apparent which direction the wind had been blowing during the storm as one side of all the houses was plastered to the rooftop with drifted snow. In fact, anything upright appeared to be partially obliterated by snow which made the homes appear smaller than they actually were. What was exposed on these tiny dwellings looked somewhat unearthly as light shone out of equally tiny windows. Some distance beyond this row of houses, I could see the tops of one or two multi-level buildings arranged in a straight line. Mr, Gaines informed me they were in the business center of the town which ran along Front Street, the main and busiest thoroughfare of the town, hugging the shoreline. Snow hid another world beneath its soft peaceful looking covering that wouldn't be exposed until spring. What I would see then would put me into culture shock.

Finally, we turned off what, I assumed, from the many buildings we were passing, was one of the main roads of the town and came to rest in front of the hospital. I knew it was the hospital, not just because it clearly said so on the front of the building, but because it looked similar to small hospitals I was used to in what Alaskans refer to as "down south" or the "Lower Forty-Eight" (states). It was the first structure I had seen that resembled a familiar looking building. It stood out with its bright yellow color and a large red front door. Further back off to the right behind the entrance and emergency department was a row of patient room windows which at present were half covered with drifted snow.

"Come into the hospital for a minute," said Miss Byrd as we climbed out of our metal carriage. "Have a quick look around before you begin to settle into the quarters." Joining some of the nursing staff on their coffee break at the nurse's station, I began to feel a rising excitement. The hospital looked very modern. I glimpsed familiar equipment in the lab and x-ray departments we passed. Here were people I would be working with. I had so many questions I wanted to ask, but they beat me to it with the number one question Alaskans ask when they meet someone new.

"Where are you from?" That from Anne, a nurse from Ohio. She had been there five months and planned to stay for only one year as she had followed her fiancé to Kotzebue when he was assigned to a year at the Air Force base outside of town. They were newly engaged, and she glowed from what I assumed was young love.

"Is this your first time to Alaska?" asked Joan, a nurse from Wisconsin. She had come to Alaska on a vacation with her parents a few years earlier and was so impressed with the flat scenery and remoteness on their one-day excursion to Kotzebue, she had decided to come work here to experience a different way of life.

"What made you want to come here?" asked Mary who was from South Carolina. It appeared her main goal in coming to Kotzebue was to save money. "There are no malls here for me to spend my money," she drawled. "And I don't have to buy food or pay big bucks for rent, so I'm hoping to save enough to buy a new car when I return home."

"How was the weather in Anchorage?" asked Sally, a lab tech who was TDY (temporary duty) and heading back to her permanent job at the medical center in Anchorage in a few weeks. Although she had enjoyed her time in Kotzebue, she was looking forward to returning to her own apartment and her permanent job.

Taking her last sip of coffee, Thea from Idaho, who was eagerly waiting to hear from her pregnant sister back home to see if she had made her an aunt yet, sighed and said:

"I hope the mail bags got on your plane; it's been a few days." And the strangest question of all, "You didn't happen to bring milk with you, did you?"

"Diane didn't ask you to bring milk?" called out a nurse heading down the hall to answer a call bell. Puzzled by the question, I answered a feeble "no," as the director stood, signaling the end of the break. The staff headed back to their duties as I and my two bags were dropped off at the residence directly across from the hospital. I was shown to my quarters and left to settle into my new home. Since my trunk had not yet arrived, unpacking two suitcases went fairly fast.

The residence for single employees such as myself was a two-story, 20-unit apartment building with ten efficiency apartments on each floor and sat directly across from the front of the hospital. It reminded me of a miniature nurse's quarters from my training hospital. Only this time I would have my own apartment and there wouldn't be as many of us as in my nursing class. It was time now to prove my worth and put into practice what I had learned while living in that last residence. My quarters were in a dominantly gray building with bright yellow splotches between the white trimmed windows of the two floors which, I assumed, were to make it appear an official part of the hospital complex with its matching shock of color to the main hospital.

The Hospital

During coffee, the director of nurses related that in winters past staff had placed a rope from the door of the quarters, lovingly known as the "20 unit" to the door of the hospital so no one could get lost going to and from work during a blizzard or whiteout. The distance was equivalent to crossing a four-lane roadway down south.

"It turned out to be a somewhat busy street," she continued. "Unfortunately, town folk who were taking short cuts through the hospital grounds, or coming to the Emergency room on snow machines, were being caught by the rope, invisible in such conditions, and yanked off their machines while the machines kept going." Being afraid someone would be badly injured, the rope guide had been taken down by the time I arrived. I weathered some bad storms in my two winters in Kotzebue but fortunately never got lost in a blizzard. I say fortunately, as I was quite capable of wandering off in the wrong direction with the danger of not being found till spring thaw!

My first floor apartment had four large picture windows allowing me to watch the flow of people and snow machine traffic going to and from the hospital. It occurred to me that the size of those windows would have covered most of the fronts of the small homes I had passed that day. Perhaps the light coming from their windows had seemed eerie because they were so small. My windows also enabled me to watch gently falling snow or witness the intensity of the storms that raged throughout the winter. Pulling the drapes to full open, I discovered a small gap on one side of the South window which was letting snow in around the edge. I put in a work request to get the window caulked but by summer I'd forgotten about it and too, it appeared, had maintenance. By the time snow began creeping inside my apartment the next winter, it was again too late to do any fixes. I just scraped it off and pulled the drapes to cover it. In retrospect snow coming into my very cozy apartment was probably the extent of my roughing it in the high Arctic.

The apartment was furnished with all the basics: a small kitchen on one side complete with stove, small oven, fridge, sink and housekeeping supplies including a broom and mop along with an ironing board and iron. The kitchen cupboards and drawers held enough dishes and cutlery to entertain a party of four. The large main room served as dining room, living room and bedroom with a dining table and chairs, a couch that transformed into a bed at night, two soft cushioned chairs and a writing desk with a hard back chair. Between the kitchen and the entryway door, was an open area containing a long clothes rack and chest of drawers in what could be called either a hallway or walk in closet, depending on one's mood of the day. It lead off the main room into the bathroom complete with tub and shower, sink and flush toilet.

"The 20 Unit" Nurses Residence

Alene, the dietician in the apartment next door, must have heard me moving things around and came to check. She was from Wisconsin and had worked at the medical center in Anchorage before transferring to Kotzebue the year before.

Alene gave me a tour of the floor which consisted of a long hallway with five doors on each side to the ten apartments. Before taking me down to the basement, she pointed out the location of the one telephone on the floor. I would soon become familiar with the main function of that phone. Then down the stairs we went to the basement where I was shown the large recreation room.

"Lots of fun times here," Alene said with a smile. "We have movies a couple of times a month. Not the latest flicks, but movies that are worth watching. Sometimes we invite some of the boys from the air base just out of town and often have pot lucks before the movies and now and then a bit of dancing after the movies."

She also showed me large freezers where residents could store frozen food and meat ordered from Anchorage. The 20 unit was for single employees who ate their meals in the hospital dining room, but who occasionally cooked and entertained in their apartments. The idea of not having to cook appealed to me but I asked what the stores in town carried and was surprised to hear that meat, other than occasional steaks and roasts from the commercial reindeer herd outside of town, was not available. Many of the staff ordered meat in bulk from a market in Anchorage. Most households in the village were still living a subsistence life style hunting and fishing for their staples. It was not profitable for the local stores to carry meat.

There were also washers and dryers off the rec room for doing laundry and a small kitchen for food prep. And so my new dwellings had all the comforts of home complete with running water, electricity and flush toilets which I had always taken for granted. Adding to the culture shock I would experience in the spring would be learning that these comforts were not "basic" in town. My new home, like the quarters in my nursing school residence, could be described as basic, functional and institutional in style but in comparison to the dwellings in town, they were extravagantly elegant. When my trunk finally arrived, I happily unpacked all my familiar belongings to make the apartment my own personal space.

Alene took me over to the hospital cafeteria for dinner where I met more staff who hailed from all over the lower forty-eight states. Not only did I enjoy hearing their stories, it was an adventure to hear different accents from the many states they came from. I was given instructions on how to order meat from the stores in Anchorage and informed about the recreation runs most evenings to and from the Air Force base five miles out of town "where," I was told with smiles and chuckles, "entertainment abounds and there are an unlimited number of men."

Diane, in Anchorage, had been right when she told me I would be meeting girls very similar to myself. Young, single, independent and very enjoyable company. Most of us living in the 20 unit were around the same age and all seemed eager to learn about our new surroundings. We were mainly women except for the pharmacist and one of the doctors. When Richard, the new sanitation engineer moved into Alene's old room next door, I learned that officer or not, if you were single you lived in the 20 unit.

"Don't you get officer's quarters?" I asked him as he was moving in.

"No," he said, "I don't qualify."

"In what way?" I asked.

"My marital status," he said with a flat expression.

"Oh," I replied, You're not married?"

"No m'am," he replied with a southern drawl and a big grin spreading over his face, "I'm happy!"

It was a long talkative dinner which extended back to the quarters over glasses of wine in one of the nurse's rooms where I was introduced to Lorraine, another Canadian nurse on staff. Slipping into typical Alaskan conversation, I asked her the time-honored question, "Where are you from?" Lorraine was from Montreal, Quebec, and her manner of speech told me she was definitely French Canadian. Back in the 60s the French and English in Canada were not getting along well. The French were demanding more recognition and threatening to pull out of the Dominion. The English, at least in Western Canada (not to sound too prejudiced), thought that might be a good idea and wondered how the Americans would deal with them and their demands. A group of very radical French Canadians were also putting bombs in mailboxes in Canada. So when I

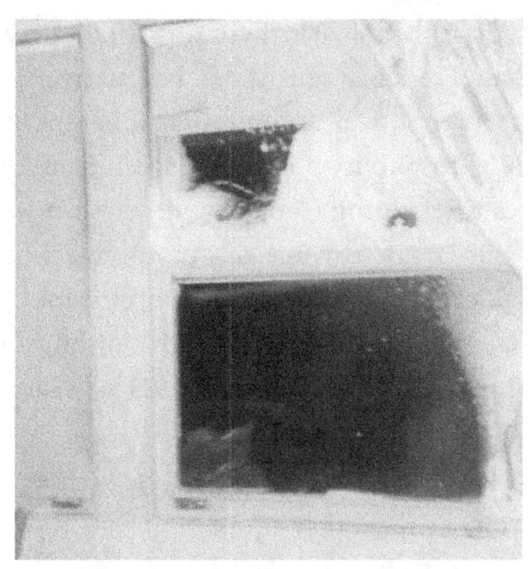

Snowy Window

My New Home

responded that I was from Calgary, there was a look between us that suggested the Canadian French/English war had arrived in the American Arctic. In spite of our political and cultural differences, Lorraine and I became great friends. In public, both being fresh from the homeland, we put up a united front defending Canada and what we were told were our "Canadian ways," but in the privacy of our rooms, which in hers hung a large poster of Pierre Elliot Trudeau, the current French Canadian prime minister, we argued the same old fight among Fracophones and Anglophones that was happening throughout Canada.

Chapter 5

The Kotzebue Hospital

The hospital was a modern 53-bed facility with medical, pediatric and obstetric wards. In addition, it boasted a fully equipped operating room, emergency and out-patient clinic, a two-person dental lab plus social worker and sanitation engineer offices. Other medical departments included central supply, pharmacy, lab, x-ray, and a radio room near the emergency department with another at the nurse's station. The radios were for communicating with health aides in the villages. Ancillary departments were laundry, stores, housekeeping, kitchen and dining room.

I had arrived at the end of the tuberculosis epidemic and so an eleven-bed isolation unit was rarely occupied. A large number of pediatric beds were empty due to a newly installed water tower that distilled sea water into clean, easily accessible drinking water, decreasing the number of gastrointestinal ailments in children. There was a water truck that delivered water to individual homes. It made me appreciate how easy my access was to water. I simply turned on a tap.

Three to four doctors were stationed at the Kotzebue hospital at any given time during my tenure. Other commissioned officers included the dentist, social worker, sanitary engineer, pharmacist and their families. If married they lived in two- and three-bedroom apartment buildings located behind our 20 unit. Married officers ordered a year's supply of food which was shipped up each fall on the supply ship *North Star*. They were responsible for their own meals and cooked at home.

Doctors rotated on-call duty for after hours, nights, weekends and holidays. They also made trips to every village in the service unit once a year for medical rounds on each villager. They were often accompanied by the dentist. They, as did all employees, rotated out on vacations. Hawaii, it appeared, was a favorite destination after the obligatory family stop in the Lower 48. Serving two years as a doctor with Public Health Service fulfilled military draft requirements. It was the 60's. The Vietnam war assured we were never short of doctors.

As none of our doctors were surgeons, the operating room, though fully supplied and ready for any emergency, was used only twice in my two years. Once to patch up a gunshot wound and once to perform an abortion one day after it became legal in Alaska. Elective surgery was sent to the medical center in Anchorage. Other emergencies requiring surgery left for Anchorage on the next scheduled jet.

There were twelve to fourteen nurses on staff from the Lower-48 states plus we two Canadians. All except one of the seven or eight Licensed Practical Nurses (LPN's) were from Kotzebue and, as permanent staff, made up the stable backbone of the nursing department. I was pleasantly surprised with such complete, modern medical facilities and living arrangements. It didn't take long for me to settle in, relax and even feel a little pampered. I had no household maintenance, shoveling snow, or window washing and had ready cooked meals in the hospital dining room. That led to a couple of new experiences.

Food seems to taste better when cooked by someone else. Under the management of dietician's Alene and later Joan, meals, just like mom used to make, were served by our wonderful Native cooks. Every now and then those cooks treated us to some of their Native foods. During whaling season, there was muktuk, the outer thick skin and oily blubber of the whale. They told us it was a treat, "like candy," they said. It did not look particularly appetizing to me, especially when I learned what it was, but I was willing to give it a try. Delicately sliced into bite size pieces, I popped the black and white morsel into my mouth and chewed, and chewed, and chewed and chewed. It seemed to expand with each bite and frankly tasted for all the world like a piece of rubber tire, a very oily rubber tire. Trying to be polite and really wanting to show I could handle muktuk, I put on a brave face, murmured a few positive sounds and kept chewing, and chewing, and chewing. Finally, feeling a total failure, I reluctantly gave up and pulled the rubbery mass out of my mouth. Embarrassed at my obvious failure, I looked at the others who had also tried it and saw I was not alone in my defeat. I had just lasted longer. And the gals in the kitchen were trying, quite unsuccessfully, not to laugh out loud at all of us. It was something, I later learned, they looked forward to, knowing how most of us would react.

Another popular Native dish they served us was fish soup. That definitely sounded more appealing than whale skin and blubber. Although I was from the prairies and had not yet been introduced to many fish recipes, I was sure I could handle fish soup. And so, once again, along with my coworkers, I gladly accepted a bowl. This time our cooks made no secret of watching us very closely as we drank our bowls of steaming hot soup. It was very good, and I kept smiling back at them until, like in a scary movie when your guard is down, my spoon emerged from the depths of the bowl with a fish eye looking up at me. I gave a shriek and dropped the spoon onto my tray, as my fellow female diners looked on in horror. Grabbing my tray, I hustled back to the serving line to show the cooks what had ended up in my bowl. Surely this ugly eye was a mistake. Turns out it definitely wasn't a mistake. The cooks and servers were waiting to see who ended up with that eyeball and what the reaction would be. Evidently, I did not disappoint.

"But nurse," Lilly, one of the cooks, said with tears running down her cheeks from laughing so hard. "The eyes are the best part of the soup." Evidently, they were looked upon as a delicacy.

"In that case," I replied, "I will auction it off to the highest bidder!" And that was the end of fish soup for me although it had tasted fine until I was eyeballed!

The hospital handled cases from every branch of medicine from pneumonia to psychiatry, accidents to obstetrics and every infection imaginable. We also had a few long-term patients that would be eligible for nursing home placement anywhere else. Nurses in the bush used all the knowledge they had learned as opposed to working on a speciality floor in a large hospital, as did many of my nursing classmates. My first week on duty had me wondering again what I had gotten myself into and seriously wondering if I would I be able to cope with such a diversity of patients.

I had only been in Kotzebue two days and not yet fully oriented to the hospital or the routine when I was called in to special, a one-on-one, with a critical patient. It was 9 p.m. and I was settled in my apartment writing a letter, a mode of communication now referred to as 'snail mail,' being used long before computers and e-mail and much cheaper than phoning. I faithfully wrote to friends and family as often as I could. After all my mother's pleas, I wrote my parents once a week. It certainly filled the hours that today we now spend watching television or texting. I was busy writing first impressions of my new home when I heard a phone ring in the hallway. That was the one phone on the floor Alene had shown me. It could be used for long distance calls to family and friends 'outside' but cost kept those calls to a minimum. Phone conversations were also open to anyone around at the time and walls to our apartments were thin. There was no guarantee of privacy and so the phone use was mainly between the hospital and the residence to call someone in to work in the middle of the night. Its ring woke everyone on the floor as it didn't stop ringing until someone answered. No one wanted to trot down the hall late at night or early in the morning to answer the phone, and whoever did, usually ended up going in to work. They could holler out the request a few times, but even they knew no one was going to volunteer. Later, I noticed people were rotating who answered the phone so that no one person got stuck twice in a row. Teamwork was apparent even off duty and in the middle of "dark and stormy nights."

Being awake and forgetting where I was, I responded like any young girl from down south who hears a phone ring. I sprinted down the hall and answered it. It would take some time before I was able to suppress the urge to bolt out my door each time I heard it ring. The supervisor was looking for an R.N. to special a woman, that is to take care of only that patient, for the duration of the shift. The patient had had a stroke while watching a basketball game at the high school gym and I was the person who answered the call. Since I was not yet scheduled to work, the supervisor convinced me I would be best suited to fill the job so other nurse's schedules would not be interrupted. I dressed in my somewhat still wrinkled uniform and headed to work. The patient's husband was in the room and was being encouraged by friends and staff to go home to family. He seemed to know the staff by name and was reluctant to leave his wife's side. He also appeared to be questioning who I was and if he should leave his wife with me. But he did go home, and I settled in for a night of special duty. Unfortunately, the worst happened. The patient, without ever regaining consciousness, died a few hours later. I felt terrible for the patient and her family although nothing could have been done to change the outcome. I hoped the husband didn't blame me for her death or himself for leaving that night. I learned the next day that he worked at the hospital. I probably carried negative connotations for him for the next two years. Not a good start to my new job. There was more to come.

After finishing my orientation to the hospital and the routine, I was scheduled to work. It was January and the weather was horrid. A storm front had hit town the night before and snow was again piled against anything above ground. It was more than half way up the windows in patient's rooms. Although the hospital was a single story, it was still a huge amount of snow piling up. The scene outside those windows reminded me of stories told of prairie blizzards in Alberta where farmers lost their way going from the farmhouse to the barn. There were not many patients and the staff was not busy. I did some exploring, walking up and down the corridor familiarizing myself with the ward. On one pass, I noticed a cold breeze coming from one of the patient rooms. When I got to the door, I saw the window pushed open. To my horror the patient was gone. Worse, he had apparently gone out the window as his outline was in the snow that at my last pass had been piled up against that window. This particular patient had been flown in from one of our villages for a mental health evaluation, and I was sure we would find him half frozen and buried in one of the snowdrifts. In a panic I ran to the nurse's station to alert the rest of the staff thinking we would all be fanning out, and by out, I was thinking outside, to retrieve our patient. To my surprise the charge nurse remained calm, picked up the phone and called the emergency room.

"Charley has bolted out the window," she said. After a minute of listening, she turned to me saying, "He's in the emergency room if you want to go get him." It seemed Charley had headed out his window in only his skivvies and a hospital gown. Fortunately, his path had taken him by the front of the hospital where the Emergency Room nurse on duty saw him loping past and rushed out to pull him back in. Charley was very apologetic as I walked him back to the ward and his room with a blanket wrapped around him and his cheeks still red with cold. He promised me he wouldn't do it again as he said it was, "pretty chilly out there, all right." The maintenance man was called to nail down his window. Again, I wondered what I had gotten myself into.

Another patient named Irena pretty much lived at the hospital. She was bedridden and suffered from severe dementia but she was a tough old gal and, although she spoke no English, was very good at letting us know what she wanted. Much of the time she wanted to make sealskin mukluks as she had done most of her active life. Native women chewed the seal skins. Their saliva softened the skin so they could chew very small precise pleats into the curves in the foot pieces before sewing them. Irena's teeth were worn down to stubs from years of chewing. We didn't often have sealskin to give her so she used whatever was available within her reach. This included the sheets and bedspreads, her gowns and anything she could get her hands on to put in her mouth. Housekeeping was constantly questioning our shredded linens. One also risked losing a finger if it got in the way of Irena's mouth. Those stubs, I soon learned, could clamp down with painful strength. She also had a strong grasp and your hand could be on its way to her mouth in a flash if you weren't careful when working with her. We all loved Irena but kept our hands at a respectful distance from both her mouth and her grasp.

It is amazing what women have done over the centuries for beauty. A few of the elderly patients we had in hospital during my stay had tattoos. Females had lines on their chins. In 1969 those traditional markings were becoming a thing of the past. Not many patients we saw had them. The ones I knew were Siberian Yup'ik from St. Lawrence Island. The tattoos were done with threads of sinew run through ash and threaded under the skin. A number of vertical lines were made covering the cleft of the chin upwards toward the lip. It must have been a painful procedure. I was recently visited by a friend from Barter Island who was proudly sporting a new chin tattoo in honor of the Inupiaq customs of her ancestors. Hers was done by a tattoo artist. I much prefer lipstick and eyeliner as marks of beauty. Another custom was placing a round piece of ivory into the base of the earlobe. I am grateful for our modern-day concept of earrings.

Chapter 6

Settling In

~

"Oh look," Mary said as she sat watching me unpack. "Your trunk made the same side trip as mine last year." My trunk had taken longer to come than anticipated. Three weeks longer and with stickers to and from Japan plastered across the top.

"You mean those stickers from some unknown place in Japan? It took a long time to get here, but do you think it actually went to Japan?"

"Of course. There must be a city there that has a spelling similar to Kotzebue," she said. "I just wish I could have accompanied my trunk to wherever that city is. Was your trunk damaged?"

"No, no everything is fine, nothing missing, nothing broken. I had a few jars of green olives tucked inside and none of them are broken, thank goodness. That would have been a mess."

"Green olives! You brought olives all the way from Canada? What on earth for?

"For the same reason Richard, the new sanitation engineer from Alabama, brought grits. We didn't think we would find them on grocery shelves in the Arctic. I love green olives and it seems grits are a staple in the South. I've never tasted them but Richard has invited me to drop by sometime and he'll treat me to a southern "dining delight" as he calls them. It seems they are popular enough to be eaten at almost every meal." My Canadian-bought green olives, nestled deep in my trunk, had become more travelled than I, and I too wished I had accompanied them on their journey. Ah well, Kotzebue in the American Arctic was a good adventure for now.

My trunk's arrival was a major event. When the call came that it had arrived, I joyfully told the maintenance crew to "bring it on over." It was my day off, and Mary and Anne, hearing me whooping it up after getting the good news, popped their heads out their doors to see what was going on. I invited them to help me unpack. My trunk was sitting in the middle of my bare, basic apartment, and I was pulling everything out as if it were

Christmas and each item was another gift. They seemed quite entertained as I explained the history of each "gift." Then the three of us discussed where each item should come to rest in my new home.

I hung two posters on the wall, the beautiful mountains of Banff National Park and one of waving wheat fields and farm buildings, both native to my home province. Perhaps they would ease any feelings of homesickness I might have. They would also prompt conversations and comparisons of where I had come from to where I was now be living.

I had promised my mother I would write once a week, and she made sure I had enough supplies for that promise under the tree at Christmas. I carefully stored those writing supplies in the desk drawer.

The largest part of my trunk contents were clothes. Each item was pulled out one at a time, laid up against me as I gave a little twirl and running commentary on the piece. There were many giggles and much laughter from my audience between the "ooh's" and "aah's," then a discussion ensued on the latest trends down south. I was told that fashion would no longer be of much interest to me as, in the Arctic, warmth trumped style.

The girls also had ideas for me to expand on the apartment basics. Mary, who was very serious about wanting to save as much as possible for her new car, did not order new household items from Sears or Penny's. She made do with what was available. She suggested I could make a bookcase out of packing crates.

"The maintenance department has some very sturdy ones," she offered. They also have wood scraps they will help you put together for any other project. If you're anything like me, you'll be expanding your library in the near future." With employees coming and going from all departments, there was an ongoing array of items for sale and give-away within the hospital campus. It seemed books were among the highest in demand.

"Keep your ears peeled for anyone having a leaving sale," Anne offered. I was advised to pay special attention when a doctor was leaving as they often had sales of their leftover pantry items. There, I was told, one could buy unusual and often pricy items like rib steaks or home baked goods and casseroles for a steal. They often had items from their yearly supply order that were not available at the local grocery store. I was glad I hadn't brought knickknacks for my apartment as there were no shelves in my room on which to put them. I was eager to purchase Native crafts and jewelry I had seen in a tourist shop in town. They carried beautiful, locally made earrings and bracelets carved from ivory, masks made of whalebone, and scenes sketched on baleen from the roof of the mouth of the bowhead whale. I decided to wait before buying, to see what was indicative of the area and what items might become special to me. It felt good to have my personal items around me again to make my apartment feel homey.

By the end of February, I was settled in. My focus in the first two months was my new job and getting acquainted with the routine and my coworkers. It was particularly nice to have breakfast and coffee each morning with an ever-changing group of people. Each day began with lively conversation in the dining room. There was always someone cheerful and talkative at meal times helping to pull others out of any doldrums they might be stuck in. I was never to be lonely in my new home. If the evenings felt too quiet, there were other people up and down the hall. Visiting, I soon discovered, was popular in the residence. Many long dark evenings were spent sipping hot chocolate or chilled wine (depending on our mood), with other residents discussing the day, the work place, or solving the problems in the world of young women everywhere. I also felt I was being educated to the American mindset. Lorraine and I both agreed the American point of view was quite different from Canadian ways of thinking. In the spring I would go through major culture shock but, by now, I had experienced two smaller ones.

The first was adjusting to the difference in American and Canadian world views. Joan, the nurse from Wisconsin, who loved to travel, had recently returned from vacation down south and commented one evening,

"You Canadians sure don't beat around the bush. Your government jumps right into things." She was referring to some news she had heard on television while at home, television being a luxury we did not have in Kotzebue. Without thinking I abruptly replied, "Yes, we say what we mean and act on it. If we say something will happen at a certain time, it does. We don't appoint commissions to study it, nor do we give you three chances to conform. We just do what we said we would and when we said we would."

Joan's mouth popped open then slowly closed again. I was surprised at my answer and how quickly it came out of me. I was defending the Canadian worldview. Though we looked and acted the same and spoke the same language, our points of view were often different.

The second little culture shock arose from living so close together. It seemed everyone knew everyone else's business. And not just in the quarters. I was coming from the store back to the hospital one day when I met up with Emma, one of the practical nurses from town.

"I hear Irena got a good bite of your finger," she said laughing.

"Wow," I replied. "Word travels fast. It just happened this morning." I had been bathing Irena when she grabbed my wrist and pulled my hand to her mouth faster than I could react. She clamped her teeth down on my finger so hard, she drew blood. We sent the bloodied sheets to the laundry.

"Oh, I heard it from Roger," she replied.

"Who's Roger?" I asked.

" Oh, you don't know him; he's related to Bonnie. You know, who works in laundry."

"Ah," I replied laughing. I taped a note for her on the sheet with a sad face on it saying, 'Sue lost the battle, Irene won,' since they keep asking about the linens from Irene's room."

"That's funny," she said. "Roger says he heard you were funny too."

"What? Who said that? Why would they say that to Roger? I don't even know him."

"Nurse, everyone knows about new people real quick around town. You may not meet them yet, but they know lots about you." That was a little unsettling to me. A definite lack of privacy. I had heard about this "everybody knows" situation that occurs in all small towns, but now I was living in one. I'd better be careful what I do and say as Roger, whoever he was, and perhaps the whole town might find out.

Working conditions at the hospital were very good. We were given more responsibility than I had experienced in the large city hospital. Although there was always a doctor to cover our actions, we were encouraged to handle many situations on our own during their off hours, holidays and weekends. I no longer had to rely on interns to start an intravenous. I did it myself.

Doctors were informed of any sick or injured persons twice a day by health aides in each village via short wave radios located in the village schools. There were two such radios in the hospital in Kotzebue. One near the emergency room and another in the nurses' station on the ward. The village aides held sick rounds twice a day then, using the radio, communicated symptoms to the doctors via "radio rounds" who then prescribed medication or treatments over the radio.

It was left to the nurse to decide whether a condition being called in by a village health aide warranted a call to the doctor or if we could offer advice for the aide until the morning scheduled radio rounds. After hours were for emergencies only, but a layman's ideas of what constituted an emergency differed greatly from the medical definition. We did not want to discourage the village health aides from calling, but gently suggested that colds, earaches and other minor conditions could be better handled at regular radio rounds during the day.

After working in a large city hospital, mostly as a student, I was aware of the hierarchy that exists in the medical field. In large hospitals, the focus is mainly on getting things done. Both RN's and especially MDs were too busy for much interaction other than work related. I was pleasantly surprised with the close working and social relationships that developed between the nurses, doctors, officers and their wives. The smaller the work environment, the more staff has a chance to come together socially, and that was certainly true in our situation. From mushing dog teams to dinners and pot lucks at the quarters, those of us who worked together formed many close bonds. Spending coffee breaks with our doctors often lead to discussions about patient conditions and treatment plans. The doctors were very receptive to our input and took time to share their knowledge and perspectives with us. But sometimes being close was also a little nerve wracking.

One of the doctor's wives became pregnant while in Kotzebue, and her husband promised her a painless delivery. I feel pretty safe in saying, as a nurse and now a mother, there is no such thing as a painless delivery unless there is a spinal anesthetic or lots of narcotics. Somehow, I ended up being the nurse in the delivery room when her time came. The doctor also wanted to deliver his own child. True to his word, he gave his wife narcotics until she no longer complained of any discomfort. I think the effect of the drugs were more "I don't care," as opposed to "I don't hurt." When the baby girl arrived, she was a very dusky purple and needed to be given narcan, a drug that reverses the effects of narcotics. Fortunately, daddy doctor had another of our docs standing by in the delivery room who had the narcan in the baby very quickly. Mother and babe were just fine. This nurse was a little rattled, but eventually I recovered.

When one of our doctors was out on vacation or away for any period of time, their position was covered by a traveling TDY (temporary duty) doctor. These doctors were generally young and eager to experience our unique area. Like our stationed doctors, they were friendly and seemed to enjoy our company. They were housed in the 20 unit where the nurses lived and had meals with us in the hospital cafeteria while we regaled them with stories of our lives in the Arctic. They too were eager to teach. One young TDY doctor who came from Anchorage got very involve in teaching me. This was shortly after my experience with the purple baby.

"I'm just not comfortable in the delivery room," I complained. It's not something we do every day, like down south. One of my classmates works on an obstetric ward and that's where she works every day. I'm worried I don't have enough experience in that area. I suppose you doctors get lots of experience before you even graduate."

"Yes, we do," he said with a grin. "And I'd be happy to show you just how we managed that. I'll try to help you get experience while I'm here. Are you game?"

"I'm not sure what I'm agreeing to," I replied, "but yes, I'm game."

His theory was that the more deliveries I attended, the more comfortable I would become. One evening shortly after that conversation, there was a knock on my door at ten o'clock in the evening. When I opened the door, I was greeted with:

"Baby on the way. Let's go and deliver it!"

Off we went to the hospital delivery room to bring a new baby into the world. Not only did he talk me through the delivery, he let me do much more than nurses generally do while assisting in a delivery. There followed a number of other deliveries at ungodly hours of the night which got me past my anxiety and able to appreciate the joy of being part of bringing new life into the world. And after each delivery, he would turn to me and say, "Now wasn't that fun?" He made each delivery an enjoyable learning experience. Not long after he left, I scrubbed in on my first set of twins. I felt glad to have been able to be a part of such joy and thankful that deliveries were no longer stressful for me (at least not until my own delivery a few years later), and thereafter I looked forward to being in the delivery room.

The Kotzebue service unit served approximately 8,000 people in 33 to 36 smaller villages over an area of approximately 85,000 square miles. That was a huge responsibility. When doctors made their village visits, not only were people's short-term problems addressed, but ongoing conditions such as diabetes, arthritis or chronic lung conditions were monitored and tended to. They, as other medical staff, had two-year contracts, so were rotating in and out frequently. These visits to the villages gave them one-on-one time with their patients: a checkup physical as well as a chance for the villagers to meet them. It was also a chance to keep each person's medical records up to date; however, it was the twice daily radio rounds with the village health aides that kept the doctors in touch with medical issues in the villages.

Unfortunately, our lack of regular radio service cut us off from much that was happening in the rest of the world. Letters from home and friends gave us some news and inklings of trends. If it was news of national or global proportions, we heard it on the armed services radio, the first moon landing, for instance. As for the Beatnik movement or the latest fashions, songs or movies, these were not discovered until our contract was over.

CHAPTER 7

The Town

~

I was also familiarizing myself with the town. The village of Kotzebue is perched on the tip of the Baldwin Peninsula, a gravel spit in the Bering Sea thirty miles north of the Arctic Circle. Three large rivers, the Selawik, Kobuk and Noatak, each with a namesake village, drain into the Kotzebue Sound from various inland locations. Kotzebue is then surrounded on three sides by water (when the ice melts). The rivers and the sea become highways in the winter for snow machines and in the summer for boats. Historically, the Kotzebue area had been a gathering place where Inupiaq people to the North and Yup'ik people from the southern Bering Sea coast came together to trade and socialize. Both groups are Eskimo, but each has their own language and customs. When the government began supplying health care and education to Alaska Natives, they placed many schools and hospitals on the coast to allow easy access for supply boats. When this happened, Kotzebue became a town populated by people from the inland villages. They came for medical care and for their children to attend school which was mandated by the government. In 1969 the Native population of Kotzebue was approximately 1,700, consisting of both Yup'ik and Inupiat people. It was the largest village in the Kotzebue service unit.

English was the language used even if there was only a single White person present and the group was predominantly Native. When I asked why more people didn't speak their Native language, one of the doctors pointed out the two different dialects. English was the common denominator for both Natives and non-Natives. That put an end to my thoughts of learning the language. Which dialect should I choose? And after listening to conversations spoken in Inupiaq, I was pretty sure I would not be a good candidate. I had barely made it through French lessons in high school, and had trouble pronouncing single, frequently used Native words, let alone learning to put them together into sentences.

Businesses in town were clustered along Front Street, the road that paralleled the beach front. Some were the multi-storied buildings I had

The Ferguson Building

seen in the distance on my first drive to the hospital that snowy day back in January. The Ferguson Building was the largest and the hub of the business area. It housed a bank, post office, movie theater, library, Tony's Restaurant and a number of apartments above the businesses. There was a small inn used mainly by the hunters that came in the winter and a hotel for tourists that came on daily Alaska Airlines overnight tours in the summer. There was one souvenir shop and two grocery/general stores offering food, clothing and Native arts.

Two other streets with homes ran behind Front Street. Throughout the town there were four churches and parsonages, a laundromat, a Head Start preschool which became a local bar the year the town went wet, a State Trooper quarters and office with a small jail, an FAA (Federal Aviation Administration) station and the airport, complete with jet runway. At the hospital end of town, there was a museum, a small library, and a community building. There was one lonely gas pump on Front Street.

The Ferguson Building After a Heavy Snowfall

When the town was wet, there were one or two bars. When the town was dry, there were one or two bootleggers. This was new vocabulary to me, as was the attempt to control social behavior by passing local laws. When John, the pharmacist, came to dinner complaining that the town was "going wet" again, I thought he was talking about rain.

"Not another storm," I complained. "I want to see blue skies a little longer, especially on my two days off coming up." Then another grim thought came to mind. We were surrounded by water. Would a storm cause flooding?

"Does it flood here?" I asked. I knew rivers overflowed their banks, and we had had plenty of snow that winter.

"That could be disastrous for the homes on Front Street," I lamented. Looking up from my plate, I saw my fellow diners staring at me with wrinkled brows and little smirks on their faces. Then Mary broke into a laugh.

"You think John is talking about water, don't you?" she chuckled.

"Think again," said John, "more about what 'wets your whistle,' not your feet."

"What on earth are you talking about? You said the town would be wet!"

After the laughing stopped, they explained to me that the term "wet" referred to the sale of alcohol.

"When the town is 'wet,' alcohol is legal. But when drinking becomes a problem, the town will often vote to go 'dry,' meaning it's illegal to sell alcohol in the town," explained John.

"You will notice a decrease in the number of visits to the emergency room when the town is dry, and in winter there is less worry about people passing out on their way home and freezing to death," said Mary. "Of course, the bootleggers become active when the town is dry. Taxi services deliver more alcohol than people during the 'dry' times."

Front Street was a well-maintained gravel road that ran the length of the town from the FAA station and airport at the south end of town, to the busy industrial area on the north end. From the road, a gravel beach dropped down to the water and was itself a constant buzz of activity during the summer. Once past the business center, Front Street continued past a long string of homes. These were small one-to-three room shacks with arctic entryways jutting towards the road. Yards were non-existent, but space between and behind residences were filled with a variety of items: sleds, spare snow machine parts, oil drums. There were often dogs chained to stakes between the homes. It seemed nothing was thrown away. Old tools, pieces and parts from broken sleds or machines and anything that might be useful to fix anything were stored close to the house. There were no hardware stores or service shops in town. Native men were applauded for their ability to apply unique and lasting fixes to mechanical or factory -made items.

The hospital complex was at the north end of town behind Front Street not far from the town's industrial area. As a city bred woman, I was never interested in venturing into that area as there were working cranes and noisy activity. Items shipped to Kotzebue on the waterways were barged and unloaded there. The sound of moving large shipments was constant.

The Lone Gas Pump

In summer, with the help of long daylight hours, work stretched late into the night.

The beach was the center of subsistence activity in the spring, summer and fall. Boats anchored in the water along the shore were constantly heading out to fish. They returned with their catch to be processed by the women. Each fish was gutted, cleaned, sliced and draped over wooden racks to dry while the men mended nets and tinkered with motors.

Non-Natives in town, who in 1969 numbered 250, give or take a few, were mostly government workers. The Public Health Service (PHS) ran all the medical facilities, the Bureau of Indian Affairs (BIA) the educational facilities, and the Federal Aviation Administration (FAA) was responsible for everything that allowed us to reconnect with the outside world. Kotzebue had one state trooper and a number of church officials belonging to various religious denominations. There were always new faces in town. New people came and went. Most positions were temporary, but there were one or two permanent residents. One crusty old gentleman had mining rights to a place called Jade Mountain located south of town which accounted for a large amount of jade jewelry in the gift shop. I didn't know him personally, but Lorraine, my Canadian counterpart, had struck up a friendship with him. She said he was a retired university professor who had moved here to escape from the hustle and bustle of city life. She referred to him as her hermit as he was not a very social person. There was Randy, the VISTA worker, a lawyer helping town people with legal matters, and Tony, who owned the restaurant and dining room in the Ferguson Building. But most non-Natives in town worked for the large government agencies and had housing provided.

The weather had been cold and very stormy since my arrival, and my visits to town were, at that point, limited to grocery runs. What I discovered hidden away on the back of a shelf in the main Kotzebue grocery store were, you guessed it, jars of green olives. What they didn't have in that grocery store was real milk, liquid milk. All that was available was canned and powdered. Yuck! Then I understood why the nurses had asked me if I had brought milk from Anchorage. Diane, the nurse recruiter, had forgotten the nurse's pleas to send milk with any new employee coming to town. On my next visit to Anchorage, she told me she had received a few strongly worded reminders. She did not forget to ask new employees to bring milk for the rest of her tenure.

The townspeople showed great respect for the nurses and doctors. I always felt safe when alone in town in both winter and summer. One evening as I was walking alone down Front Street there was a group of young Native men in front of me. They were having a great time bantering back and forth and teasing one another. For a brief moment I wondered if they had been drinking and if it would be safe to keep going. We were the only people on the street at the time. Then the recreation truck from the Air Force base arrived and stopped just in front of us. As the boys from the base piled out the back of the truck with loud raucous voices and not so steady steps, it was apparent that THEY had been imbibing a little too much. In an instant the scene in front of me changed. The town boys became very quiet, moving into a semicircle in front of me, extending

Houses with Dogs in Yard

Front Street Fish Racks and Boats

to the side of the parked Air Force truck, reducing the space between the airmen and myself. The young Native men kept that formation until I was past them, then turned off down a street and were gone. There was no doubt in my mind the boys from town had been protecting me. No eye contact, nothing spoken, but they were definitely watching out for the nurse.

And as I became aware of the privileges I enjoyed as a nurse, in comparison to what was available to the townspeople, such as large comfortable living quarters, running water and electric lights and a well-paying, full-time job, I did not perceive bad feelings toward me or resentment for what I had as a result of my position. I would soon discover that what I had far exceeded that of most people in town. As I began to know more townspeople and visit homes in the village, I often wondered how I would fare living in town without the conveniences I had in the hospital quarters.

Charter pilots did a thriving business in winter flying hunters north of town to hunt polar bear, the massive white kings of the Arctic. These hunters were mainly older gentlemen of sound financial means. They were no doubt used to much higher standards of living than was apparent here. Once in a while one of them became ill enough to be brought in to our hospital to be treated or stabilized before sending him south. They were always understandably nervous at being taken ill so far from home. Often, they were not too subtle in communicating their doubts about our little hospital or our ability to adequately care for them. One hunter had a heart attack out on the ice where the hunting occurred. He described it as "the middle of nowhere" and was sure he was going to die in our "small outpost hospital in the wilderness." We tried to convince him otherwise, but he remained apprehensive and agitated. Afraid he was going to talk himself into another heart attack before we could get him home, the doctor gave him sedation to relax until we could start him on his long trip.

Planes on the Ice

Aside from the charter pilots used by the polar bear hunters, Kotzebue had their own Native born, pilot, Don Ferguson. The hospital used him for flying staff and patients to and from the villages. He was an excellent pilot. I flew with him many times doing patient transports. For someone who had only flown twice before arriving, I quickly became adept at taking care of patients in small single engine planes, and in a variety of weather conditions ranging from extreme cold, to severe rain, wind, and snowy conditions. On calm clear days flying to the many villages allowed me to see the arctic landscape in all its glory. I was having many new experiences, and flying was certainly one of the most exciting ones.

Chapter 8

Differences

~

"Good evening Miss Sue," drawled Ed the lab technician in his soft quiet voice as we sat down for dinner. "And how are y'all this evening?" he cooed, smiling at the others sitting beside me. Till now I had never heard a southern accent spoken except in old movies like "Gone With the Wind." To my ears it sounded put on and phony.

Our nursing staff came from all over the United States. I was enthralled with the many different accents, especially those from the South. To my surprise there was more than one type of drawl. Apparently, each southern state has its own version. All of them sounded surreal to a prairie girl from Canada. Mary's soft-spoken drawl was from South Carolina, Rick, the new sanitation engineer, came to us from Alabama, and Ed, the lab technician, was from Georgia. At meal times, when the staff came together in the hospital cafeteria, I had to listen carefully to the conversation as I sometimes had trouble understanding what was said, even though it was in English. And I thought the language barrier would only be from Eskimo to English.

I did not understand why Ed kept referring to me as "Miss Sue" and that evening I casually but somewhat indignantly responded to him by saying:

"Ed, my name is just Sue, and everyone knows I'm not married!"

I immediately suspected I had made a terrible mistake, as silence enveloped the table until someone, breaking the uncomfortable lack of conversation, said:

"Sue, it's a southern thing. Ed is just being a southern gentleman." When Ed headed back to the residence, Mary, the nurse from South Carolina, was quick to inform me that Ed had been using very polite southern discourse.

"That is how we talk and what he said is the normal way of polite greeting in the South."

I was embarrassed and made a point of apologizing to Ed that very evening on the way back from supper. I realized I had to be careful not to blurt out my sometimes ignorant impressions of something new or foreign to me. The gals from New York and New Jersey were hilariously funny to listen to. I had never in my life heard people talk with that intonation. I often found it hard to keep a straight face listening to them and watching their flamboyant theatrics accompanying their speech. They constantly referred to everyone as "y'ouse guys."

Of course, I never once thought I had an accent until I was told it was obvious that I was from Canada. I was quite surprised.

"Is it because I speak the Queen's English very precisely and clearly?" I asked in an indignant tone.

"Oh no," said the gal with a southern accent so thick one could cut it with a knife. "It's the funny way y'all say your o's…like 'oot' and 'aboot.'" I avoided her for a few days in case I might again offend another southern coworker.

Evidently, I also had an annoying speech habit. It was the Canadian idiosyncrasy of saying "eh?" at the end of a sentence, turning it into a question. I was not aware of this habit. The Americans who ate with me every day were not only aware, but annoyed by it and conspired together to break me of it. In unison, every time I said "eh," which appeared to be at the end of most sentences, they all cupped an ear, leaned toward me and said a long, drawn out "ehhhh?" in loud voices. And while they were changing my pattern of speech, even the Native staff I worked with joined in so that no matter where I was, at work, in the cafeteria or in the quarters, I was ganged up on until I was rid of the "annoying habit" or, as I complained, I had become Americanized. Sometimes you don't hear your own quirks until you yourself have lost them. When I next went back to Edmonton for a nursing reunion, I found myself in a room full of women constantly saying "eh," and experienced firsthand how I had sounded to the Americans. Slowly over the years I have lost my "accent." No one tells me I am Canadian anymore.

The hospital compound was a small community in itself. Between the residence and hospital, all one's needs could be met with the occasional trip to town for groceries or small items for the apartment. What was not available was television or regular radio. There was a huge difference from the rest of the country on how people communicated with each other in rural Alaska. The lack of good phone service and diminished means of connecting, led to feelings of isolation. There was an Armed Services radio station which was not very entertaining but kept us accurately informed of the weather. That news was not always good news:

"Present temperature is minus 20 degrees with a wind chill of minus 50 degrees. Expect more snow flurries and stronger winds."

Basically, what was being said was that anyone who ventured outside that day was crazy. To put a positive spin on that kind of news, I would quietly thank the announcer for warning me not to plan anything beyond my cozy apartment for the day.

But once a day the station offered a message service to the surrounding villages known as the "Mukluk Telegraph." Now THAT was entertaining! It was also a vital link for villagers to get messages or announcements to family or friends in other villages. Most places had only one phone in town located in a public place, like the town store. That option was very expensive and open to anyone around to listen in.

"To the Jones family in Kobuk. Johnny will be arriving sometime on Saturday. Keep a lookout for him on his snow machine.

"To Issac in Kotzebue from Ben in Noorvik: the motor arrived in good shape and thanks for sending it. Check for you coming in the mail.

"From Iva to Mary in Shungnak: Anna had her baby. A girl. She will be coming there with the baby in one week.

"To Willie in Kotzebue; come now to Pt Hope. whaling starting in 2 days."

I was convinced that everyone near a radio in both Kotzebue and the surrounding villages, was tuned in when the "Mukluk Telegraph" was airing. If they weren't and a message was for them, the rest of the town would soon let them know. It was easy to imagine every household in each village across the vast tundra landscape linked together by radio as one big family, a family where everyone could learn everyone else's business. Coming from a big city where privacy was valued and easily maintained, forfeiting it was at first difficult for me to get used to, though the practicality and convenience was apparent.

In as much as our accents were different, our reasons for living and working in the Arctic were also different. All but one of the nurses were single. All were adventurous types keen to see a different way of life and experience the arctic environment. Other than avoiding the draft, the men were eager to try new hunting and fishing experiences. Some staff were there for the good salaries and a chance to save money. There were also one or two who were "getting away from it all" and in some cases "all" included a spouse. But for our many differences of origin, accents, and reasons for being there, everyone came together in both work and play. There were a variety of ages and personalities but we worked at getting along and tolerating our many differences. Although we worked together and lived in close proximity to each other, we were able to retreat to our own apartments to avoid those who at times we might find a little annoying. Being so far removed from family and friends, we were fortunate to have such interesting people with whom to socialize. And the group was constantly changing as the two-year contracts were vacated and refilled by new arrivals.

And socialize we did, in a number of different ways. Any reason was a good one for a get together or party, sometimes in each other's apartments, other times in the recreation room in the basement. Homemade pizza parties were accompanied by guitars and singsongs, fancy dinners with one or two friends (often from the air base), and the occasional potluck. A spontaneous invitation to share someone's fabulous new desert was looked forward to at any time. Differences in regional cuisines came to light at these social functions; I was introduced to grits and biscuits and gravy. You still don't find either of those in Western Canadian cuisine. There were movies, birthday parties, one bridal shower, bon voyage parties and welcome back get togethers. During Christmas those who hadn't left due to their work schedule came together to celebrate the holiday. We became each other's families. There were also get togethers with staff from town.

Another difference I was forced to face living in another culture was my position in the life of the village. My first year I spent a lot of time thinking about the fact that I, as a non-Native, was a minority in that town. I had, of course, heard about the problems faced by minorities the world over. I did not feel like a minority although I wasn't too sure how one should feel. I was young and idealistic and not very aware of how things in life worked. I was somewhat ignorant of social class and social disparity. Later, in conversation with those older and wiser than myself, I realized that being a minority in numbers was not the same as being a minority in social position. I was not yet seeing that wealth and power divided people. I had never heard the term "white privilege." As a nurse, I had a much needed service to offer and held some respect in the town. My position had influence on the physical well-being of people. I was a single young woman with a job, financial security, a warm, and by town standards, large, comfortable home with running water, flush toilets and electric lights. As this reality began to dawn on me, my privileged lifestyle gave me a feeling of guilt. It certainly made me aware of the hardships faced by so many of our country's less fortunate and very thankful for my position in life.

CHAPTER 9

Snow Machines

"Why don't any of you have a snow machine?" I asked the other nurses during a get together in Anne's room. Snow machines, referred to as snow mobiles in the Lower-48 states, were the most common means of transportation in the Arctic during the winter months. The snow had finally stopped blowing sideways and the gleaming white canopy that lay over the town was calling me to outdoor activities.

"What better way to get around than using a snow machine?" I had been contemplating buying one, but anything new was far too expensive. I was looking for something second hand.

"Well, I'm only here for a few more months," Anne responded. The only place I want to go in my spare time is to see Brad at the base and their rec run truck gets me there."

Brad was her fiancé stationed at the radar site five miles out of town and his year in Kotzebue was almost over.

"Why spend money on a snow machine?" asked Mary. "I'm saving my money for a car when I go south. It's too short a term for such an investment. And I will be leaving before you." She had a point. We had all come at different times. One of us would have to buy out whoever left first. But I really wanted a snow machine.

"Don't you want to do more outdoors? Ride over the open tundra? Explore farther away from town? The guys all have them," I said, hoping to move someone to my way of thinking.

"And that's why we don't need them." said Thea. "If they plan a trip, we get to ride on the back of one of their machines or in their sleds. All the fun without the cost or responsibility. Didn't you go on the last picnic upriver?" she asked.

"Yes," I replied. And that's why I want a machine of my own. I don't want to have to rely on the guys to go anywhere."

"I heard Mr. Barton is selling his," offered Sally. Mr. Barton was the social worker who was scheduled to leave the next month.

"He wants $500 for it. It's not one of those big powerful noisy ones. He wasn't into hunting. It's been around for a while, but seems to run good," Sally continued. "And it's a good size for you."

"That is exactly what I have been looking for," I said, with hope mounting. And the price was affordable. "What kind is it?"

"Don't know the brand but it is smaller than most you see around town. Those really go fast, which is what the guys are looking for. They say they are good on hunting trips. The one I'm talking about is red, so it would be easy to see coming. You know, to warn anyone in your path! Just kidding! I wonder if it's anything like driving a car?"

"Anyone want to go in with me to purchase it?" I asked. "It's safer to travel in twos and more fun if you have a companion to explore with." No takers.

"What's wrong with all of you?" I whined. "I thought we were all here to experience new things. I've been watching the guys having fun on their machines. Now I want my turn."

I could not understand why the other girls didn't feel as I did.

The next day I connected with Mr. Barton and had him show me his machine. It sounded good (no rattles or bangs), and, after a very smooth ride on the back of the machine with him around the town, I was sold. I knew nothing about mechanics or snow machines but they say, "ignorance is bliss," and so, in an excited state of bliss, I sealed the deal with a down payment. I couldn't come up with the $500 he was asking just then, but after my next paycheck I became the proud owner of a very old red skidoo snow machine. I named her "Little Red." It was a steal at that price, and I was sure I would have no problem selling it when I left. In the end it was one of the best purchases I made during my time in the North.

I wanted to see as much countryside as I could before spring break-up, but it took a while to get comfortable driving "Little Red." The day I bought her, I was given a quick "how to": how to pull the cord to start it, how to squeeze the right handle bar to go, the left to stop and how to fill the gas tank from that lonely pump on Front Street. I was told I just needed to practice to become proficient at handling my new toy. I knew nothing about engines or maintenance or specifically, snow machines.

My biggest problem was getting it started. No electric starts, just a cord slightly too long for my short arms. It took a fair amount of strength combined with speed to pull it hard enough to spark the engine into action. I spent an inordinate amount of time getting that darned engine to turn over. Will, our wonderful x-ray technician and, for me, master snow machine starter, came to my aid during the days he was at work. He watched my failed attempts from a window in his department at the hospital, then out he'd come, pulling on his parka. Will was from town and owned a very large Arctic Cat, one of the big machines the hunters preferred.

"Stand in this place." he would instruct me. "Lean into the machine, like this. Now pull fast all the way, no stopping." I did just as he said, but by then my arms were tired from too many choppy tries.

"My arms aren't long enough Will," I'd whine.

"You can do it. Try again!" But I had him there and I was going to use him.

"My arm aches from so much trying," I'd say.

"OK, then just watch again how I do it. Next time you'll get it." And next time he'd show me again as he started it for me. With just one strong pull from Will, "Little Red" fired up ready to go. Will always came to my rescue.

After a few short circles around the hospital complex, I headed to Front Street for my first solo ride. Front Street followed the shoreline with houses and stores on one side and the ice of Kotzebue Sound on the other. There had been snow and blowing wind earlier that morning, and the plow had not yet made it around town but that's what snow machines are good for: going where snow plows have not. What didn't show on the white landscape were drifts on the road created from snow blowing between the houses. As soon as I turned onto the street, I hit one of those drifts and was air born. The shock of flying through the air overruled my logical thinking causing me to lean forward and squeeze hard on both handlebars. When I landed with a hard whump on the snow-covered road, the gas trigger won control. The machine's treads caught the snow, and in a minute, I was roaring up and over the next drift. It happened so fast and took me by surprise both times. It took a few drifts before my brain caught up and I was able to relax my grip, slow down and regain some control. There were two elderly Native men sitting on a bench outside a house, and as I roller-coasted by on my first run, their eyes grew big as saucers as they watched my machine fly up and off the drift in front of them while charging down the street. On my way back they jumped up to attention, probably thinking they might have to run for their lives. Again, not in full control, my machine flew off a drift landing hard on the road in front of them. They clapped and laughed and waved their arms about as I passed. At least I was entertaining!

I suspect they were muttering "dumb tunic!" to each other. "Tunic" is the nice word for white people. I was jokingly (at least I hope it was jokingly) called "dumb tunic" by my close Kotzebue friends so many times when I did something out of context or irrational to them, or asked a question that only an "outsider" would ask, that I began to think of it as my second name. I had a lot of "dumb tunic" moments during my time in the Arctic. Shaking of heads and rolling of eyes would be followed by a logical explanation of what I had done wrong followed by hearty laughs. This was never done in anger, nor did they give up on me. Most of my "dumb tunic" moments were explained to me. What did a city girl know about hunting and gathering ways when her food had always come from a Safeway grocery store? There was a family I became close to in town, especially the mother. I began to call her my "Eskimo Mama." It was her husband who kept me well informed of my ignorance to their way of life.

"You eat that? Is it cooked?" I would ask my Eskimo mama. To which her husband would reply, "Sure, don't you know intestines are real good to eat?" or "It's not cooked, can't you tell that?" Then he'd shake his head and turn away from me muttering, "Dumb tunic," when I stopped eating what had been given to me when I discovered it was not cooked.

Other times there were Native ways versus White man ways. When I visited people in town, long stretches of silence were difficult for me to understand and deal with, and our use of time where activities are assigned to a specific time on the clock did not mesh with Native ways, which were based on their environment. For example, you hunt when the animals are present, you sleep in the long summer days, only when one is tired. In reality, it was the townspeople who were constantly adjusting to our ways, but when I was doing things with them in their environment, the feeling appeared to be, "when in Rome." It was a steep learning curve for a city girl.

I did eventually become a good snow machine driver. That opinion was based on my estimation, as there was no driver's education program. One didn't need a license to drive a snow machine. I saw many teenagers buzzing around town and felt I could hold my own with them. Good common sense seemed to be the rule of the road. I parked my machine under the window of my apartment, out in the open, no cover, no lock and never a worry about someone stealing it. People drove to where they were going, hopped off and left the machine where they had stopped, sometimes leaving it running while they ran into the post office or bank. Theft did not appear to be a problem.

Me on "Little Red"

Waiting for the Race to Begin

CHAPTER 10

Snow Machine Adventures

I had many adventures on Little Red. In winter, groups of us took snow machines and sleds on trips up the rivers. The gals packed lunches, everyone brought thermoses of hot chocolate or coffee, and all enjoyed the camaraderie of a winter picnic. It was a great feeling of freedom skimming along the snow on my snow machine, feeling the wind rush by and enjoying the barren but beautiful winter scenery in its simplicity. There were no trees in the Kotzebue landscape, but the light play on stretches of snow created a wonderland of shadows and sparkling white. If it was a sunny day in spring, before the snow melted, I wore sunglasses so my eyes would not be damaged by the glare off the snow. In earlier times the Native people wore similar protective eye wear made from slices of caribou hooves with slits for the eyes and straps made of hide to tie behind the head.

I basked in the joy of my new found sport and felt proud of my ability to handle a snow machine until, on one trip with other hospital employees, without warning, my machine came to an abrupt stop. I had broken down a very long way from town and had no idea why.

After much tinkering and consultation by the men, it was determined that Little Red was going nowhere until something was replaced. Since no one had that vital part with them, my machine was lifted onto one of the sleds and towed back home while I rode behind the pharmacist on his large powerful Arctic Cat. So much for freedom and independence. Although it was a warm (by Arctic standards), clear day, and I had lots of support, it made me realize how easily one could get into trouble far from town with no means of getting help except on foot. In this time before cell phones, people who travelled away from the villages had to be prepared with extra parts, tools, food and water for being stranded on the tundra or a forced landing while flying over those same tundra landscapes. Their physical safety depended on it. Having my survival kit packed and ready to grab on my way out the door when heading to the airport for a village medivac, or out on a snow machine trip, gave me a sense of security. As it turned out, a false sense of security, as I did not have any spare parts, and if I did, I had no idea how to install them. Owning a snow machine gave me not only the pleasure of driving myself on group outings, but allowed me to travel around town in comfort and speed. It helped me to feel connected to the rhythm of the town. And soon Little Red began opening up new adventures for me.

There were two young brothers from town who came to our quarters now and then to play cards with some of the nurses. We played a game called Snerts, which I had never seen played before, nor since. On one such occasion, they were busy planning a trip to bring ice from a lake not far from town to replenish their family's spare water supply.

"Don't forget the rope this time Ernie" said Daniel. "I want big chunks so we don't have to do so much sawing".

"We'll bring the big tarp if that's what you want to do," said Ernie. "Think two loads will be enough?"

"Mom said the tank is empty. Wish we had one more sled. Then we could make just one run."

I had been concentrating on the card game we were playing, but my ears perked at Daniel's last statement.

"Another snow machine? You need another person with a snow machine?" I said in a loud voice. "I have a snow machine," I exclaimed excitedly. "I could probably borrow someone's sled too, and I have a day off tomorrow. I'll go with you. Could I?" I saw the look that passed between them and hastened to reassure them I would not be a burden.

"I'll just follow you and let you load my sled then follow you back to your place so you can unload. I won't get in the way at all. Promise."

They pretended to look at their cards, but I saw Ernie glancing at his brother a few times and finally Daniel, being the older and decision maker, said reluctantly:

"OK, if you can find a sled and are outside the back door at 11 o'clock tomorrow morning, you can come."

I was so excited I could barely concentrate on the cards. In my head I was busy planning what I would wear as the weather had been very cold. If the wind was blowing the chill factor would make it feel much colder. I didn't know what to expect, but I knew it would be a learning experience.

It was one of the reasons I had bought my snow machine.

When they left, I hurried down the hall to John, the pharmacist, to ask if I could borrow his sled. He did not seem too eager to let go of his beautiful handmade prized possession. After giving me detailed instructions on how to hitch it and drive with it behind my machine, and after more than one reassurance from me that I was capable of driving with a sled behind me (he didn't need to know I had never driven one before), and after more promises that I would be careful, he finally agreed to trust his sled to this begging of an eager nurse. He was stretching his trust level by turning over his sled to someone who might not measure up to the standards.

At eleven the next morning, the sled was hitched and I was waiting. Other than overcast skies, the weather looked good. I was traveling with young men from town so I felt safe. They assured me it wasn't too far, and I had a full tank of gas. They checked over my equipment and told me to stay close as we headed out of town. Off we went, the three of us, driving our snow machines and empty sleds in a straight line. I brought up the rear feeling proud to be included and excited for the new experience. We headed a few miles out of town to a frozen lake. They directed me to a spot away from where they would be working, telling me to stay there for my safety.

After looking over the ice and picking a spot, Daniel cranked up their chain saw and began cutting two squares from the edge of the lake of approximately the length and width of the sleds. When the chunks broke loose, they pulled them on to land. Straining muscles to their limits, using long handled ice picks, they pulled the pieces onto land then cut the two large chunks into more manageable sizes.

It was cold and sitting on my snow machine made me feel colder. I walked around stomping my feet and clapping my hands. I needed something to do to keep warm and wanted to help. I snuck in behind them and began lifting a smaller chunk of ice for the sled. I was surprised at how heavy it was. Once I had a good grip, I lifted it and headed toward my sled. Instantly my right foot hit a patch of ice and slid out in front of me, knocking me off my stance. My arms jerked out trying to help maintain my balance. The chunk of ice dropped from my arms landing within inches of my foot. Turning to see what was going on, Daniel sprinted to my aid.

"What did we tell you?" he shouted shaking his fist after seeing there was no damage. "Not gonna look good for us if we crush the nurse's foot under a block of ice! Stay there and don't move till we're done. This is men's work anyway," he said giving me a side glance to see how I would react to that statement. But I had learned my lesson. I was happy now to leave it to the "men." Perspiration dripped from their foreheads as they covered the ice with tarps, securing them with rope to each sled. They had obviously done this many times before and had a system that worked. The chunks of ice they had cut fit neatly onto the sleds, and when they were secured, we started back to town.

The temperature had warmed. The wind was picking up and blowing the snow in swirls on the ground. As we were preparing to leave, it began to snow. Soon the ground snow along with the falling snow was being whipped to a frenzy, blurring my vision. Shortly after we began heading back, the boys stopped and placed me between their two sleds before continuing on. I focused on keeping within eye sight of the back of Daniel's sled without ramming into it. I worried that Ernie would crash into my sled if I had to stop suddenly. I quickly lost any sense of direction as our incoming tracks were fast being covered with new snowfall. The swirling snow was blocking any vision and making me a little dizzy as it swirled soundlessly around me, making it hard to see even the sled in front of me. We seemed to be traveling forever. I had also lost sense of time. I began to wonder if we were going in the right direction back toward town or if we would even see the town if we were too far from its outskirts. I was afraid we would drive right on past until I saw the water tower loom up in front of us. It was a familiar landmark and I knew, as soon as I saw it, that we were in town and close to the hospital quarters. We continued on to Daniel and Ernie's house where they unloaded my sled and had me follow one of them back to my quarters. Hauling a sled full of ice through a blinding snow storm was a firsthand experience in how quickly the weather can change, and another in the need to always be prepared. We had left in ideal weather and within a couple of hours we were in the middle of a blinding whiteout. Even so close to town, in those conditions one's sense of place and direction could fail. It would be easy to get off course. The boys had a compass and had used it to help them back to town. I was very happy to be back at the residence that day.

"You did real good for a white girl," Daniel said next time they came to play cards. We gonna give you an Eskimo name. "Seekatauruq," he said laughing. "Yep, "Seekatauruq."

They told me it meant "go get ice." And I had!

Another time on my snow machine during a blizzard, I was struggling to drive back to the hospital from town. Although I might have run into the side of a house or a building in such a storm, there wasn't the same danger of getting lost as there was outside the town perimeter. I never ventured out of town if the weather was anything less than clear, but if I did, it was always in a group or accompanied by someone from town familiar with traveling in adverse conditions. We listened to weather reports on the Armed Services radio before heading anywhere.

Winter was the time for snow machines and, as with all fast-moving vehicles, there were races. I didn't pay much attention to the details of snow machine racing, but it was fun to watch the start. Our big winter race was 250 miles, from Kotzebue to some of the surrounding villages and back. The racers were from a number of our local villages and as far away as Nome. Midmorning on the day of the race, people and machines gathered on the ice in front of town. Women, visiting in bright colored parkas, many with babies on their backs. Men talking everything snow machine, predicting weather and hedging bets on which driver was capable of what. Children running their own two-legged races. We were between storms and the sun was peeking longer over the horizon. It was a thrill seeing the machines lined up on the ice, with the townspeople gathered around them. Feeling the tension in the air, even the dogs tied up in town were howling their excitement. When the starter gun went off, the snow machines seemed to spring from zero to 60 mph in minutes, throwing sprays of snow behind them, and the young boys attempting to run after them. The roar of the engines dimmed as the machines got further away and was soon overpowered by shouts and well wishes of waving bystanders until every machine was out of sight. People gradually broke up and headed home until everyone was gone and it was as deserted and quiet as it had been early in the morning. A few days later when news of the progress of the riders filtered back to town and it became apparent the racers were returning, crowds again gathered on the ice to welcome them home. People strained to see who was coming first. Many had binoculars eager to holler the names of the drivers as they appeared. As each snow machine arrived, it was swarmed by friends and relatives eager to hear their contestants' stories. The crowds lingered for most of the day waiting for all to cross the finish line. Winners were announced and everyone headed home to prepare for the awards banquet. The race remained the talk of the town for many days. It was one of the highlights of winter.

Surprisingly, after I left Kotzebue, I never again owned or rode a snow machine, even though I lived with snow in winter. My snow machine days were relegated to the North and to its miles of open tundra.

Finish Line: Waiting for the Winner

City living is not conducive to snow machines. Here in Alaska, there are Iron Dog snowmobile races each year, but those are for young, speed-lusting men and a little too aggressive for my taste. I prefer the real dogs of the Iditarod Sled Dog race held each year in March from Anchorage to Nome to commemorate the serum run of 1925 during the diphtheria epidemic in Alaska.

Snow machines had definitely replaced dogs in the Arctic by 1969, making subsistence activities and travel easier. Outlying villages could be reached in a day with a snow machine. The same trip traveling with dogs and sleds could require a night of camping on the trail and packing food for the dogs. My friends told me they would start out "real early" in the morning with the dogs to reach the village before night.

A downside to replacing dogs was the cost. The rural Alaska economymade buying and maintaining these modern machines expensively difficult. Gas to power them was also expensive.

There were not many paying jobs in the small villages. Sharing was a way people survived in rural Alaska. I suspect families went in together to purchase machines that were shared. Excellent maintenance by the Inupiaq men kept machines working long past their normal lifespan. I doubt they had any special training, but they seemed to be very good at figuring out any problem and were gifted in their ability to fix it. There were no service stations or parts stores. Everything had to be ordered from larger centers. Thus, the reason old relics remained in yards awaiting the need for some part to be removed from it to fix the current machine. Native food remained traditional, but the way of getting it had become mechanized. Snow machines had found a permanent place in village life.

CHAPTER 11

Village Health Aides

"KIK 764 Kivalina calling KIK 735 Kotzebue Hospital." The VHF radio at the hospital nurses station crackled to life as I turned to answer the call. It came from the health aide in the small village of Kivalina north of us on the Bering Sea coast. Someone needed medical help. As the nurse on duty at two o'clock in the morning, I would be her first response. It was up to me to assess the condition of her patient and decide if the problem required a doctor's response or if I could give her enough assistance to carry her to regular morning radio rounds with the doctor. If the condition was critical, our doctor on call would arrange for a plane to bring the patient to hospital for treatment. Fortunately, this call did not require a doctor. The young male patient had a cough, sore throat and painful ear that was keeping him awake. I gave the standard treatment plan of Tylenol for the fever and discomfort and to call in on morning rounds for further treatment. I suspected the little fellow was going to get a shot of penicillin in the morning.

Little is known of the health and welfare of the Inupiaq people before Western contact, but we do know it was the shaman, the spiritual healer, that tended to many medical needs in the society. First contact with the outside world came from interaction with New England whalers as early as the 1840s and 1850s and again with Navy sailors around the 1880s, according to Dr. Robert Fortuine in his book *Chills and Fever*. At the time of contact, people were living in unsanitary conditions. Sem-subterranean homes were crowded, smokey, poorly ventilated and lacked a clean water supply. There were also periods of famine resulting from changing animal migration patterns and weather conditions. Infectious diseases swept through the Arctic after Western contact. Especially deadly were the 1918–1919 flu epidemic and the rapid spread of tuberculosis that caused a large decline in the Native population throughout Alaska.

In the 1890s, medical missionaries began setting up hospitals in larger villages. A hospital was built in Kotzebue in 1939. In 1955 the

United States Public Health Service (USPHS) took over Native health care from the Bureau of Indian Affairs. In 1956 tuberculosis patients were prescribed a number of drugs to take in their home villages. By the 1960s, a need arose for one person in the village, called a chemotherapy aide, to dispense these drugs and other medications to patients as well as keep the doctors informed of medical emergencies.

These aides were mostly female and bilingual so they could converse with the elders who often did not speak English. They had very basic training on how to take vital signs and obtain a medical history. As time passed, aides began providing primary health care. Even without substantial medical training, the village aides took on a larger amount of responsibility: they were available 24/7 in case of an emergency, they held sick call twice a day weekdays, often going to the patient's home to collect information, and they participated in scheduled radio rounds with a doctor at the Kotzebue hospital. Rounds were held twice a day, mid-morning and again at five p.m.

The doctors in Kotzebue, recognizing the importance of the aides' roles, and their need for further training, used their own service unit funds to teach the aides how to improve reporting and how to best handle the drugs. It was not until 1969 that the Public Health Service received federal funding to train and pay salaries to local health aides. The title Community Health Aide (CHA) was chosen to reflect village involvement and to stress the emphasis on health care. This brought better understanding and communication between the health professionals and their patients, especially elders who did not speak English. By selecting village residents, especially those with village approval, the system reduced cultural barriers and offered more effective health care. I was excited when the health aides came to the hospital from the villages. We were so happy to meet them and put a face to the voices that came over the radio to us in the late evenings and during the night when the doctors were not at the hospital. Some of them brought carvings to sell. I acquired a beautiful ivory carved dog team and sled with the driver riding the runners as they chased a polar bear in front of them. The carvings sat on a small fossil ivory sled runner. The woman I bought the runner from told me it was one used to lash an umiak to in order to haul it to an open lead where it would be launched to hunt seals.

Although the doctors visited each village once a year to do medical rounds on every person, the day-to-day and emergency needs were handled by radio rounds. In most cases the only radio in the village was located in the school. I was very interested in this method of long-distance medicine and spent my first year sitting in on the 5 p.m. radio rounds with the doctor of the day. They were an hour before dinner so I came early each day to witness a unique health care delivery system. The doctors became used to me being in attendance and let me handle the radio while they took notes and gave out treatments. Each evening the rounds with all the villages in the service unit began the same way:

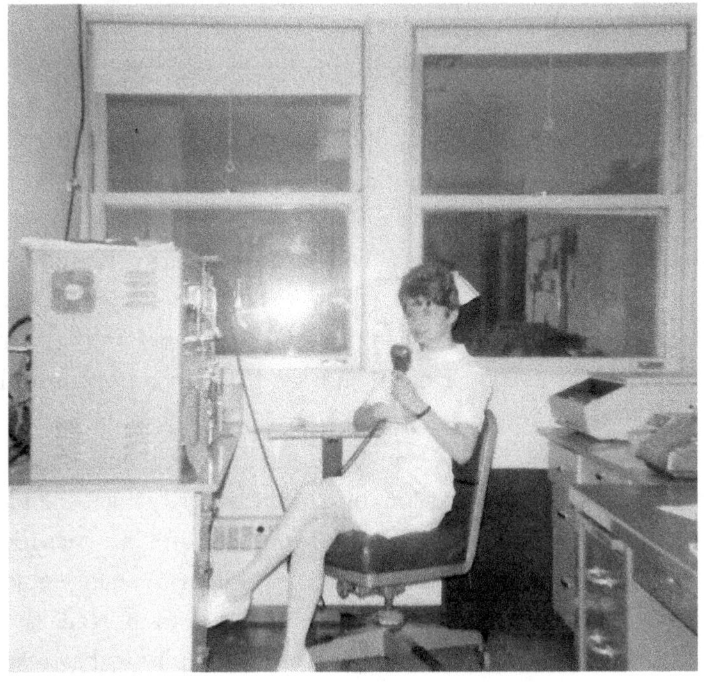

KIK 735 Kotzebue Hospital
Author assisting with radio calls

"KIK 735 Kotzebue hospital calling KIK 764 Kivalina."

The health aide would identify each patient by age, gender and symptoms. For patient privacy, names were not given over the air:

"We have: (giving us each patient's symptoms one at a time):

"41-year-old male with bad cold, sore throat and chest. He's coughing up green stuff now. Temperature 101."

"14-year-old girl with cut on her lower arm from a knife she was using at fish camp, now has a red streak running up from the cut. Temperature 99."

"7-year-old boy with right earache, his ear is draining, temp 100."

And the doctor, to the best of his ability, would diagnose and prescribe medication or a treatment. Treatment very often involved inter-muscular antibiotics, (generally penicillin), to cover the many bacterial infections. Some doctors, because of its high usage, worried some patients might become resistant to it.

There was another radio at the nurse's station that the nurses monitored evenings, nights, weekends and holidays. Many times the radio crackled in the middle of a night shift to the familiar call:

"KIK 735 Kotzebue hospital this is (village name). We have an emergency." I would feel my blood pressure and anxiety rise before answering the call, anticipating a worst-case scenario. Would I be able to handle the situation or would I have to wake the doctor? As it took time for the doctors to dress and fight the elements before they arrived, it fell to the nurse to keep the aide calm and obtain an accurate history. After a time, I began to recognize not only the voices of each village aide, but the manner in which each one responded to emergencies. Some were very precise in relaying critical symptoms. Others were panicked and needed calming down and prompting before getting any useful information. Often the doctor would send a plane to a village to bring in an emergency, only to find the patient's condition not as serious as had been reported. There were also some under treated patients for lack of proper physical assessment by the aide. Before any training had occurred in and after 1969 for the village aides, it was up to the nurses to decide the severity of a case. Often it was the pitch or tone of the aide's voice that provided a clue as to the severity of the patient's condition. These women were not medical people and nurses were their first line of help after hours. How frightening to be first responders to accidents and crisis situations with no training nor any medical support in the village. That kind of help was available only if the planes could fly.

And often the patients they were treating were friends or relatives, adding a level of stress that often made it difficult or embarrassing for the aide.

One radio call I received in the middle of a stormy night was from a very upset health aide who had attended the delivery of a baby by the village midwife. Most villages had Native midwives that handled home deliveries. Only first babies or problem pregnancies were flown in to deliver at the hospital. This delivery was the patient's third child. The delivery had gone well but after the birth she began bleeding more than usual and it was not slowing down. The aide had come to the school radio for help from the hospital. She sounded out of breath, as if she had been running, and had trouble giving me an accurate account.

"Slow down Doris; sit down and catch your breath."

"OK nurse, but she not doing good. I know. I've seen lots of deliveries. This is too much."

"Too much what Doris?"

"Too much she bleed, something's wrong."

I instructed her on proper fundal massage, a technique to firm the uterus and slow down the bleeding. Back she went to the patient's home. Soon the radio again crackled to life.

"Not working nurse, still too much bleeding. I keep pushing into her tummy and rubbing but not get hard. Please tell me what else to do."

The aide was getting extremely anxious and I was feeling very helpless. I called the doctor over but he too was limited in what he could do without being there. The aides had a small supply of medications on hand. The intra-muscular medicine needed to help the uterus to clamp down to stop the bleeding was not one available in her supply. Perhaps the patient also needed manual evacuation of any blood clots that would stop the uterus from doing its natural job. But the aide had no training on how to handle a post-delivery hemorrhage. The doctor had attempted to get a plane to the village to bring the patient to hospital but the pilot told us it would not be safe to fly. Finally, after numerous trips from the home to the school to update us, the health aid, in barely audible tones and with a catch in her voice said simply, "she died," and broke into sobs. The patient had been her cousin. I felt so helpless and sad and couldn't begin to imagine how she and the midwife were feeling. Those words haunted me for a very long time, knowing that this tragedy would probably not have happened in the Lower 48 where medical help was readily available.

With the implementation of the 1969 Federally funded training program for the village aides, things began to improve. Aides became more proficient in reporting. One year after I left Kotzebue, federal funding became available to build clinics in each village. These clinics provided a place to store a larger supply of drugs, equipment, their own radio and space for medical records. It allowed the village aide to separate home from work. In some villages the health aide position was one of the few paying jobs available. In providing a paying job for a woman, her husband could devote more of his time to subsistence activities and, because sharing was a traditional Inupiat way of life, one man's catch could benefit many who otherwise might go hungry including elders, widows and their children and others who had no access to the spoils of the hunts.

It was always exciting and sometimes challenging to go on medical (mercy) flights to the villages. One never knew what would be waiting at the other end. My first mercy flight occurred a couple of months after I arrived and, although thrilling, was also nerve wracking. It was dark and I had never flown in the dark in a small plane before. I was looking for some reassurance.

"Boy it really is pitch black. I can't see anything. How do you know where you are going?" He mumbled something I didn't understand.

"I sure hope there aren't any other planes flying around. We'd see them, right?"

"No one else crazy enough to fly in this weather in the middle of the night nurse," he quipped.

"Oh, right. You're the only one doing mercy flights, right?"

"Relax, I've been doing this for a long time. I know what I'm doing. You're safe.

"Right. Sorry. No offense intended."

Then, all of a sudden, I saw two strips of light appear in the distant darkness. Even to me it was apparent it was where we were going to land.

"Wow, their airport lights sure light up the runway," I said with relief.

"There's no runway, just ice and snow. We're landing on a river."

"But the lights," I sputtered. And he began dropping our little plane down towards them. In the darkness of winter, villagers on snow machines were lined up to simulate a runway. When the plane was heard approaching, headlights were turned on to mark a landing strip.

Sometimes the trip only required a nurse. Sometimes there would be both a nurse and doctor. And always snow machines would whisk us off to a building with the patient and waiting health aide. In a dire emergency, the patient would be waiting in a sled by the runway, loaded onto the plane upon landing, and we would be back in the air as quickly as possible, with snow machine headlights still blazing the way.

Flying out to villages posed some risks, especially in harsh winter conditions. One of our doctors helped us put together survival kits to carry with us when we flew anywhere by small plane including extra socks and mittens, a flashlight, matches and a recipe of "survival bars" we made involving nuts, grains and honey, that were every bit as good as modern-day protein bars. I never flew anywhere or travelled away from the village on snow machines without taking my kit with me. It became habit to pick it up as I headed out the door.

As much as we, in our modern hospital did for the health of the people in our service unit, it was the health aides that were the medical eyes and ears in villages throughout the Arctic, keeping us informed of the health status of each village and their inhabitants.

Chapter 12

Traditional Medicine and Religion

One afternoon the doctor on call alerted me to a male patient being flown to hospital from Point Hope, one of the larger villages north of Kotzebue. The patient had a severe nosebleed that showed no signs of letting up. The health aide had been instructed to pack his nostrils with gauze which she had informed us had needed to be replaced several times.

"I keep putting in lots of gauze," she told us, "but pretty soon it's full and blood drips out again. This is the worst nosebleed I ever saw." The nose continued to bleed and the patient was authorized to be flown to the hospital.

"I put something else in his nose, and his nose doesn't bleed anymore and he says he's not swallowing blood either. Maybe I cured him our Native way."

"What do you mean "Native way?" the doctor asked.

"I hear plane landing now," she said. "Better get him ready to meet the plane."

When the patient arrived, I settled him on a stretcher in the treatment room. The color had drained from his face. He was also exhausted and kept mumbling and pointing to his nose. I covered him with a warm blanket and encouraged him to relax so the doctor could remove the packing. It didn't seem to want to budge. The doctor had trouble grasping and latching on to pull it out. Upon closer examination, all we could see was a large flat black mass inside the nostril.

"That is not old blood," said the doctor as he prodded and attempted to get a grip on the unidentified mass, "and definitely not gauze. What does it look like to you?"

"Well, its black and moist and apparently slippery," I responded as his forceps kept slipping off the end of it. I dug into a drawer and pulled out a tweezer-like instrument with a jagged end.

"Whatever it is, it seems to have stopped the bleeding," I said trying to hold the patient's head still and keep his hands away from his nose. He was trying to tell us something but didn't speak English. He kept waving his hands and pointing to his face. And the more we dug at the object in his nose, the louder he became. Finally, the instrument latched onto the mystery object and it began to slide out. As it did the patient hollered, "muktuk!" Sure enough, out of his nostril came a perfectly sized triangle of whale skin and blubber along with a trickle of blood.

"Muktuk?" we both said in disbelief.

"EE," (the Eskimo word for yes), "EE, muktuk," the patient said, grinning from ear to ear. "Work good huh?" he said in his broken English.

We were shocked into silence as we stood looking at this piece of traditional medicine. The black outer whale skin had put pressure on the nostril while the oil in the blubber kept the mucus membrane moist. Unfortunately, the nostril again began to ooze, then trickle, then to bleed profusely. The doctor attempted to put lubricated gauze packing into the nose but by then it was bleeding so much that each packing quickly became saturated with blood. Finally, we both agreed the whale had done a much better job, and the doctor stuffed the muktuk back into the patient's nostril. Again, the bleeding stopped. The "Native way" worked perfectly. The patient was put on an Alaska Airlines flight to the Anchorage hospital to have a vein sutured to stop the bleeding. A ruptured vein was a fairly rare occurrence for a nosebleed, but not the first I had experienced. The muktuk cure was definitely new. Later that evening, we got a call from the doctor in Anchorage wanting to know what that vile stuff was in the patient's nose, and should they be giving him antibiotics in case it was infectious. Our doctor, with a straight face and in a calm, somewhat condescending voice said:

"I can't believe you're not familiar with our famous muktuk nose plug. Works better than anything we've ever used for a nosebleed. Want us to send you some to keep on hand?"

The Anchorage doctor respectfully declined our offer!

The environment of the northern Inupiaq people is one of the most severe in the world. From the Brooks Range in the south, to the Arctic Ocean in the north, winters are long with extreme cold. Summers are short and cool. These conditions make survival a constant struggle against the elements. Living in the Arctic allowed me to see firsthand the dangers dealt with in an environment the Inupiat continue to face on an ongoing basis.

As a nurse, I wondered how medical conditions and healing had been dealt with in traditional times. From books I had bought in Anchorage, I learned the village spiritual healer had been the shaman. He was a powerful person being both a religious leader and healer. He was the cohesive force who dealt with the religious and psychological needs of the people. Religious beliefs were heavily intertwined with health care. Taboos and social codes prescribed by the shaman were to be followed to avoid illness and ensure good health.

The Inupiaq believe that all living things possess a soul. The soul or Inua of animals were, and still are, paid great respect, for instance, by pouring water over the mouth of the killed animal to offer its spirit a drink of water. It is believed this act of respect pleases the animal's spirit so it will return to earth to replenish man's food supply. The shaman alone was the link to communicating with the spirit world. There were also taboos to follow so as to not anger the spirits whom they believed controlled their world and could cause illness. The shaman brought the society together in a common belief system. After reading about traditional shamanism in the Native culture, I began to believe the shaman was not only a highly regarded spiritual leader, but a much better psychiatrist than our current-day versions for dealing with the mental health of the people. Hopefully they had better outcomes.

Traditionally, illness was looked upon as being either physical or spiritual. People recognized some conditions had a physical cause and could be treated by anyone. A broken limb could be splinted with whalebone or driftwood. Certain plants could provide relief from gastrointestinal ailments. Blubber from sea mammals was used to treat burns and some rashes, and heat along with salves made from plants could relieve aches and muscular pains. But other illnesses not having an apparent physical cause, or ones that lingered over a long period of time, were thought to be spiritual in nature and curable only by the shaman. He alone had power over the spirits. The downfall of the shaman was the direct result of contact with Western civilization.

As early as the mid-1800s, the northern Natives were exposed to White whalers and traders. Whaling stations were established in the Arctic between 1890 and 1910 at Pt. Hope and Point Barrow. Whalers sought baleen, a hard black substance from the whale's mouth used to manufacture corset stays. To them the whale meant economic gain. To the Inupiaq it meant physical survival. The whale provided the bulk of the coastal Native food supply as well as heat and light where whale oil was burned in homes. The Native people also provided baleen for cash to the whalers to help purchase new technology being provided in the form of guns and outboard motors. The shaman imposed many religious taboos on Native whalers to ensure they showed the utmost respect to the whale's spirit.

In his book *Fifty Years Below Zero*, Charles Brower, a White whaler who established a trading post at Point Barrow at the turn of the century, describes the conflicts shamans had with the whalers. In his book he gives an example of how quickly the Natives forsook the shaman's authority. The shaman informed the White whalers of their taboos. For example, if they drank tea while camped on the ice during a hunt, they would offend the whale's spirit, and the whale would not give itself to them. The whalers ignored these taboos and drank tea continually during the first trip. They also landed three whales. The Native whalers who followed the shaman's taboo of not drinking tea did not land any whales. The next trip found Eskimo whalers drinking tea. Unfortunately for the shaman, they also landed a whale. The shaman's authority was undermined in many such ways. Because a shaman practiced alone and was in competition with other shamans, they did not band together or put forth a united resistance to the American intruders who quickly eroded their power.

Not only was the shaman's religious authority assaulted, his role as medical practitioner was also challenged. When the Eskimo population came in contact with the Europeans, they were exposed to diseases previously unknown to them. Epidemics of smallpox, influenza and tuberculosis swept through villages. Having no resistance to these new diseases, Native populations were decimated as a result of the epidemics. Although the non-Native healers were unable to slow the epidemics, nor stop the alarming number of deaths they caused, it was the shaman's reputation and authority that suffered the most for his inability to stop the sickness. He lost the trust of the people over such devastation.

The role of healer was also taken from the shaman by a new Western contact, the medical missionary. Many missionaries sent into the Arctic were trained doctors and nurses who could offer effective treatment for many ailments. This mimicked the shaman's role of addressing illness with both religion and medicine. People readily took to medical technology as those treatments offered cures without rigid taboos or the chance of falling into debt to a shaman. Fear of the spirit world was not part of Western medicine, and modern drugs and treatments were so successful in controlling so many conditions, that the shaman, rather quickly, lost his importance in the society.

Health and religion were tied together through the belief in spirits. Before the mission groups flooded into Alaska, churches came together to carve up the territory between different religious denominations. Two results were that Kotzebue was initially given to the Friends Church, and Southeast Alaska went to the Presbyterians. Over the years, other churches crept in, so that by 1969, Kotzebue hosted the Friends Church plus the Catholic, Episcopal and Baptist faiths. Although the missionaries had good intentions, they, along with the whalers, did things that undermined the culture and spirit of the people. For instance, stopping Native dances, one of my favorite activities and, judging from what I saw, also a favorite traditional pastime. Dances were a time to come together during the long dark months of winter to visit, share laughs, news or gossip and see how the new babies had grown. All cultures have ways of gathering together for entertainment and celebration. It saddened me to learn that missionaries forbade their songs and dances. Because these practices were different, they were thought to be a bad influence. Different, however, does not equate with wrong.

I became upset realizing what missionaries had done to destroy traditional lifestyles, not only by removing songs and dances, but also changing people's Native names to English names and taking away their language. Because of this, I did not support any church mission programs for many years. I realize that what happened was due to the mindset of the times, but for me, it did not justify the damage that was done to the well functioning Native cultures. It is not hard to see how missionaries felt these groups had no religion, so they worked hard to acculturate Natives to Christianity with different sects battling for the most converts. Although the missionaries were focused on religion, their messages unraveled many cultural threads, subduing many traditions besides language, songs, and dances. Years later when a friend from Barrow was visiting me, I showed her an article in *National Geographic* about whaling that featured her brother. The magazine cover said in big bold words "People of the Lost Spirit." The next day as she walked past the magazine, she slapped her hand on the cover and said indignantly, "We haven't lost our spirit." And indeed they have not. In place of shamans, there are now Native ministers and the spirituality and reverence for all life is as strong today as it was hundreds of years ago. God works in many different ways.

This does not mean that traditional medicine was lost. People continue to use what has always worked, and traditional medicine has been carried down by traditional healers. Our doctors respected those healers in the Kotzebue service unit. Patients would come to us if traditional medicine was not as effective as they had hoped, but most times the patient presented first to the hospital for treatment. Modern medicine is not always black and white. There are many grey areas. Traditional healers knew the people, culture and land intimately. Because of this knowledge, they had the ability to heal mental as well as physical conditions.

The most prominent healer during my stay in Kotzebue was Della Keats. She was respected by the people she served and by the medical community. In fact, she became a very well-known healer. Della passed away in 1986. The University of Alaska, Anchorage now offers a health science summer program and scholarships in her honor for Native or underprivileged youth interested in entering the medical field.

Another use of traditional medicine came to our attention when treating a patient who was afflicted with gonococcal arthritis. This condition arises from untreated gonorrhea. It is a painful condition of the joints. Our patient was flown to the hospital from his village whenever he had a flare up. The doctors would admit him and run a course of intravenous antibiotics. If his pain was not brought under control, upon discharge he saw Della Keats. She had a Native tea and ointment she gave him which relieved the pain in his joints. Our patient always came to us for the antibiotics and the doctors always gave their blessing to his visit to the traditional healer afterwards for non-narcotic pain relief. It was modern and traditional medicine working together for the best patient results.

The psychological benefits of the shaman are no longer available. I believe that our mental health system is less effective than traditional shamans dealing with the stress and anxiety of everyday life in communities. Something vital was lost with the demise of the shaman. Often it is the management of mind mixed with cultural values and positive self-esteem that works best to make people stronger.

Chapter 13

Arctic Winters

As I became comfortable in my new workplace, getting to know the people I lived and worked with, my horizons broadened outward to the town. Most of the LPN's (Licensed Practical Nurses) and a large part of ancillary hospital staff were from Kotzebue. It must have been difficult for them to adapt to the constant turnover of doctors and nurses. As a new-comer I was made to feel welcome. I had been working at the hospital for about four months when Agnes, an LPN I worked closely with, said:

"So, how long do you plan to be here Sue? When will you go back to Canada?"

I was surprised at the question and she sounded a little sarcastic in the way it was said.

"It's a two year contract." I answered. "Isn't that the norm with the nurses and doctors that come?"

"Yes, but some of them don't last that long. Guess they don't like it here. Or maybe they don't like us." Agnes and I had worked together nu-merous times, and our work schedules seemed to often coincide. We got along well. She had a great sense of humor and was not afraid to speak her mind. We joked back and forth a lot. I felt comfortable with her, so her question and the tone of it came as a surprise.

"Well," I replied, "unfortunately you will be stuck with me for the full two years. Got a problem with that?" She burst out laughing, then be-came serious when she answered:

"It's hard you know. You guys are always coming and going. We are just getting to really know you and like you, and then you are gone. This happens all the time. Barbara is leaving next month and I really liked her. We've even spent time doing things together after work, like you and I are doing. It's just hard to develop such friendships then you go, and we never see you again."

"Well, you may never want to see me again after working with me for two years. If you like, I'll try hard to make you glad to see me go." She laughed again. Her laugh was loud and infectious and she laughed a lot. She also teased us about some of our ways, pointing out cultural differences between us with accuracy and humor. If we were doing something that was not to her way of thinking, she would let us know.

"This is how we do it," she'd say. "Pay attention. Maybe you could learn something." Everyone liked Agnes. She was fun to be around and we did learn from her. She showed us how to do things in ways more acceptable to our elderly patients. She was constantly telling me to "calm down," when I'd come begging for her to translate my needs to a patient that did not understand English. By the time I engaged her help, I was frustrated at all my failed attempts to get my message across.

"You need to slow down and not talk so fast," she would say. "And you're getting that squeaky voice again. That gonna make the poor patient scared. We only talk like that when something terrible is happening. You White girls always sound excited. Makes me tired just listening to you. And slow down. OK if it's an emergency, but when you go into someone's room, especially an elder, just for patient care, give them time to get used to you. Maybe wait a minute before getting to your point. When you go in talking fast right away, it makes people nervous." She gave me a glimpse of myself from a different cultural point of view. It made me realize how gracious the townspeople were in accepting and befriending us, knowing we would not be around too long. They were forever "breaking in" the new girls. Through my work as a nurse, I was meeting more townspeople and getting to know some on a personal level. If I was invited to someone's home, I never missed the opportunity.

And as my time in the outdoors increased, my city attire was not warm enough, especially when riding my snow machine. I began to look for more weather appropriate clothing. "When in Rome" became my mantra, and I began asking around where I might purchase a fur parka. Not long after, one of our doctors returned from a village trip with a beautiful second-hand parka that was just my size and within my price range. The body was made of silver muskrat bellies with a beautiful wolf and wolverine ruff on the hood. Wolverine fur prevents the moisture of one's breath from freezing. It is worn directly next to the face for protection and is attached to the wolf fur extending beyond it. The sleeves were trimmed with beaver fur. Along the bottom of the coat was a black and white calfskin flower design with beaver fur trim below. It was a perfect fit and most important, it was very warm. I wore it constantly during my two winters in the Arctic.

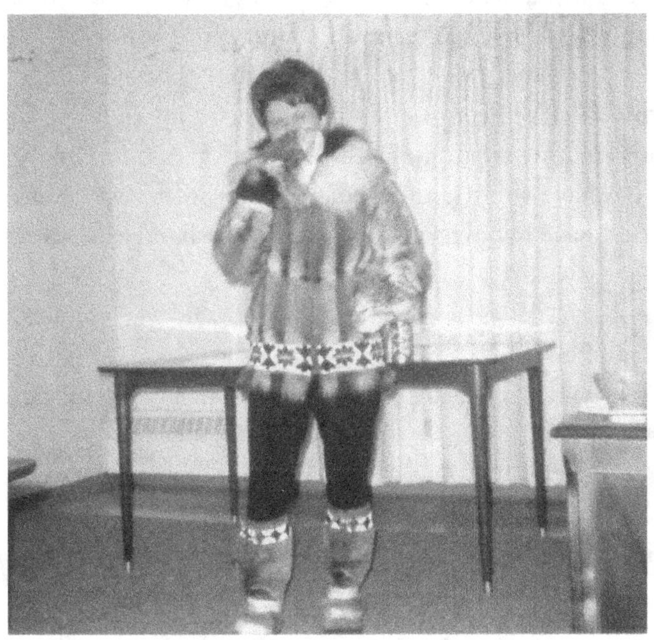

Muskrat Belly Parka

Next came mittens. I had been listening to one of the ladies from town talk about making rabbit skin mittens and had asked her how I could make some for myself. She brought me a pattern and sent me to the store where I could buy rabbit furs. I was told they were partially tanned but I could soften them by scraping them more. I had my own scraper. It was a round piece of metal pipe fitted onto a piece of wood carved and sanded down to fit my hand. Using the pattern, I cut out the pieces and set about softening the skins. I then sewed them together. Traditional sewing was done with sinew, the tough fibrous tissue from animal tendons. After being vested from the animal, the sinew had to be dried and separated into thread-like strings. Dental floss was replacing sinew. It was just as strong and sold in large quantities in the store in town. It was my choice for sewing my mittens.

Mary and Joan, two of my fellow RN's living just down from me in the quarters, stopped by as I was scrapping the skins to make them softer and more pliable.

"Now what are you doing?" asked Mary as she looked at me sitting on the floor of my apartment scrubbing as hard as I could without putting holes into the skins. I was concentrating on getting just the right amount of pressure.

"I think you've been spending too much time in town," she scoffed. "Is someone training you to do their work for them now?"

"These have been tanned but need to be softened some more," I replied "See, I have my own scraper." Betty's husband made it for me to fit my hand for easy use."

"I heard that urine is used to tan hides," said Mary as she bent down to sniff at the skins."

"Yes," I said, "I heard that too, but I'm Just using oil. See how soft they are getting?"

"So what are you going to do with them when you're done?" asked Joan.

"I'm making mittens. My hands get cold when I'm on my snow machine with just knit mittens or gloves, so I decided to get something warmer."

"You know you can buy fur mittens at the store? You don't have to make them yourself," said Joan.

"Where is your sense of adventure?" I asked. "Don't you want to try new things and learn new skills while you're here?"

"I'm quite content to buy the finished product made by the experts to take back home to show friends and family. I have no desire to tan and sew it myself. Besides, I'm not good at sewing," she replied.

Later that week they stopped by to see my progress and I had to agree with them that I too, was not so good at sewing. But sew them I did. To my great disappointment they were not very warm.

"No, no," said my teacher Betty when I showed her my finished product. "These are only liners. The fur side goes against your hands inside some heavy skin mittens."

And so I took my hunt for warmth to the store where I purchased a pair of wolf head mittens made from the hide and fur of a wolf's head with beaded eye holes and beaver fur around the wrists. They were attached to knit cords that rested on my shoulders and ran down the sleeves of my parka to keep the mittens in place so they could be slipped off to dangle from my wrists for any chore, then quickly slipped back on when done. I turned my rabbit skin mittens inside out and used them to line the wolf heads. Now I was ready for anything the arctic climate could throw at me.

The other challenge in winter, along with adjusting one's outer wear, was the long dark days and nights. When I arrived in January, it was dark almost twenty-four hours a day. If I worked the day shift, I missed the few hours of twilight where some remnant of light peeked over the horizon. I was slowly adapting to constant darkness, but nurses are also, unfortunately, blessed with shift work. After working a week or two of days, the next two weeks on night shift, then switching to evenings, any sense of time soon became blurred. On one occasion I came home tired from a busy day shift and decided to take a nap before dinner. Slipping out of my uniform, I fell into bed and into a deep sleep. I awoke with a start, looked at the clock and saw 7:30. I was sure I would be late for work which started at eight. I threw on my uniform, brushed my teeth, ran a wet cloth over my face, a comb through my hair, pulled on my parka and boots and ran out the door. Knowing I wouldn't have time for breakfast, I rushed past the cafeteria, which seemed awfully quiet. Come to think of it, I hadn't seen the emergency room nurse on my way in either, but I was in too much of a hurry to process the obvious. When I got to the nurses' station, I apologized profusely for being late. When they asked me what I was late for, I began to realize that perhaps the 7:30 was p.m. not a.m. and, in fact, that was the case. It took a long time to live that one down.

"Here she comes" they'd say. "I wonder what time she thinks it is?"

"So Sue, are you here for the day shift or are you late for the evening shift?"

And I would smile and say, "I'll be happy to go back home if you don't want me." And they would laugh and tell me they'd take me on for any shift. They just enjoyed reminding me of my moment of total disorientation.

People's reaction to the extended darkness varied. One or two of the girls fought constant feelings of fatigue and napped frequently on their days off. Their constant yawning could make the most alert and active of us feel sleepy. I tried to avoid them if I had plans that day, lest I, too, ended up napping on my couch.

"Hey Jean," I'd ask at lunch, "want go to the base with me this afternoon? The movie sounds great and the one o'clock rec run can take us." Jean was a California girl and liked to socialize and party.

"Sounds good," she would reply, "I'm just going to take a short nap, but I'll be at the door by one." And that would be the last I saw of Jean for the afternoon. At dinner she seemed surprised she had slept so long.

I was gifted a cat named Missy from one of the departing nurses. I think Missy was used to a new owner every couple of years, as she adapted to both me, and my apartment, very well. The year she was with me she made her bed in a corner under my clothes rack in the bathroom hallway. My lap seemed to be her favorite place to sit when I was home. She provided warmth and companionship during long winter evenings. She was no longer a kitten, but did have some wild moments where she would tear around the apartment in circles. Her presence was widely known in the quarters, so I knew she would be returned to me if she escaped into the hallway. But I was careful to keep her contained as I knew she would not survive if she were to get outside. Someone mentioned it was against the rules to have pets in our apartments, but Missy was declawed, I suspect by a doctor in the distant past. And two of the doctors had dogs, so I did not feel any guilt over my friendly, loving cat. I did not, however, attempt to clarify the rules.

Darkness and storms kept us inside a good part of the time. Having my snow machine was an incentive for me to be outside as often as possible, but I also kept busy reading and letter writing on stormy days. I too felt the occasional darkness fatigue, but getting out of the quarters helped me keep a normal night-to-day schedule even on days off. In spite of the lack of daylight, I managed to spend a considerable amount of time outdoors exploring around town on my snow machine.

I began visiting people in town although doing so caused me to step out of my comfort zone. Since there were no phones in town, I could not call ahead. I'd arrive at their door unannounced. From my upbringing, dropping in was not good manners. Were they home? Were they busy? Would I be interrupting something? But I would gather my courage and knock on the door anyway. Someone would holler "Come in." That caused even more discomfort. Never did anyone come to answer the door. And that was the inner door. I learned I had to step into the arctic entryway where outdoor paraphernalia was kept, and knock on the inner door in order to be heard in the house: past the coats, boots, guns, shovels and all manner of things used outdoors. Being so close to guns made me nervous. Being asked to come in when they obviously didn't know who was knocking, always amazed me. People were so trusting. I was always greeted with smiles and offered tea. I drank many jars of tea with new found friends. And I do mean jars. I was served tea in jam jars, pickle jars and other unique sized jars. I am happy to report, tea is just as good in jam jars as in fancy teacups. More important is time spent visiting with friends.

But then, without fail, once I was given tea, a long silence ensued. I would try to strike up a conversation but for the first fifteen or so minutes I was always unsuccessful.

"How are you today?"

"Good."

"Pretty nice day today. No more snow."

"Yep."

"I'm looking forward to spring. Seeing Kotzebue without snow."

"Uh, huh."

"Not so busy at the hospital this week. Sent everyone home."

"mmm."

"Glad to see you got better so quick. Still doing OK?"

"Yes. I'm good."

And I would give up and start an internal dialogue with myself:

"Maybe I've come at a bad time."

"Maybe I'm interrupting something"

"See, my mother was right. Never visit without a head's up. Maybe I should have sent someone ahead to see if it was a good time."

"Maybe they are uncomfortable with me. Maybe I'm talking too much."

"But they did say to come by for tea. Maybe they were just being polite

and didn't think I'd really come."

I did not understand the silence that occurred every time I visited and had an even harder time enduring it. I strived to fill the silence with endless talking or, as my Scottish grandfather called it, "endless blithering." I was good at that. But my words were met with stoic silence. My babble was countered with polite but silent smiles and questions answered with one or two syllables. Feeling terribly uncomfortable, I would quickly drink my tea, thank them and start to leave. Their reaction told me that wasn't right either, as they looked quite surprised at my leaving. One time as I was preparing to bolt, Iva, the mother of the family I was visiting said:

"You're leaving? But you just got here."

That gave me a hint that whatever the silence was, it didn't mean I should assume the worst and leave. I found it interesting that I continued to feel the need to cling to my learned cultural ways and manners. If there wasn't phone service, calling ahead certainly wasn't a prerequisite for visiting. It had nothing to do with manners. In the middle of the dark and dreary winter months, people were happy to have visitors.

So I began to tough out the silence and, low and behold, after what seemed to me an eternity, people would start a conversation and I would have a wonderful visit. I just had to make it through the silence. In my culture, we often finish each other's sentences and sometimes we all talk at once. Here a person's actions seemed to speak volumes. In the Native culture, silent observation appeared to be a way of getting to know you and to assess your mood by your demeanor at that particular time. I could see that perhaps, in my culture, if we spent more quiet time with each other, we too would sense more than words alone can convey. Maybe silence is golden.

CHAPTER 14

Surviving Winter

My first winter in the Arctic introduced me to cold as I had never experienced. I was from the prairies but lived in a large city where the blowing snow was subdued by tall buildings and disposed of by many snowplows. Calgary weather was cold enough to require my dad to plug the car into an electrical outlet to make sure it started in minus temperatures, but the chill I experienced in the Arctic was a bitter cold that penetrated to the bone. Winters back home in Alberta were punctuated now and then with warm Chinook winds. These dry winds, after depositing their moisture in the Rocky Mountains, swept across the prairies warming the temperature and melting the snow. There were no Chinooks in the Arctic.

In the information pamphlets I was given before coming north, the snowfall was described as moderate to heavy, but when the wind is blowing and the swirling snow all but blinding you, especially when sitting on a snow machine, there appears to be more snow than is measured. Snow blew endlessly across the tundra until it hit town and piled in huge drifts against anything in its way. Blizzards and severe snowstorms often led to whiteouts where visibility was reduced to zero. Those conditions brought the town to a standstill. The frightening thing about whiteouts is that all sense of direction is lost. This happens whether one is on foot, a snow machine or in a vehicle. Wind also affected one's perception of cold. To me, 20 below felt just as cold as 40 below but if the wind was blowing, as it most often did, the windchill made one feel much colder than the actual temperature on the thermometer and could become unbearable in a very short time. Blowing wind causes the body to lose more heat.

There were three young fellows from town who decided to construct an igloo. They did it for the fun of it and to prove they had the skill to do it. Igloos were not used as permanent housing here. Occasionally they were erected in an emergency, for instance, when out hunting and a storm arose. The young men acquired quite a crowd, and I was right up in the front. They made a very large cylindrical igloo and allowed people to crawl in and out to experience it. I gave my camera to another nurse and in I went. As I came crawling out, I had her snap a very posed picture. I sent it to my folks and my mother told me the next time she ran into Mrs. Smith, my friend Lynne's mother, she pulled out the picture and showed it to her saying:

"Look, here is a new picture Sue sent. How do you like her new home?"

Mom was not prepared for her explosive reaction.

"Oh my goodness, you can't mean she is living in an igloo? How could you let her go way up there and live like that? Doesn't she get cold? Why would she even want to stay there? You need to talk her into coming back."

Mom was shocked at her reaction and quickly let her know she was just teasing her and that I lived in a very modern apartment. We had a good laugh. Mom pulled that picture out frequently but never got that reaction again.

Emerging from an Igloo Built for Fun

Until I could recognize individuals by their colorful parkas, I had no idea who I was passing on the street. Fur ruffs and scarves covered all but the eyes and most eyes were pointing down to keep the blowing snow out. Those weather conditions were best spent in my residence reading books, listening to my reel-to-reel music and writing letters to friends and family.

I loved attending the Native dances. It was one of my favorite activities during the dark days of winter. In summer the town dance group put on a nightly show for the tourists. In winter, dances were for themselves, to keep in practice and for the sheer joy of it. Dancing was a fun way to be socially and physically active during those dark cold months. There were two ladies I worked with who seemed to know when a dance was planned, but getting that information was not an easy feat. It was in the way I was told.

"Maybe tomorrow night," they would say, or "Maybe on Friday." It was never a firm date or time but I learned that even though they said "maybe," it meant the dance would occur on that day and time. It was a glaring difference in communication styles. In my urban lifestyle, by necessity, life rhythms and activities are set by the clock. Traditional Native rhythms are set by the seasons and the animals they rely on for subsistence. It was explained to me that since no one could predict the future, any number of things could change before any event. Hence the vagueness so often expressed. When we set dates and times, we expect them to happen when planned, barring an act of God. Well, God did act one night!

It was Saturday and the dance was scheduled for "maybe around 7 p.m." I was off duty and eager to attend. I looked forward to dancing with the group. I was becoming less shy about joining in on invitational or common dances where everyone is invited to join in. There were also story dances, but there were rules about who owned those dances and therefore who could dance them. Often the ownership belonged to a specific village. The common dance was open to everyone. For me, moving in rhythm to the beat of the drums was exhilarating.

It had been snowing all day. After dinner the wind picked up and the weather turned nasty. It was minus 20 degrees with a wind chill that made it feel much lower. I was proud that I was able to start my snow machine. I arrived at Cudd Hall, where the dances were held, only to find the door locked and no one in sight. I had been told "maybe 7 o'clock" and was disappointed no one was showing up. I waited 20 minutes in the cold and stormy darkness before heading back home. Next Monday, at work, thinking maybe I had got the dance date or time wrong, I asked my source what had happened. She looked at me as if I was joking, or maybe a little crazy, and said:

"You were there?"

"Sure," I said, "but no one else showed up." She looked at me another minute in utter disbelief then leaned in to me and quietly said:

"We don't go out in a blizzard."

Another "dumb tunic" moment. It was around that time that I set weather limits on when I'd venture out.

Entertainment in my apartment and dancing to the music of my own culture, was harder to attain. I essentially missed out on two years of pop culture including beatniks and hippies. I also missed the music of the day and ordered a large free standing tape recorder from J.C. Penny's. I then visited the homes of two coworkers in town to tape the latest music from their teenager's tapes. Even their songs were not the latest breaking hits. My tape deck became popular at get togethers in the quarters. We practiced our dance steps now and then and once had a dance down in the recreation room with some of the boys from the base. I was finding ways to keep myself entertained on winter evenings at home.

There were no computers, no Internet or instant messaging and the cost of phone calls home limited them to special occasions. I wrote my parents once a week and made tapes of the dogs howling and the drumming and singing from town dances to send them. I also wrote frequent letters to close friends, two of whom sent my letters back to me after I returned home, suggesting that I write about my experiences. Now, fifty years later, I am finally doing it, reliving those amazing two years and reaffirming how very special they were to me.

I kept my ears open for events in town that I might want to see or take part in. My coworkers from town were a wonderful source and willing to invite me to things they knew I would enjoy. But opportunities came from many sources. One day, Lorraine my Canadian counterpart came banging on my door.

"Sue, have you seen a polar bear hide yet?" Lorraine, like me, was also interested enough in town life to visit people. As a result, we were often invited to see and do interesting things we would otherwise not know about. Lorraine bought a motorcycle, so between the two of us we had the ability to travel out of town most any time of year. Spring breakup being the sloppy, slushy exception.

"I thought the bear hides went from the ice pack to the planes and were taken outside by the hunters," I replied. It turned out the hides were cleaned and tanned by ladies in town before the hunters took them home. Lorraine had found one such lady and had been watching her work on a hide in her home.

"You won't believe it," she said. "This hide is as large as her living room. You've got to go and watch Selma working on it." I did not know Selma and did not want to go knocking on someone's door I didn't know.

"Could you take me please?" I asked her.

"I've just spent time there. I'll tell you what house it is." I did not want to go alone. It was time to up my whiny voice.

"Oh please come with me. Don't make me go alone. She doesn't know me and it could be awkward."

"For her or you?" Lorraine quipped. "Buck up, go on, you can do it." It was time to bargain hard.

"I'll let you borrow my snow machine if you come with me now," I begged. "Please!"

"Twice." she said with a grin on her face. "Let me borrow it twice."

When I agreed, she caved. Off we went to Selma's house.

As we entered, Lorraine introduced me to Selma who smiled and waved her bloodied hand from an equally bloodied hide at us in greeting. There were two small children in the kitchen doorway watching their mom. After we settled in, they began watching us, as they huddled close together talking in their Native tongue and giggling nonstop. Selma was scraping and tanning the biggest polar bear hide I had ever seen, both standing and not standing on four legs. It was larger than the total floor area of the main room of her house. Granted the room was small, but it made the hide seem enormous. She was on her knees hovering over the hide, scraping hard and fast. She had a rhythm going and moved from one area to the next, scraping with her ulu in rapid succession. An ulu is a semi-circular blade inserted into a handle made of wood or bone. It is manipulated back and forth with a wrist flicking action that separates tissue and fat from the hide. When the scrapping was finished, the tanning process to smooth and soften the hide began. We watched in awe as she cleaned the bits of fat and flesh away. I was sure she would be spending more than one or two days of hard arm work to finish such a large hide.

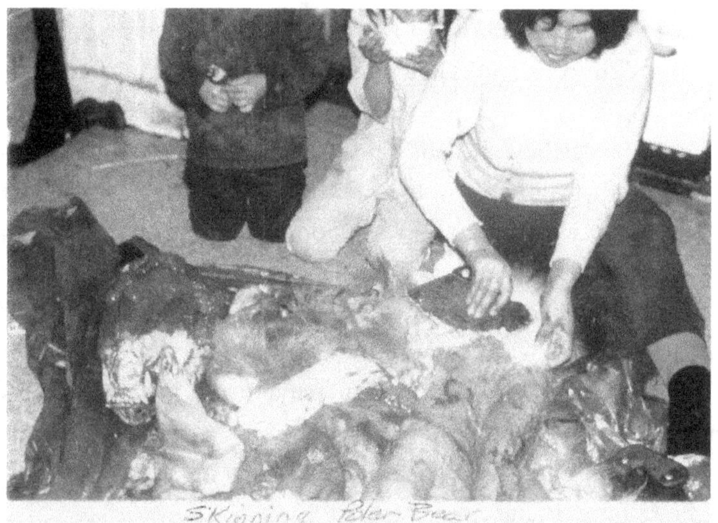

Scraping a Polar Bear Hide

I had scrubbed the rabbit skins for my gloves with a tanning tool consisting of a metal cylinder attached to a wooden handle that would soften my skins. I had also obtained my own ulu. On a day in late winter, as I was passing by a coworker's house in town, I saw he and his wife Anna busy working on some very large sea animal. Curiosity stopped me in my tracks.

"What is that Will?" I said. "And what are you doing to it?"

"It's an oogruk and we're skinning it," he replied. An ugruk is a large bearded seal.

"Wow, can I help?" I asked.

"Don't have another ulu," he replied.

"I do," I practically yelled. "I have my own and I'll run over to quarters and get it. Then can I help?" They both started laughing.

"Sure," said Will. "If we teach you real good, maybe you can do all of it and we'll just watch."

"OK!" I said, and ran as fast as I could to retrieve my ulu and join them. Anna very patiently showed me what to do, the angle to hold the ulu, the amount of pressure to apply and how to tug at the loosened skin to keep the ulu going forward to evenly separate the flesh from the hide. Soon I was picking up speed and better yet, I was making clean slices between the skin and blubber. In other words, I was becoming accurate. Willie nodded and smiled and Anna assured me I was doing well. I must have been as they continued to let me help. After a long stretch of working, we broke for lunch. I thanked them for letting me help, washed up in my quarters and headed to the hospital dining room.

I was very proud of myself and couldn't wait to share my accomplishment with others.

"You'll never guess what I've been doing this morning," I said with a cunning grin.

"Do tell," said Norm Gaines our hospital administrator.

"I have been helping Will and Anna skin an ugruk. It was huge and I got pretty good at it. I have my own ulu." I was bursting with pride, and of course I was sure they all would be envious of me.

"Well that explains it," said Mary.

"Explains what?" I asked.

"We wondered what that strong odor was coming from you."

Totally deflated, I slunk back to my apartment to shower and change.

Dog Team

CHAPTER 15

Dogs

The transition from traditional dogsleds in Arctic Alaska to snow machines began during the 1950's. By the time I arrived in 1969, snowmobiles were the choice of transportation in winter. Boats on the many waterways were the choice in summer. People often lamented they missed traveling by dogsled. They also claimed dogs were less trouble than modern day machines.

"Dogs' don't break down," said Wilson, one of the hospital maintenance men. "And dog 'fuel' is cheaper. They like fish and my Mrs. is good at catching lots of fish," he boasted. In winter, people went ice fishing off Front Street for dog food as well as people food. There were plenty of dogs in town, but they were not so much seen, as heard. These were not the impressive huskies depicted in photographs with heads held proudly high and tails curved upward on muscular bodies. Nor were they cherished pets that children ran and played with in the streets. I honestly don't know why the dogs were kept. Someone suggested it was a hold on to the old culture. Even though most people in town no longer ran dogs, many kept them around. Perhaps they felt they were insurance in case the "iron dogs" failed them. These were scrawny, often snarly dogs tethered to stakes in yards. They were spaced apart to avoid any fighting with each other. Sometimes, after a storm, they were completely blanketed in snow and not seen at all. As a newcomer, I was warned not to take short cuts through yards. The dogs were not people friendly; in fact, they could be quite ill tempered. No one wanted to surprise them by stumbling into their snowy beds behind or between the houses. Those who did often ended up in our Emergency Room with severe dog bites.

Among the junk that accumulated in people's yards in summer, the dogs ate, slept and existed. As I walked by them heading back from town to quarters, they would rise to a standing position to gaze at me with droopy eyes, straining on their restraints to get closer to me. These dog's tails did not wag and they did not jump up and down with anticipation. It took just one dog to begin a dismal sounding lament before the rest joined in. Their sad sounding wails followed me down the street until I was out of sight. It made me feel sorry for them as they seemed to be crying for attention. From time to time, the town had a curfew. When the siren sounded each evening, it set off a chorus from every dog in town. I wondered what it was about the sound of the siren that caused such howling, and what they were trying to say with their racket. More than once I fell asleep to the mournful strains of the dogs. It made my spine tingle to hear, and I would be thankful to be indoors under warm covers. Whatever they were trying to say, it left me with an eerie sad feeling.

Huskies love to run and were bred for the purpose of hauling sleds filled with equipment, supplies and people. Since the dogs had been re-placed with snow machines and didn't often get the chance to do what they loved, perhaps their howls broadcast how abandoned they felt. The dogs became excited and animated when their owners brought sleds around and began loading them. They began yipping, barking, jumping up and down and working themselves into a frenzy. Their excitement was palpable. But when the sled was hooked to a snow machine and driven away, that excitement ended abruptly and they again began their soulful howls. There was no mistaking that message. They knew they had been replaced and were expressing their sorrow. My heart went out to them.

Occasionally, a dog would break loose from its tie down and trot victoriously through town, taunting the other dogs. That victory lap definitely set every chained dog in town howling protest to their lack of freedom. Along with upsetting the other dogs, they could become a real problem. Loose dogs tended to join wild wolf packs. In time these dogs became wild. Newly freed dogs associated food with the towns they came from, often returning. It was not unusual for them to be followed by wild dogs, either directly into town or close enough to be a danger to those traveling to and from town. People worried about children being attacked. The danger from wild dogs or loose dogs that had spent some time with wild packs was rabies. This was a real health hazard to everyone in town. Villages would keep these dogs in check by running them out of town, but if they returned and became a nuisance, they were shot. The head was removed and sent to Richard, our sanitation engineer, for rabies testing. It was fun to hear his yelp followed by a few choice words when he opened a box with a dog head inside, at least until he became suspicious of any box he received and prepared himself for opening it. We teased him to no end. Fortunately, this did not happen too often.

"Well, you'd holler too if you opened a package to see lifeless eyes in a dog's head looking up at you. And I mean looking, as with the eyes open, staring at you as soon as you open the box. Makes me feel the rest of him is hidden underneath and he's going to jump out and attack me any minute. I wish they would shut the eyes when they package those heads, and wrap a cloth around it so it isn't right there staring at me when I open it. Better to think it was sleeping than ready to bark and bite you in the next second."

Dog sledding or mushing, as it is called in Alaska, has become synonymous with northern culture. One of our doctors went to great lengths to have his own dog team. He owned a large handmade wood sled and, in addition to his beloved German Shepherd, borrowed four dogs from a man in town whenever he wanted to run a team. I eagerly expressed an interest in his newfound activity.

"You're mushing dogs? When are you going again? Where do you go? What do I need to do for an invite to join you? Seriously, what!" He graciously invited me to join him the following Saturday, and I promised to babysit next time he planned dinner out with his wife. The day arrived. In preparation, I filled my thermos with hot coffee, packed some cheese and crackers, my survival kit and extra gloves. I was ready for a new adventure.

Getting dogs ready for an outing is tedious work. They need to be harnessed, placed in two lines side by side, with one lead dog in front. There are other formations, but this was the only way I saw it done in Kotzebue. Often fights would break out between the side-by-side dogs during or after harnessing, which required disciplining. This was done by the doctor, but after he had them hitched, he went back into his house for something, leaving me alone with them. Two of the dogs, started nipping at each other, then snarling until they sounded like they would kill each other. When sled dogs fight, their harnesses become twisted and tangled, sometimes so badly one has to undo them and start over. And if two dogs decided to argue with each other, it didn't take long, if not quickly stopped, for the other dogs to join in, causing disaster in the whole team. We were ready to go, and I did not want to waste time redoing harnesses. My reaction was fast and wild.

"Oh no, no you don't!" I yelled at the top of my lungs, rising from my sitting position on the porch stairs. "Hey, stop, whoa, break it up!" I screamed and jumped behind them grabbing their harnesses with both hands to pull them apart. "Hey, knock it off dogs!" I hollered, pulling so tight on their strands I was almost choking them. Sit! Sit!" I hissed as I knelt between them to keep them separated. They began to calm down. I'm not sure who was more surprised, the doctor, as he came dashing out the door to see what the commotion was, or the dogs I had descended upon yelling and screeching like a crazed animal myself. The doctor took over, and just in time, as my energy was fading fast.

"Whatever possessed you to jump between two snarling, dogs," he asked when things were back to normal.

"It took so long to get them ready to go. I just didn't want us to have do it all over again," I replied.

"But I'm the one that did it. You just sat and watched," he said.

"And now we're still ready to go. You can thank me later," I replied.

"I'll have to be careful not to cross you at work," he said with a grin. "Now that I've seen what you're capable of!"

I had kind of surprised myself and realized, once things calmed down, that my reaction could have had serious consequences for me. I was careful not to be the one breaking up any more dog fights. I hadn't thought it through before leaping into action.

At first, we took turns sitting in the sled and standing on the sled runners. A good musher is not bashful or quiet spoken, although I think the dogs were so eager to go, that anything out of the driver's mouth would have them leaping into action. My favorite position while mushing that day became riding the sled runners. One felt every bump riding in the sled. There was a blanket lining the bottom of his sled, but we didn't have the soft thick caribou furs I had seen on Native sleds to cushion the blows.

"Since I saved us time back there," I said, "I think I should ride the runners."

"You're sure you don't want to sit and rest after such a vigorous workout?" he chided.

"No, no, you harnessed the dogs. You deserve a rest."

And so I was happy standing on the two long narrow wood runners that extended out on either side behind the sled. In this position one could shout commands to the dogs. The driver controls the dogs with sharp commands: "mush," to get going, "gee," to turn right, "haw," for left turn and "whoa" to stop. In order to not jar one's spine, the person on the runners needs to keep their knees unlocked so they can gently bend from their knees as the runners hit bumps in the trail. Since we were seldom on established trails on these outings, we frequently needed to holler directions to the dogs. They responded best to strong sounding authority. I used my loudest and gruffest voice to send my commands. When going at a slow enough pace, the person riding the runners can jump off and jog along behind the sled holding tight to the handles, ready to jump back on board if the speed picks up or the legs get tired. That meant paying close attention. It was a lovely day. The sky was clear. The snow was packed from so much activity on the ice in front of town. I had jumped from the runners and was comfortably jogging behind the sled when something small and fast darted in front of the dogs, catching their attention. In an instant they picked up speed. Although I maintained a tight grip on the handles of the sled, I was jerked forward and was being dragged from the waist down before I realized what had happened.

"Help," I hollered. "HELP, HELP, STOP THE DOGS!" I cried. Thankfully the doctor had realized something was wrong when the dogs lurched forward. He began hollering "whoa" at the top of his voice. I sputtered everything except that magic word to stop them. Fortunately, I did not loosen my grip on the handles. Doing so would have left me far behind and flat on my face in the snow. When they finally stopped, the lead dog turned to look at me. I swear he was grinning before he snapped his head to face front while I called him out. Running the dogs allowed me to experience a time when dogsleds were the only means of winter transportation in the Arctic.

One clear, chilly sunny day as I was driving my snow machine down Front Street wearing my newly acquired fur coat and gloves, I passed two men with a very large camera talking to one of the town elders who was standing on the ice beside a sled and team of seven husky dogs. I recognized him. He was one of the few men in town that actually ran his dogs now and then. It was a wonderful sight and once or twice I had stopped to watch them moving over the snow and ice. One of the men came running after me, catching up as I parked Little Red in front of the post office.

"Excuse me ma'm," he said huffing and puffing from running down Front Street.

"I'm from *National Geographic*. We're here filming a documentary on life in the Arctic. Mr. Tupuq has kindly hitched up his dog team and will be running them across the Sound off Front Street for us to film. You have on a fine fur parka, oh, and your gloves are beautiful too. Would you consider being in Mr. Tupuq's sled while we film?" I was delighted, and back I went to join the group.

I was introduced to Mr. Tupuq who agreed to let me come along. As I was settling into his sled, complete with a caribou hide draped over my legs and another to sit on, the man with the camera knelt down beside me.

"No offense," he whispered, but would you mind pulling the hood of your coat up over your head enough so it covers your face a little?"

"Of course not," I replied. "You want both the wolf and wolverine of the ruff to show don't you?"

"Actually, he replied, I just don't want your face to show.

"What," I sputtered. "What's wrong with my face?"

Then Mr. Tupuq leaned down and laughingly blurted out, "Not brown enough nurse. Face too white. If people see, they gonna know you not the 'real deal.'"

We had a good laugh over that. So, if you ever see a National Geographic film with a dog team, a Native man riding the runners, and a young lady in furs sitting in the sled, it just might be this White girl in Native dress.

And so the beloved dogs of the North have been replaced by iron dogs. Technology brings improvements but there are always tradeoffs. Change in one area often affects in other areas. Gas is expensive but harnesses were challenging. No more dog fights but jobs are needed to pay for machines and gas. Since the dogs have been mostly relegated to yards, it appears that snow machines have won the popular vote. A way of life has been replaced.

Dog Team and Snow Machine
(the old and the new)

CHAPTER 16

The Base

Perhaps the biggest outlet for entertainment for the nurses during my two years in Kotzebue was the Air Force base, an outpost located five lonely miles out of town. After passing the airport and Federal Aviation Station on the edge of town, the view was either flat scrubby tundra, or in winter, miles of undisturbed white snow as far as the gravel or snow plowed road took us. There were two interesting visual distractions on that road on our way to the base. One was a jet, the same size as those still coming and going from town every day. It was sitting on the side of the road just feet past the town's city limits. The story was that it had landed with its tires still retracted. No one was hurt and the plane was still intact. This had happened some time before I was there. I questioned a couple of gals from town, but they didn't seem to want to talk about it.

"So what airline was it, Alma?"

"Don't know."

"How could anyone not know. It says so on the side of every plane and the markings are different for each airline."

"Yeah, but that got painted over real quick. We were asked not to take pictures of it before they painted over the airline name, and were asked not to talk about it even though we knew who it was. The truck came and guys on ladders painted off the name and markings. Then pretty quick they tow it out that road and leave it there. It's been there for long time now." And she never did tell me which airline it was. Although it was pretty apparent to me, it was not important enough to me to push for an answer.

One place that became humorously visible on our trips to the base when the darkness of winter subsided was the Kotzebue National Forest. It was a forest of one tree that was planted by servicemen beside the road to the base in the 1950s. It was surrounded by a little white picket fence with the sign declaring it a forest. There are no other trees for miles in Kotzebue.

Kotzebue National Forest

The base was a radar site, part of the DEW (Distant Early Warning) system that stretched across the top of America. This site monitored air traffic in the area. Russia was where the eyes, or rather the radar, of the base was trained. I was told by more than one airman that some years prior a Russian MIG (Soviet military fighter aircraft) had flown undetected under our radar and was not noticed until the pilot requested clearance to land at the Fairbanks airport. The airmen at the Kotzebue base took their jobs seriously. If any foreign or unscheduled plane breached our border, American military planes were dispatched from Galena, Alaska, another base further southeast of Kotzebue, to escort the "lost" pilot back into his own airspace. I was led to understand this happened on a number of occasions. The Russians were constantly testing our powers of observation, our capabilities and definitely our response times. I had the exciting pleasure of being smuggled into the radar room one time where I watched the afternoon scheduled jet arrive and a small plane fly across the screen while the officer who smuggled me in explained the workings of the system and what they were on the lookout for as I huddled at the base of his work station.

For the nurses, the base offered music and dancing, often with a live band, movies, and NCO and Officer's clubs. It was also an ongoing education in the social habits of the opposite sex for all the nurses, including myself. Since the base was out of town, it was the only place to go for a drink when the town was voted "dry." If we wanted a bottle of wine in our cupboards for personal use or entertaining, there was always a "friend" at the base who would be happy to gift us one from their PX. And the men always brought us a bottle of something when they were the recipients of our home-cooking. They were our very willing dance partners, both at get-togethers in our residence and at the base.

I made the trek with whoever else was off duty any particular evening of the week, with weekends being the desired evening we all wanted to go as the non-commissioned officers' club was always full on a Saturday night and music and alcohol flowed constantly. The base housed a hundred men and was rated an isolation post. As a result, the attention paid to the nurses when we arrived for an evening was somewhat overwhelming. It certainly bolstered our egos and made us feel like celebrities. I soon realized that my popularity was based on the fact that I was one of very few single white females in the region. I could have been an ugly duckling with an annoying habit or two, and would still have been popular. Although that realization burst the celebrity illusion, I wasn't about to deny myself all that wonderful attention. And most of the time it was wonderful.

I was privileged to attended a U.S.O. show held at the base: wonderful live entertainment, and a treat for everyone. The comedian was hilarious but some of his jokes reminded me of my misguided impressions of Alaska and Eskimos before I came to live here. Turns out they don't live in igloos and they don't kiss by rubbing noses. There was lots of singing and dancing and the costumes were beautiful. There were also lots of girls in the performances and the boys at the base were eager to entertain them when the show was over. We nurses definitely dropped to second place that night, so we took the rec run back to town after the show and let the boys impress the visiting girls.

Whenever you have a hundred isolated men away from family and friends, things can go many different ways. When a high-ranking married officer began making advances toward me the first winter, it put a damper on my trips to the base. I noticed the enlisted men took many of their cues from the officers and when they were rowdy or aggressive, so were the men. The turnover time at the base was just one year tour of duty, so with a change in officers the next year, there was also an attitude change for the better in our interactions with enlisted the men. It helped when I later began dating Jim, one of the lieutenants. Dating an officer took me out of reach of excessive attention from the enlisted men.

Many of the men sought out Native girls from town for companionship. I wanted to warn those girls to be careful. They too were the objects of very lonely men who could offer them things that some of their own men might not be able to. These men had a job and pay checks. Most young men in town did not. A number of girls over the years had married men from the base. Many returned with the same sad story. They went south with their new husbands to places so very different from their home and had problems adjusting and fitting in. The culture shock and loneliness they experienced was too much to deal with and they ended up divorced and back home, often with one or two little ones to care for on their own.

After my initial uncomfortable experiences at the base, new men arrived and most of the ones I came to know my second year were polite and fun to be around. We enjoyed getting to know them and invited many to dinners and get togethers in the recreation room or in our quarters. The older married men were always appreciative of someplace to go off base for female company, good conversation and a home cooked meal. Of course, some of the young married men forgot they were married, and there were those who were a little too aggressive and a source of annoyance and aggravation. We nurses tried hard to avoid their advances. More often, from an offhand comment, it was the older married men we had befriended that quietly came to our aid, and when they did, those who were bothering us were never again a problem.

The base ran rec runs, large trucks for their men to go to and from town. They also transported civilians to activities at the base. That first year the nurses travelled mostly in groups. Some planning had to be done before going to an evening at the base. For me it was a decision whether to drink hard liquor or beer. If I had those wonderful mixed drinks, many that I was sampling for the first time, I ran the risk of losing good judgement if the sampling became one too many. If I chose beer, I would inevitably be spending a lot of good conversation time in the washroom (bathroom, as the Americans call it). The other problem was that when we first settled in at the NCO club, someone would ask us what we wanted to drink and for the rest of the evening there would be a never-ending line of what we had ordered placed in front of us. It was easy to overdo when there was an unlimited supply. At first, being somewhat naive and not wanting to hurt anyone's feelings, I made a valiant attempt to finish them. I wasn't much of a drinker and no one listened when I'd say "that's enough thank you." Later, I realized that perhaps those drinks were lavished on us for a purpose other than generosity and had no qualms leaving them untouched. I was learning quickly and had a few good friends with me to watch out for my best interests. Or maybe it was just that we were in survival mode. Occasionally I'd ask for a glass of pop, but the fellows didn't seem to hear that either.

The criteria for whether or not we went to the base on any given weekend was based on whether the rec run showed up in town and in front of the nurse's residence. If the base truck was running, we went. Perhaps we should have checked the weather first, but consensus was if the vans were running, that was safe enough for us. The storms would shut down the runs when it was deemed unsafe to drive, but the temperature caused other problems.

A number of times the pipes in the base's main floor restrooms froze and left the only functioning bathrooms on the second floor where the men resided. When that happened, we would be escorted to the bathroom by at least two airmen. One would go in and clear the room of any men, then they would both stand guard while we were inside. We never knew when it would happen, but it was something we asked about each time we went, as frozen pipes would definitely rule out a beer night. Frozen pipes would swing me to the fancy drinks for the evening.

Once I got stuck at the base. Now one might think that being stuck at a remote Air Force base with a hundred men would be any woman's dream, right? Well, it wasn't. It happened during the daytime. I don't remember why I was there, but in the middle of the afternoon, war was declared. War games that is. I was told it was to simulate a real attack and how the base would respond. I'm sure it was a bit more complicated and provided training for the men, but I was a civilian and a foreigner at that, so what did I know. What impressed me was how quickly the status quo at the base changed and how the men morphed from every day laid back guys into very serious military men. The officer I was visiting was quickly sent to the radar room when the alarm sounded and the loudspeaker spat out orders. One being:

"Any civilians on site report immediately to sick bay. Repeat, all civilians to sick bay."

Base Tracmaster Run: Pickup at the Hospital

I was promptly escorted there. When I arrived, the officer in charge looked happy to see me.

"Good" he said. "A nurse. You can help with the casualties."

"Just how long is this 'game' going to take?" I asked.

With a deadpan face he informed me, "Till we win."

"Well," I replied, "I am scheduled to work an evening shift at the real hospital in town with real sick people and I need to be there by 4 p.m." Unfortunately, he was not impressed with the credibility of my real job situation and informed me that I had better call for a ride because soon no one would be coming in or going out of the base grounds and sometimes these "activities" went on for days. I called the hospital and arranged for the hospital driver to pick me up. Apparently, he didn't meet the deadline because soon thereafter an airman came and drove me to the perimeter of the site where we waited for the hospital truck. When it arrived, I transferred from the base vehicle to the hospital truck, feeling for all the world like I was a hostage being led to freedom. I was very thankful to have been scheduled to work that evening.

My second winter I dated Jim, a lieutenant from Florida who was experiencing winter for the first time. Coming from the prairies, it never occurred to me that there were people who had never experienced snow or ice. I knew many had not experienced blizzards, whiteouts and minus 50 degrees temperatures that were occurring in Kotzebue that winter. Even for me the severity was more than I was used to, though snow and ice had been a large part of life where I came from. Jim, it appeared, had experienced none of it. As I mentioned, he was an officer and so was able to requisition a truck and come to town himself to pick me up. On one fall trip to the base he became quite animated and began pointing to all the ponds along the way that were freezing over.

"Look at that!" he kept saying in his deep southern drawl, "Just look at that!" and he would pull over to the side of the road to look at a shiny pond with a new coat of ice.

"Oh, for heaven's sake," I finally said, after we had stopped for the umpteenth time for him to jump out and check the ice like it was something miraculous. "Have you never seen ice before?"

"Of course I have," he replied, "In my drinks!" That was when I realized there were many cultural differences among even the non-Natives I was surrounded by. Our ways of talking, the places we came from, and the very diverse life experiences that shaped how we looked at the world and others were all culturally different.

Chapter 17

Springtime and Culture Shock

Kotzebue had a mixture of not only Inupiaq and Yup'ik Eskimos but also a few Siberian Yup'ik from St. Lawrence Island just thirty-six miles from the Russian coastline. Native people hunted sea mammals in the waters between Siberia and Alaska until the iron curtain came down in 1945. Sadly, those who were hunting on the Russian side did not come home. In 1991, after the Cold War, the curtain fell and trips in skin boats were arranged for people to reconnect and visit lost relatives.

But this was 1970 and some things never change, one being the seasons. Eventually winter loses its chilling grip and the weather slowly begins to warm, the ice to thaw, and snow to melt until there are puddles and slush and mud everywhere. Early spring in Kotzebue is not a pretty sight. As the protective cover of snow disappeared, what was underneath became a reality jolt for me. Although I had been living in Kotzebue five months, I had romanticized the white arctic landscape, not fully registering conditions in the town. I had seen only a fairyland of snow covering everything.

By early spring I had suffered a major culture shock that truly affected me more than the two smaller ones I experienced not long after arriving.

This was the difference between my living conditions and those of the townspeople. When the snow melted, this reality could not be ignored. Even though I had done some visiting in one or two homes in town, I had been focused on the people and our very different ways of communicating, but in town, the houses I had seen on my first ride by in a tracmaster the day I arrived in Kotzebue, were now fully exposed as the snow melted. Spring thaw and melting snow in Kotzebue laid the ground bare and visible. No city parks or landscaping here. An area around each house had collections of what I could only refer to as junk. The houses were very small and dilapidated. Many were just one or two room shacks. Friends I often visited that summer were a family of five who lived in one room. Another family of four that I was close to lived in two rooms. There was no running water, no plumbing. The water truck delivered water from the new water tank but many still cut ice from the surrounding lakes for washing and bathing. Large industrial sized buckets, referred to as honey buckets, with a toilet seat on top served as home toilets. A honey bucket truck regularly collected and emptied them, taking the waste far out onto the ice to dump and await dispersal during spring thaw. The largest flush toilet for the town was the ocean and it flushed just once a year at spring break up. Not sure how it was dealt with after spring thaw.

Almost every home had an arctic entry where outside gear was stored. Perhaps that is why no one answered the door. No one wanted to brave the cold of the arctic entry when a loud "Come in" would yield the same results. And so I would enter and knock on the inner door where, after another loud "Come in," I was always warmly greeted. I made an effort to meet people in their surroundings even when the reality of their living conditions finally registered. That was when I experienced my major culture shock.

Culture shock is defined as the feeling of confusion and disorientation when confronted with a way of life different from one's own. Life in Kotzebue was vastly different from anything I had experienced before. The majority of small-box like homes throughout the town spoke to poverty within thin, poorly insulated walls. Interior furnishings were bare basics: a table, a couple of chairs, a mattress. The second time I went visiting in town I came back feeling shocked and sad. I sought out Joan, the dietician, a neighbor down the hall, to talk with.

"Have you been to visit anyone in town?" I asked her. Joan had been in Kotzebue over a year and I thought she would have more insight than I.

"Oh no," she said, "I really don't know any of my kitchen staff outside of work and I manage to keep pretty busy at work."

"I just came from having tea and a visit in a one room shack with mom, dad and three kids age two to ten. In one room, Joan! With a small table, a big mattress, two chairs and not much else.

"Must have been a stove if you had tea," she said.

"No. There was a two-burner camp stove on the table. How can anyone live like that?" I saw two pots and a fry pan hanging on hooks on the wall and a towel on a hook on another wall. There was a box under the table that looked like it had a lot of things stored in it, but just a bare mattress. The husband makes beautiful jewelry from ivory and baleen but neither of them have regular jobs. The last place I visited had two rooms although I just saw the one. It did have a stove and a bigger table and a counter with a couple of drawers and jars of things like flour, sugar and cereal on the counter top. I think the back room was a bedroom. There were four people living there. And the husband was a good hunter and the mom had a job at the restaurant. Still, I just don't know how people can live like that."

"Well, I suppose it is better than a partially underground sod hut like they used to have," she offered.

"I don't know," I said. "I think they were probably warmer in those. But maybe you're right. Maybe they are used to living in small spaces."

Still, I could not justify or come to grips with the level of poverty that I saw. This was so far from my way of life that it left me feeling sad and, in a way, angry at what I was witnessing. The lack of accessories which we tend to refer to as basics such as cupboards full of dishes, drawers of cutlery and more cooking utensils that one needs for any one meal, made these homes appear cold and bare. They also made me feel guilty for the excess I had. Even my apartment was larger than most of the homes I visited and the apartment was just for me.

I did not want to stay in my comfortable quarters and only socialize with the hospital staff. Some, such as the married doctors, reached out to the other government workers in town to extend their social circles, especially couples with families. I enjoyed meeting teachers and FAA people, the State Trooper and the ministers, but it was not my reason for coming so far away from home. I often wondered if I would have been as free to enjoy myself or as comfortable, if I had to live in town. I may have been living in a totally different place but I was still surrounded by the comforts and perks of my own culture. I decided that I would not fare as well had I been living in town. But I had come this far to see and experience and learn new ways, and so I worked through my feelings of guilt and discomfort, and continued to put myself in situations that, in the beginning, were a little trying. Things like visiting people who did not speak when I arrived, and enduring the silence even though I did not understand it.

On a trip home to Calgary, I visited friends who took me out back of their house to see their new motorhome. That motorhome was larger and better equipped than any home I had seen in Kotzebue. It had running water from taps and shower heads, electric lights, soft comfortable couches and chairs, a kitchen with cupboards, modern appliances, matching dishes and cutlery, and beds for all four of the family. That motorhome was just for their vacations around the province.

The BIA school and the PHS hospital were the two largest government agencies in town and their buildings and living quarters were also the most modern in town. They provided the setting for much of our entertainment, but I did attend a movie or two in town. The Ferguson Building on Front Street housed many businesses and apartments as well as the movie theater. The films were old and many of the seats were wooden boxes. The reactions of townspeople were often more entertaining than the movie itself. The movie I remember most was a good old cowboy and Indian film. Whenever the Indians were winning the theater audience would cheer. Not so much when the cowboys were killing the Indians. I went once or twice then opted for movies shown in our residence or at the Air Force base. Although the atmosphere at those places wasn't as entertaining, the films were current and the surroundings definitely more comfortable.

The place to go before an evening of entertainment was Tony's Cafe, also in the Ferguson Building close to the movie theater. Tony, a hard-working Italian man, ran one of the two cafes in town. There was also a dining room in the back which was THE place to eat out. That summer I decided it would be fun to work at the cafe on my days off. Not only would it be a new experience but a chance to meet some of the tourists and construction workers who came to town in the summer. As it turned out, I was not very good waitress material. I wasn't too organized. If I had more than four customers, I had trouble keeping the orders straight. I think the only reason Tony kept me on was because I was working for tips only. I learned that running a restaurant in the Arctic was quite different from down south. Getting supplies in was the largest challenge. Weather often grounded planes for days. And getting fresh vegetables and fruit was always a toss-up. Supplies came from Anchorage or Fairbanks and the extra time it took to reach the Arctic pretty much deleted the "fresh" from any produce. Sometimes we just ran out of things, like tomatoes and lettuce for the hamburgers,

"There's no lettuce or tomato on this hamburger Miss."

"I'm sorry sir, we have run out, and our order isn't yet delivered from the plane you came in on. We have not had any produce delivered for a few days. It happens quite often."

"Well then you need to knock a few bucks from the price. This is not what was expected for this exorbitant price."

When once we ran out of hamburger buns, Tony had to use bread. That didn't sit well with the tourists who gave me quite an earful.

"What the H—- is this? I ordered a hamburger, not a sandwich."

"Sorry, we ran out of buns and our local grocery store has too. We are waiting for our grocery order from Anchorage, but the planes have been booked with tourists with very limited room for extra cargo. It happens a lot in the summer. In winter the weather dictates how quickly we get our orders in."

They weren't too sympathetic with our problems of supply and demand and, compared to down south, the cost of a hamburger in Kotzebue was pretty pricey. As a nurse, I became irritated at the tourist's complaints. This was not the Ritz and they were complaining about things we had no control over. I have immense tolerance for complaining patients. They were ill and upset with the turn of events that put them in my care. But if you are on vacation, just checking out the "local wildlife in such a strange little place" (as I once overheard it described), my patience quickly ran out. Unfortunately, the conversations with these visitors were sparse. I was only working on days off and it was not as enjoyable as I had hoped. I only lasted a month.

For a short time one winter, Kentucky Fried Chicken had a franchise in town. I would leave their establishment with a hot takeout chicken dinner stuffed inside my fur parka. By the time I was back home, it would be cold. That eatery didn't last very long. I assume fried chicken was not as desirable to the locals as caribou steak.

KFC Kotzebue

In Kotzebue one did not find convenience stores or drive-throughs that were common down south. No speciality stores and, as my mother had predicted, no latest fashions. Fashion was not something on the minds of the nurses in Kotzebue. Eddie Bauer was a staple in most of our closets.

As spring became summer, boats were tied up along the shore of the road I roared down on my snow machine in winter. Between the road and boats bobbing on the water were racks laden with strips of freshly caught fish cut and hung to dry in the sun. There was an influx of people from outlying villages with much visiting and preparation for subsistence activities. Summers were food gathering and preparation times. Spring was just the beginning of summer subsistence.

Chapter 18

Summertime in the Arctic

After the dark days of winter and spring melt, summer daylight was welcomed. Most summer weather was pleasant. Once or twice the temperature reached a high of 70 degrees. Kotzebue was a windy place and, although the wind kept the bugs at bay, it dropped the warmth. Rarely did I go anywhere without my light cotton summer coat called a kuspuk, complete with a hood providing protection from the constant wind. Kuspuks had two large front pockets outlined with colorful rickrack. They were either hung straight or were gathered below the waist in skirt-like fashion. They varied in length from slightly below the hips to below the knees. More rickrack was placed on the hood, around the waist gatherings or along the bottom. They were worn for all summer activities from fishing to berry picking. I had a second coat for the cooler days of early spring and

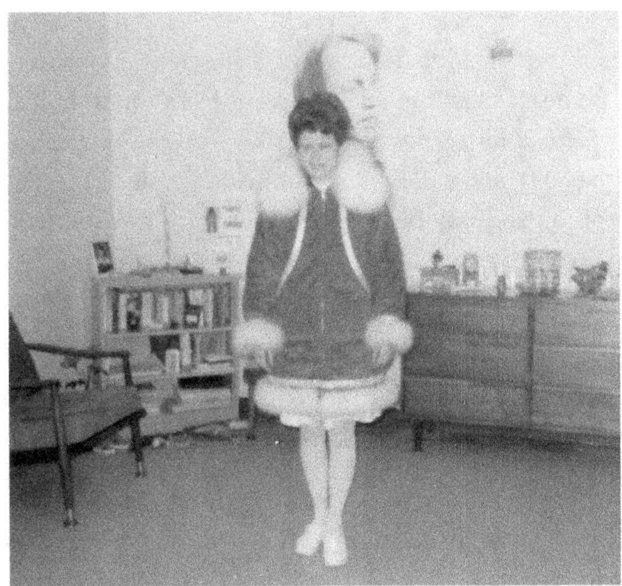

Coat for Spring and Fall

late fall made of corduroy with a white arctic fox collar and a zipper up the front. Summers were mostly dry with August being the rainy month.

I should mention the mosquitoes. Almost every place deals with mosquitoes in summer, but Arctic mosquitoes were the largest blood suckers I have ever encountered. They liked to attack in swarms. Other nasty insects were black flies and no-see-ums. The flies were big and mean, the no-see-ums hardly visible, but bites from each left welts and itchy bumps on necks, arms and other exposed skin. There were times when they were so annoying I wished for winter again. Although I used copious amounts of Off and other anti-bug sprays, it seemed the attacking insects were always the victors. Bare limbs wore the battle scars.

Summer is opposite winter in ways other than just weather. Hours of daylight in summer are as long as the hours of darkness in winter. Continuous light plays tricks on the body. Twenty-four hours of daylight did not make me as tired as did the same amount of darkness. Instead, the never-ending days gave me a boost of energy which could lead to burnout from overactivity. When the sun was up, it was hard to think about going to bed, and so I tended to keep busy until I dropped from lack of sleep. On a bright, sunny day off, I often cooked my own breakfast as I was awake and hungry long before the hospital cafeteria was serving. I managed to fill the sunshine hours with busy activities: baking to keep my sweet tooth content, cleaning my apartment from top to bottom, laundry, a trip to town for a few groceries, a walk through town to see what was happening that day and take some pictures, a visit to a friend in town, check my mail on the way back home and answer any letters I received. If Hanson's store had caribou steaks for sale, then I just might purchase a couple and invite someone, also on a day off, over for dinner. By evening, I was beginning to think maybe I should slow down but that is the time for visiting in the quarters. If you had the next day off, those visits could last till the wee hours of the morning. Sometimes it was my work schedule that slowed me down to an eight instead of sixteen-hour day. Even the children in town played outside until tiredness overtook them, which might be three o'clock in the morning. I often fell asleep in summer to sounds of children's laughter while playing in the midnight sun.

One very long weekend for me started as an evening at the base that turned into 48 hours of wakefulness for myself and two other nurses and our dates from the base. We danced and watched movies late into the night at the officers' club then headed to my apartment in town for a night of homemade pizza and cards. Mary cooked breakfast for all of us in her apartment the next morning after which we drove one of the base trucks all over town, had the boys help us with some furniture rearranging, had dinner at Tony's Cafe and again visited and played cards at the quarters until morning. Somewhere in the middle of all this I worked an eight-hour evening shift then returned to join the card game. Nurses are used to working long hours, sometimes double shifts and being up all night, but never before nor since, have I stayed awake for two days straight. The constant sunlight told my mind it was the time of day to be active, but after forty-eight hours of activity, my body screamed sleep. I did just that without any alarm to wake me. After twelve hours it was a full bladder that got me out of bed. Constant sun can definitely trick your biology.

A cultural difference between Natives and non-Natives lies in interpretation and use of time. For Natives, whose lives were tied to the land by subsistence lifestyles, nature more often determined time. The time to hunt is when the animals present themselves. Women pick berries when nature ripens them. Fishing occurs when each species runs. For town people not yet inserted into our ways, bedtime was when you were tired. For me a set time on my clock dictated my sleeping and waking. The sounds of happy children filtering through my open window day and night reinforced this difference. The society I came from was driven by schedules and clocks that mark off segments of time. In nature the amount of time for any task is set by how long it takes to get it done. For the town people adapting to our way of life, it became difficult to mesh these two very different uses of time. A nine-to-five job could interfere with the need to hunt when the animals presented themselves.

Summer months were tourist months. Every day the two airlines servicing Kotzebue brought planeloads of tourists to town from the Lower-48 states and around the world. Wien Air tourists wore bright colored parkas provided by the airlines. Those parkas distinguished the outsiders from Kotzebue residents. Tourists were loaded onto buses that drove them around town and out to see the commercial reindeer herd.

They were also treated to a Native dance and talks and demonstrations on Native culture. I often thought it would be fun to sign up for a tour just to see what the drivers were saying and if it matched what I, as an outsider, was experiencing. The tourists were fun to watch as they witnessed different surroundings and a different way of life. They were eager to talk to anyone they saw and had lots of questions to ask. Their bright parkas alerted us so we could avoid them if we didn't want to be interrogated with the same questions time and again.

"How come you not want to go where they are?" asked Dolly, one of my Native coworkers as we were walking to town. "Maybe someone from Canada, like you."

"They ask a lot of questions," I replied. "Some pretty funny ones too," I laughed.

"Yeah," said Dolly. "Just like you when you first come."

Directly across the Sound from town was a place called Sesaulik. Many people lived there in the summer months while engaged in subsistence hunting and fishing. More than one tourist asked me if it was Siberia, and this was long before Sarah Palin.

"Dolly, a tourist asked me where the igloos were the other day," I said, hoping she would realize I wasn't as ignorant as our visitors.

"Did you tell them we don't live in igloos, never did. Just make them for emergency hunting shelters when the weather turns bad. Those white people think we all live in ice and snow huts," she said.

"Dolly," I said with a deep sigh, "It's the middle of summer. Where did she think there would be anything made of snow in the middle of the summer? Dumb tunics," I said as if I was an old timer and had a right to laugh at the tourists.

"I remember after you and doctor went sledding with the dogs, you asked Joe from maintenance where the Inuksuks were to mark the trails. He said you must have got real lost because we don't have them on any of our trails: 'Maybe you guys mushed all the way into Canada.'" Inuksuks are large stones piled on each other to resemble a human shape and were used to mark trails or food caches and sometimes the women herded reindeer through them to drive them towards the men who were waiting to hunt them. They are found all over the circumpolar north, the majority being in

Canada where the Inuit identify closely with them. But there were none in the Kotzebue area. I blushed remembering how the Native staff had a good laugh from that. And also when I reacted to the eyeball in my fish soup. "Dumb tunic" indeed! I was squarely in that category.

Along with the tourists from all over the Lower-48 states, there were those from many different countries. Not only were they tourists, but one time they became hospital employees. Lisa and Mary were two nurses touring the United States. Mary was from Scotland, Lisa from Ireland. They wanted to see the Arctic and needed to work for a few months as they were running short on funds. Mary was quickly hired by PHS and came to Kotzebue to work. She was a delightful person with a fun accent we all loved listening to, a hearty laugh and was a good worker. Listening to her converse with the Southern gals was hilarious to me. She had only been with us a few weeks when one day she was just gone. She did not show up to work, her apartment was empty of all her possessions and a quick check with the airlines showed she had left town on the early morning flight. We later found out from the nurse recruiter that her friend Lisa from Ireland was not able to work for our government due to some political legality with Ireland. She was leaving Alaska and Mary wanted to continue traveling with her, hence her hasty and secretive departure. So much for contracts. We missed her. Lorraine and I, as Canadians, remained the only two foreigners working at the Kotzebue hospital.

Another summer event was hauling freight to the surrounding villages. A barge brought yearly supplies to Kotzebue in the summer months and pilots from the larger airlines flew freight to the villages in Twin Otter planes. My first summer I met Pete, a Wien Air pilot who did weekly rotations from Fairbanks to fly the Otters.

"How exciting," I said showing as much enthusiasm as I could muster. "You are so lucky to be able to see all the smaller villages. I often wonder what my patients' home towns are like. I can't imagine living in places smaller than here." That got me an invitation to fly with him and his co-pilot on my days off. The Twin Otters were larger than most of the planes used to transport patients. Those flights had been in the dark of winter and my attention had been on patients, not the towns. Twin Otters can fly lower to the ground, as the pilots demonstrated, causing me some anxiety. It took the expression "skimming over the landscape" a little too far for my comfort. The pilots said the Otters could land on a dime which made them good for small air strips. Every time we landed in one of the tinier villages, I wondered how people could survive in such a harsh and barren landscape. I was definitely a city girl. Even though I had grown up on the prairies with small towns scattered between the cities, unlike the prairies, these places had no waving wheat fields or herds of cattle to sustain them. The Inupiaq had survived for centuries living off a land that was not as barren as it looked. And I was discovering that a caribou roast from the arctic tundra was just as good as any Alberta prairie beef.

In the early 1960s a group of hippies had gone into the Arctic wilderness to "live off the land." From all reports they would not have survived the winter without the guidance, help and kindness of the Native people from the closest Inupiaq village. I guess a centuries old way of life was not as easy as the young city hippies thought it would be.

A very surprising part of the landscape we flew over a number of times, was the Kobuk Sand Dunes. The dunes were twenty-five square

Midnight in July

miles of golden white sand southeast of Kotzebue above the Arctic Circle. Flying over them seemed like an optical illusion, a trick of nature. The dunes were the result of the grinding glaciers from the Pleistocene era which began over a million years ago and lasted until 10,000 years ago. The dunes were formed by wind that had piled the sand in some places to 100-feet high.

In the evening Pete, the Wien head pilot, visited me in my apartment, or we would go to dinner at Tony's Cafe. I was growing fond of him until my Eskimo mama, a lady from town who I visited often and had become close to, and who apparently knew my pilot better than I, said, "You two make a nice couple. You remind me of his wife." That was the end of my friendship with the Wien pilot and my trips in the Twin Otters. Fortunately, I had seen many villages in our service unit and had flown over much of the landscape out of Kotzebue before it ended.

John, another pilot in town my first summer, was from Ontario, Canada. He was flying for Shell Oil Company trailing instruments off the back of his small plane as he flew grid patterns over Kotzebue sound

Midnight in December

looking for oil deposits. It was the beginning of Alaska's oil boom. Oil had been discovered in Prudhoe Bay and infrastructure for the huge oilfield was being built. I had no idea in 1969 how important that would be for Alaska's economy and how the profits from it would benefit me throughout my life. John told me there was definitely oil in Kotzebue sound and I secretly hoped it wouldn't turn Kotzebue into another Prudhoe Bay. So far it has not.

To celebrate summer solstice my first June in the Arctic, I joined a few other hardy hospital staff to wade into the freezing waters of Kotzebue Sound. I made it up to my thighs and quickly scurried back to shore wrapping up in a thick towel to dry off and get back into my clothes. Once was enough for me, but I could honestly say I had dipped my toes into the Arctic Ocean. The next year I was one of the ones on shore holding the towels for the new girls.

There was always something happening outdoors in the short summer months, and I spent as much spare time as I could participating, knowing the long days of darkness would soon be back.

Chapter 19

Fun In The Sun

My parents and brother Greg came to visit me my first summer in Kotzebue. Greg was fifteen years old, a high school boy who was mesmerized with all he saw and experienced in my new home. I enjoyed taking them around town and watching their reactions. We ate dinner at Tony's restaurant with prices that shocked my father so much we only ate there once.

"Hope you don't eat here very often," he exclaimed.

"Seems you could have a new outfit for the cost," my mother added. But they were both impressed with the taste of reindeer steaks which they declared were "just about as tasty as an Alberta beef steak." That was a top compliment coming from my father. We strolled Front Street often to see the boats tied up and the fish drying on racks. They especially enjoyed watching boats come and go and seeing the fish being prepared to hang. Being from a vast prairie landscape, the water and boats captivated them. They had never tasted dried fish and declared it very tasty, at least my mother and brother did. My father was not a fish lover and it had not been served very often when I was growing up. My brother took the challenge to help out when one of my coworkers from the hospital cajoled him into helping her cut and hang fish. I was proud of his efforts to learn. He seemed proud of his results.

It was fun seeing my family's reactions to sights and sounds so very different from a big city. Dogs did not howl in evening serenades in Calgary, and the sun did not shine through the wee hours of the night. They met many of my new friends while we were out strolling and my mother, in particular, wanted to talk with the ladies. She had many questions to ask them, especially how they prepared whale and seal meat. My dad and brother were interested in the wooden sleds they saw in the yards and the snow machines beside them. As I explained life in Kotzebue to them, I realized how much I had learned in seven months and how much I was enjoying my new home, my work and especially the people in my new surroundings.

I also took them to see the Native dances. The dance group in town performed most evenings in summer for the tourists and I went as often as possible. As my family watched me dancing the invitational dance with the group, a dance everyone in the audience was encouraged to join in, a tourist, observing that mom and I were together, leaned over and asked her if I was Eskimo. My mother thought that was pretty funny, but I felt a sense of pride to think an outsider thought I danced as well as the Native ladies. Although my parents enjoyed watching the dances, I could not entice them to join in. Brother Greg jumped at the chance and did an excellent job. My family was pleasantly surprised at all they saw and experienced in my new home. They said they were relieved to see for themselves how happy I was in my new surroundings. They stayed for four days. They had driven up the ALCAN Highway to Anchorage and planned on a visit there, then down to Kenai and Homer, Alaska before returning home. Now they would be able to picture the places and some of the people I talked about in my letters. My brother thought I was brave to travel so far away and experience a new world. He thought maybe he would like to do something similar when he got older. I was sad to see them leave but glad they had come so far to visit.

Summertime offered opportunities for new experiences. The most exciting opportunity I experienced was riding in a kayak. Not a store-bought kayak, but one made from ugruk skins by a Native man in town. Ugruk are large bearded seals. Kayaks are extremely durable and I was told they would right themselves if they capsized. They have been used for hunting in the high Arctic for thousands of years. Women tan and sew the hides then waterproof them using melted animal fat rubbed over the skins and seams. The men then stretch the hides over a light narrow wood frame they build. The lashings are made of sinew. The kayak I was offered was a one-person design. I became nervous while climbing in as I was told they were "pretty tippy alright," and that I should be "very still." I didn't venture out too far or too long as I didn't relish doing a 360-degree rollover in the water. I again was assured the kayak would right itself, but to me there was always the chance my mouth would open at some point of the rollover to scream. I would then inhale water and drown. No long kayak trips for the prairie girl, but at least I experienced the thrill of paddling a kayak. Small accomplishments made me happy. It was not till long after I left the Arctic that I learned that kayaks do NOT right themselves, but when they roll over it is easy enough for the rider to slip out of the portal, place themselves in the middle point of the kayak and pull it gently towards them in order to right it.

Me in the Kayak

The other form of new transportation I experienced was riding on the back of a motorcycle. Lorraine, the other Canadian nurse, had acquired one before I arrived. It did not look very sturdy to me but it did run. When I rode with her, we managed to terrorize a few people on the streets of Kotzebue as she drove the bike at breakneck speed through town. The next time we rode together we tackled the five miles to the Air Force base. The road was rough gravel and there were many skids and slides putting us at frightening angles before she got her speed under control. Although the trip back was less exciting, I never did feel safe. The whole time I clutched tight around her waist focusing on the road ahead instead of the landscape we were speeding through. Thankfully, we made it very close to the edge of town before we ran out of gas. We walked and pushed the bike the rest of the way back to the hospital. That was the last time I rode with her. A sad lack of courage on my part.

Another new experience for me was celebrating the American Fourth of July. To my surprise, it was a very big event in Kotzebue. The whole town turned out and probably, judging from the size of the crowds, that included many people from other villages. I don't know why it surprised me. Perhaps because, not being American, I had never experienced a Fourth of July and didn't recognize it as such an important national holiday. Or maybe I thought people that were experiencing such cultural upheaval and change as a result of encroachment by White culture, wouldn't be so keen to celebrate the origins of the present-day government. But I was wrong. I will always remember celebrating my first American Fourth of July with the wonderful people of Kotzebue.

Events that special day were quite different from those I had experienced during Canada Day in my youth. There were foot races for the kids and a very popular muktuk (whale blubber) eating contest, and a beauty contest in which the young women wore traditional fur coats and mukluks. The winner would go on to participate in the Miss Alaska contest. There was also a baby beauty contest with adorable little ones also dressed in traditional furs.

Beauty Queens

Other events tested men's strength and endurance. These contests of hunting skills had been practiced for generations. Today these survival skills are celebrated each summer at the World Eskimo Indian Olympic (WEIO) competitions in Fairbanks. Competitors from all over Alaska come together to celebrate their Native games. On the Fourth, in Kotzebue, there was the ear pull, where a band was wrapped around the ears of two people sitting face to face. Whoever pulled the hardest and dislodged the band from the other's ear won the pull. The one leg and two leg high kick were fun to watch. A skin ball the size of a large baseball was dangled from a pole as competitors tried to kick it from a standing position. When it was done with both legs it was even more thrilling to watch. After each successful kick, the ball was raised higher.

High Kick

The seal (knuckle) hop looked painful as the competitors "hopped" using their knuckles and toes as the only landing spots of their bodies when they hopped. Another test of endurance, the four-man carry involved four different men carrying another man by his outstretched limbs while he was in a horizontal position. Accompanying these feats were cheers of encouragement and gasps of amazement when a new record was set.

The event I enjoyed the most was the blanket toss, in which even the women participated. It consisted of a huge round "blanket" made from the skin of seals with hand holds around the outside edges for people to grasp and lift it. The blanket was lowered for someone to climb on then those on the outside pulled outward till the blanket snapped and propelled its occupant skyward. They then relaxed their pull and just as the person

Muktuk Eating Contest

landed, they once again pulled out, snapping him upwards higher and higher with each pull. Traditionally, this was done to allow a hunter to see further out to sea to spot whales. The goals for the person being flipped were to stay over the blanket, bend the knees when coming down, land upright on the feet, then straighten the knees for the upward thrust. Not as easy as it sounds and a little frightening to find one's self hanging in midair with the knowledge that what goes up must come down. Looking down to see if you will land on the blanket could put you off balance. One just trusts that the group handling the skin blanket will make sure it is under you when you land, especially if your trajectory isn't straight up. It was a thrilling sensation. I was fortunate to have been given a try at it, and was proud when I landed on my feet for two or three pulls and that I hadn't screamed too loud on the way up. The wind was blowing and maybe cut off the sound coming from my mouth but the hospital dentist said he could have done a full mouth dental extraction on me when I hit the highest point of the upward flip.

Blanket Toss

Once we had a sweet little four-year-old girl named Dalia in the hospital for a number of weeks while the doctor adjusted medications for her growth problem. I often brought her over to my apartment to spoil her. I took her to my second Fourth of July. Seeing it through her eyes made it very special for me. Dalia also loved pop. Not being a mother and not tuned in to the pattern I was setting, I made the mistake of giving her a pop the first time she came to the apartment. Every time thereafter her first question was "You got soda pop?" and I would melt and give her one. My head nurse asked her why she liked to go to my place all the time and in a loud joyful voice she replied, "Soda Pop!" And I had thought it was just because of me. I received a rather stern lecture on the evils of feeding sweets to the little ones, especially soda pop.

In summer, both men and women occupy themselves with subsistence activities. It is a time to store food for the long winter months. Men hunt sea mammals such as seals, both ringed and the larger bearded seals called ugruk, and walrus along the coastal areas. Also muskrat, which are equally comfortable on land and in water, are hunted and provide wonderful fur for parkas. The largest sea mammal hunted in the Kotzebue area is the white beluga whale. The beluga whale is smaller than the humpback whale hunted further north in Point Hope, Barrow and Wainwright, Alaska. The waters of Kotzebue Sound and the major rivers that flow into the Sound provide numerous species of fish including salmon, sheefish, and Dolly Varden trout. The most hunted land animal is caribou which not only supplies food, but also hides for blankets and clothing. Smaller land animals including fox, squirrel, wolf and wolverine are also hunted. These animals also provide fur for parkas. Birds such as ducks and geese are hunted, generally later in fall.

Women also fish, either alone, with a friend or with their families. Women are the ones responsible for preparing the catch to hang for drying or smoking. Dried fish is a staple that ensures there is food to eat year-round. There were no fridges or freezers. Huge quantities were dried and put away to last through the winter. The fish are gutted and sliced into two halves almost to the end of the tail, then scored and hung on hand made racks for the sun to dry and the wind to keep the flies away. Women are also busy putting up game brought home by the men, prepping the skins for tanning and sewing in the darker days of winter. Women spend many hours picking berries in season. The berries range from salmon berries as the first to ripen, followed by blueberries, blackberries, cranberries and lingonberries or low bush cranberries. Each family claims their own picking areas scattered far and wide across the tundra. They also pick a variety of greens, dig for edible roots and look for bird eggs. Summers are busy, but also a time for families to spend time together while they gather food. Many families have fish camps along the river banks with each family member helping in the subsistence activities both on the surrounding landscape and on the water.

People in town passing by on warm summer days stopped to say hello and visit with their friends and neighbors. Without heavy fur parkas and ruffs protecting their faces, you knew who you were passing in the street and were happy to see them and stop to chat. And there were more invitations to "come see us." And I did. I always enjoyed visiting people in their homes. The Inupiaq people are known for their smiles and wonderful sense of humor. Laughing and joking was a way of life in the villages. It was uplifting to spend time with my friends in town. During the summer there were fewer trips to the base as more time was spent outdoors during time off work. The weather allowed us to explore places that in winter were inaccessible under layers of snow and summer days allowed me to become more familiar with the surrounding landscape. We walked out onto the tundra picking flowers and looking for bird nests. The land was alive with color without the layers of snow.

In summer the town bustled with activity and new faces, but by the end of the good weather and long hours of daylight, those new faces disappeared, and we prepared for the peace and quiet that descended on the town in the long winter months. Summer time had given me the opportunity to once again expand horizons and experience the outdoors in a new way.

Chapter 20

Arctic Nursing

It felt as if the majority of my two years in the Arctic was experienced during long, cold winter months when snow and freezing temperatures were the norm. It allowed me to see the difficulty of arctic living. Work kept me busy no matter what the season or temperature.

The winter of 1970 brought a harsh strain of flu to town. It was particularly hard on the elderly and sadly there were a few deaths. As a nurse, experiencing the death of your patient is hard no matter where or when it occurs, but in a small hospital in such a small town, each death, especially of an elder who has been an important link to the past history of the culture, becomes more than personal. It is a loss for the whole town.

There was also an increased number of severe storms and bad weather that winter. At the height of the flu epidemic, the doctors were kept busy day and night with the influx of patients and, due to the inclement weather, there were times people couldn't get to the hospital to pick up their prescribed medicine. I volunteered to use my snow machine to deliver antibiotics and other medications the doctors ordered for people in town. I was given instructions as to where to deliver them when I picked up the prescriptions from John our hospital pharmacist, but finding homes in a small town without street signs or names proved challenging.

"Sue, this package goes to the Williams. The senior Williams that live down past the trooper's house."

"I'm not sure which house it is."

"Their place is two doors down from Lena's house. Lena lives right next to the trooper in the little green house." Lena was one of our practical nurses and I knew where she lived so I knew exactly where he meant. And if you got the wrong house, the people there would point you in the right direction and probably even invite you in for a cup of tea. And always Will, the x-ray tech, made sure my snow machine started. Off I would go, Sue Barton of the North! Sue Barton books were a series for young girls about an adventurous nurse. In my youth I had read every one of them, probably twice. Since Junior High (Middle School), I had wanted to be a nurse and by golly I had finally made it. Who knew that RN title would lead me to such new and exciting places full of adventure and delivering medications on a snow machine during storms in the high Arctic.

Ear infections were prevalent in the children, especially during the winter months. Getting them to dress warm or wear hats, especially the young boys, was a never-ending battle. Kids will be kids wherever they are. The treatment, besides antibiotics, was to flood the ear with hydrogen peroxide. It bubbled and foamed and softened the crusted drainage allowing it to be suctioned. Not so easy a task with squirming, crying, unhappy little ones. There were so many of them, each to be suctioned four times a day. I tried to give them hugs when I was done but after a few treatments my popularity would hit an all-time low.

"Let me give you a hug Jesse."

"You do dis me again?"

"I have to Jesse, make your ears better."

"NO! No hugs!" And all I would get was a betrayed look.

Nursing was our first and foremost responsibility. Because there were a limited number of medical personnel, we were reminded frequently that other nurses were dependent on us to stay healthy so there would not be any staffing shortages. Perhaps if they had left us on one shift for a longer period of time instead of changing them every week, we would have been less tired and prone to illness. Between the extremes of seasonal daylight and darkness and frequent shift changes, I was often left wondering what day, and what time of day it was. And napping was common in the dark winter months.

Then there was the "weathered in" day on the tail end of any trip outside. I came back two days before my scheduled shift instead of the day before, in case weather prevented me from returning, forcing another nurse to work overtime or an extra shift.

I went to Dillingham, Alaska my first winter as a recovery room nurse at the Kanakanak hospital. Dillingham was the trading and fishing center for the Bristol Bay area of Western Alaska. In summer the population exploded with fishing boats and seasonal cannery workers. The thirty-eight bed PHS hospital was located six miles out of town at the old village site of Kanakanak. Anchorage periodically sent surgical teams to their outlying hospitals to do surgery clinics for patients. I seem to have been out of town for the one held in Kotzebue, but for two weeks I worked in the recovery room for post-operative surgery patients from the Dillingham service area. During the first week, I cared for children who had their tonsils and adenoids removed. The following week I cared for adults who were having minor surgeries. It was a pleasant change from the general nursing I was doing in Kotzebue. Since Kanakanak was out of town, I spent most of my time at the hospital site. The accommodations were cozy. The apartments were only four to a building and felt homey and less institutional. I enjoyed getting to know the nurses and staff at another PHS facility. It was also a break from the routine in Kotzebue. At the rate I was going, I figured if I stayed working for PHS in Alaska long enough, I might make it to all their hospitals in the state. I had not seen much of Dillingham as I had remained on the hospital premises for the duration of my stay. Hearing my complaints, coworkers took me into town the night before I was to leave and gave me a guided tour ending at the Willow Tree Bar in town, which was probably their intended destination at the onset. It was definitely a place to relieve pressure and blow off steam. And in my honor, on the jukebox, they played John Denver's song by Peter, Paul and Mary, "Leaving On A Jet Plane" over and over. The next day I did leave on a jet plane, with happy memories and more than a slight headache from the evening before.

I flew out to a number of villages to escort sick or injured patients back to the hospital. On all escort flights, I took my survival pack of warm clothes and a few of my survival bars with me. It became a habit to pick up my pack as I headed out the door.

Medivac flights to the smaller villages were always exciting and sometimes challenging. One never knew what might be waiting at the other end regardless of what we were told on the emergency radio call. There were times when the term "emergency" held different connotations to the health aid and the medical responder at the hospital. Our health aides were not medically trained and sometimes a patient's condition was judged to be worse than it was. A severe cold is not the same as pneumonia but sometimes the aide's description left some doubt as to the severity of the patient's condition. As medical personnel, we had to err on the side of safety, so sometimes a patient was flown to the hospital when his symptoms could have been treated effectively in the village.

Each medivac trip was a new learning experience and gradually, with experience, I became more confident in myself to handle whatever might arise during the trips. On one particular, trip I cared for a man who was growing weaker by the hour. The larger muscles of his legs and arms were the first to become weak. By the end of the day, he had trouble walking. By evening, he was beginning to have trouble breathing, and I was flown to his village to escort him back to the hospital. No one was sure what was wrong with him, and I was alarmed at how quickly he was losing strength in his muscles. It had taken both myself and the health aid to walk him to the plane and help him into a seat. By the time we arrived in Kotzebue, less than an hour later, it took two strong men to move him off the plane and into a vehicle to transport him to the hospital.

The doctor was baffled. What was causing these strange symptoms? It was frightening to watch him struggle to breathe. His chest was not expanding. We used our intermittent positive pressure (IPPB) machine, the most effective piece of breathing equipment we had at the time, but in the end, breathing could not be sustained. Even the sanitation engineer became involved. As he was heading home past the emergency room, he overheard the doctor talking to a second doctor he had called in to help diagnose the illness, and became interested in what was happening. He asked the doctors a few questions and left. Instead of heading home, he went back to his office and did some quick research. We were surprised when he came rushing back to us saying, "I do believe this man has botulism." He was right. The doctors were relieved to have a diagnosis but sadly we did not have the cure. Botulism is caused by a bacteria which produces a toxin attacking the brain, spinal cord and nerves, causing muscle paralysis. When the chest muscles become affected, the patient can no longer breathe. We did not have the antitoxin on hand to counteract this process. The nearest dose was in Anchorage and the last jet of the day had left town heading back to Anchorage. The patient died before the drug could be transported to us. We were devastated. Watching this man struggle to move, then to breath, and not have the means to help him left us all feeling frustrated and, in the end, defeated. Officials in Anchorage were notified and a team of scientists were sent to the village to determine the source of the botulism.

Botulism is a bacteria that can live without oxygen. It can occur in canned foods but in this case, it was in a Native dish. The patient's home village was preparing for a whale feast and the wife was making a favorite meat dish by soaking it in whale oil. The family had been traveling and arrived back to the village shortly before the feast. In order to render the particular dish to the taste desired in a short amount of time, the wife had not stirred it each day which is normally done, thus not exposing the meat and oil to the air. Of course. the people in the village were not aware of the problem that not stirring the dish could cause. Because the dish did not have enough air exposure, the botulism organism took hold and grew.

The affected man, the only one in the family to sample a taste of his favorite food, had ingested the bacteria. The village was not happy with the findings of the medical team as to the cause of death. This was a Native food that had been made without problems for as long as anyone could remember. That those outside their culture were criticizing their means of preparing a traditional dish was upsetting. It took a while for them to see it was the rushed version of not stirring the dish each day that had caused the problem, not the normal way of preparation.

On another occasion, I medivaced a three-day old boy diagnosed with pyloric stenosis to the medical center in Anchorage. In this condition the pylorus, which connects the stomach to the small intestine, has a restriction that does not allow food, even baby formula, to pass into the intestine. Babies with pyloric stenosis have projectile vomiting after a normal feeding, and if it continues, can lead to death from dehydration, electrolyte imbalance, and starvation. The cure involves surgery to widen the pyloric opening. Until they have surgery, these tiny patients need frequent small feedings. I love babies, but in 1969 my only experience with them had been in a hospital nursery. I had never travelled with a sick baby and all the paraphernalia they require. For a while all went well. No throwing up and no crying, until I had to change planes in Fairbanks. I headed to the ladies' room with my little one. Apparently, he did not like this change in status quo. He began to verbalize his unhappiness at the top of his lungs, causing me a fair amount of stress. In the ladies' room my efforts at changing diapers and keeping tabs on all the baby gear drew a fair amount of attention. I received a lot of unsolicited advice.

"How old is that poor baby? Don't you think he's a little young to be traveling?"

"Aren't you brave traveling alone with such a young baby."

"He's crying because he's hungry dear, you're not feeding him enough."

"He must have colic. Maybe you fed him too much?"

"Did you burp him?"

If I had been his mother, I would have felt totally browbeaten. I wanted to tell them to mind their own business, but nice young nurses on medivac trips don't do that. Instead, I smiled, thanked them for their concern and explained the situation. With that I became a hero on a mission of mercy and the advice turned into questions about his condition, giving me an opportunity to do some public education and restore my ego. Both baby and I survived the trip. He made a full recovery from his surgery and returned home to his village and his worried mother a week or so later.

I was always willing to be an escort to Anchorage. There was the lure of a quick shopping trip before heading back home. These trips happened on short notice with the only preparation time being just before the next plane was due to depart south. It left very little time to plan, or to worry about what could happen en route. Often, the nurse on duty prepared not only the patient, but any equipment or supplies needed during the escort. As the escort, you were given the diagnosis and a brief report on the patient's condition as well as a written doctor's report to be handed to the receiving doctor in Anchorage. Any time I got the call, my anxiety level was on high alert until my patient and I were settled on the plane and on our way. At that point, my nursing instincts kicked in, and the anxiety disappeared. Most times the flight went smoothly, but there were times that the unforeseen happened or the patient's condition worsened. Not all mercy flights had a happy ending.

One of the patients we sent south died en route. He came to us from his village with late-stage kidney failure. The doctor felt if he could get him to the Anchorage Hospital and on dialysis that perhaps he would have a fighting chance. The patient became confused and at one point combative. Because of this, he was sent to Anchorage on Alaska Airlines escorted not by a doctor or nurse, but by a local man who worked in the hospital maintenance department. He was chosen because he was large and very strong and someone the patient knew, which the doctor felt would help keep him calm. The flight had one stop in Nome. Just after departing Nome, the patient died. So as to not upset the passengers, it was decided to leave him sitting in his seat until arriving in Anchorage. Airline rules stipulated the patient could not be removed from the plane until seen by the coroner. Unfortunately, neither could the other passengers. I worked the evening shift that afternoon and received the sad news when the coroner called wanting information on the patient's condition. He needed to know the patient's diagnosis and if he had anything contagious. It took me a minute to recover from the surprise of hearing of his death, then I assured the coroner the patient was not contagious and explained why his escort, the maintenance man, couldn't give any medical history. Shortly after this incident, Alaska Airlines began requiring lengthy medical questionnaires to be filled out on any patient flying to or from any medical facility on their planes. It was the first time we had encountered such regulations for transporting patients, and I am convinced it was our patient that brought them about.

Once, while coming back to Kotzebue from vacation, I was asked to escort a patient back from his stay at the Medical Center in Anchorage. It was a trip I doubt either of us shall ever forget. The patient had had minor surgery in Anchorage and was returning to his home village of Kivalina located along the coast north of Kotzebue. He was quite nervous about flying. By then I had become a frequent flyer and had the utmost faith in the comfort and safety of modern air travel. But that day, on takeoff from the Anchorage airport, the jet banked into a turn and side slipped, which means it literally slipped sideways and downward reducing altitude but not gaining speed. That generally occurs as a result of the plane banking too steeply. All of a sudden, the wing out my window appeared much closer to the ground, and I had felt every inch of its decline before it righted.

Instinctively, I grabbed the arm rests and so did the poor man I was escorting. He did not react quite as fast as I, but when he did, his large, strong hand clamped down over mine in a death grip. Fortunately, the pain of that grip took my mind off the terror of slipping downward through the sky, redirecting my scream of fear to an "ouch! ouch! ouch!" of pain. The plane quickly righted itself and continued to climb but I literally had to pry the man's hand off mine. He was so tense I feared he might pop some stitches, and I focused on calming him down as I myself quivered in shock. It was a long tense flight to Kotzebue that day.

It was also common practice to send patients to the medical center in Anchorage for conditions not necessarily deemed emergencies. The hospital there provided more patient options, more intense treatments, surgery, and education about chronic conditions. For all the medivacs and scheduled travel to the city, many of our older patients showed reluctance to go to the hospital in Anchorage. From the 1950s to the mid-1960s those who tested positive for TB were sent to the Alaska Native Medical Center, a tuberculosis treatment hospital that opened in Anchorage in 1953. Many did not return. Patients who were drug resistant or with a condition too advanced for a cure died there. The government did not send the bodies back to their relatives. It's no wonder there was fear and mistrust even though policies had changed and trust was slowly coming back. Fortunately, I saw no fear or reluctance to be treated in our local hospital.

Toward the end of tourist season one summer, a gentleman from one of our villages was admitted with a bleeding ulcer. At first the bleeding was medically manageable. A few days later he again began to bleed and was in need of a blood transfusion. Our director of nurses was protective of her limited number of staff. She did not want us doing anything that might weaken us or make us sick and cause us to miss work. She would not allow us to donate blood. Instead, at ten o'clock at night, she took two nurses to the local hotel where tourists were overnighting before flying back to Anchorage the next day. Our nurses knocked on every door asking people with our patient's blood type if they would come to the hospital and donate blood. And they did. The patient needed to be medivaced to Anchorage for surgery, but needed blood before leaving, plus extra blood to take on the plane for his trip south. He was sent out on the same plane as the people who had donated blood for him the night before.

Patients needing transport to Anchorage who were stretcher bound were placed on three folded down seats at the back of a commercial flight. The only privacy was a small screen placed at their head. The accompanying nurse sat at their side. Transports had to be arranged around the airline's scheduled departures. In summer the planes were full of curious tourists wanting to know details about our patient. As the nurse, I felt very exposed. One could barely talk with the patient without the conversation being overheard by some of the passengers. Confidentiality was compromised. The stewardess peaked in frequently and nosey passengers paraded past us to access the bathrooms behind us. Today there are special medical jets for the sole purpose of transporting patients. They are equipped as well as a hospital emergency room and privacy is assured for both patient and nurse. No more changing baby diapers in an airport restroom. The patient can be transported when they need it, not at the mercy of a commercial carrier's schedule. And tourists can enjoy their commercial flights without the stress of a very sick passenger being transported on their flights. Traveling for treatment will always be stressful, but today one can count on speed and expertise and privacy in case of emergencies.

Chapter 21

Travels

There were three distinct types of travel from Kotzebue that were expressed in different ways for different destinations. For example, if someone was going to one of the villages in the service unit to assist the doctor with medical rounds, the name of the village was given as the destination. "I'm accompanying the doctor to Point Hope tomorrow." If one was going on a medivac or a weekend of R&R to Anchorage, it was referred to as "going out." "I'm going out for a few days to do some shopping and to visit with Sally." But when it was travel that took one out of Alaska, it was referred to as "going outside" or "going south."

I kept two items readily available to grab whenever I was called on to escort a patient to the Anchorage hospital. Traveler's checks were tucked into a desk drawer ready for a short notice shopping spree. Next to the checks lay my constantly updated shopping list. The list varied depending on my current needs, but always included a trip to J. C. Penny's department store to view and perhaps purchase the latest fashions. For me, medivacs and shopping went hand in hand, but each time I had to adapt to big city shopping again. The sheer variety of items and array of colors in the ladies' clothing department was overwhelming. First find the slacks area, find your size group, then sort through all the colors and try to remember what you wanted to match them with to make a coherent outfit. After "going out" to the big city a few times, I learned to blitz the department store in record time to complete my list of needs.

There were two requisites to being selected for a medivac. The first was that you were not on duty for any shift the day of the medivac. Our director of nurses made sure we were available to leave without interrupting the work schedule. Second was one's willingness to accept the care required for the patient. Generally speaking, being willing to do medivacs was not a problem as most of the nurses looked forward to a free trip to Anchorage. Travel arrangements were made by our hospital travel clerk in conjunction with the travel clerk at the Alaska Native Medical Center in Anchorage.

They arranged for our pick up at the Anchorage airport by either ambulance or van. After arriving at the emergency room, giving my detailed patient condition report to one of their nurses or doctors, and leaving my patient in capable hands, my obligation was over, and I was off downtown to shop before returning to the airport that evening or next morning for the return flight. I carried a soft-sided folding bag stuffed into my main suitcase so I had an extra bag for purchases and a couple of cartons of milk for the return trip.

On these visits to the big city, I went through a little reverse culture-shock. The number of people in a city seemed overwhelming after living in a small, remote village like Kotzebue. It felt that every one of those city folk were in a rush. But it was the noise level that made the biggest difference. After living away from the crowds and traffic, the constant hum of city life was intimidating. A few times when my trips to Anchorage were just for rest and relaxation or R&R as we called it, or I had days off after an escort and wanted to cover more ground in the city, I would rent a car at the airport. If the large number of people in the city unnerved me, the number of cars was downright frightening. Making left hand turns across traffic was more than I wanted to handle, so I limited my driving to right turns only. Not the most efficient way to get to one's destination. Nevertheless, long spells of village life broken by medivac diversions were like a shot in the arm, giving me a city boost to hold me until the next opportunity.

Vacations and "going outside" were anticipated with great enthusiasm. These trips most often took us back to family and friends, involved multiple airlines to get to our destinations and lasted a few weeks. I did not take a vacation until my second year. In the spring of 1970, I headed back to Canada to visit family, stopping at new destinations and historically interesting places along the way. My first stop was Fairbanks, Alaska which, in 1970, was where workers from the Prudhoe Bay oil fields headed to unwind on their long stretches of days off. Fairbanks was the nearest city to the oil fields and seemed to always be full of men ready for a party. A little too eager for my liking. Downtown the bars were full, the music loud and the streets humming with activity. The kind of activity that, as the night wore on, could make a young girl blush. The Nordale Hotel, where I stayed, was in the middle of all the activity. Each time I visited, I requested a room on an upper floor facing the street so I could spend the evening watching the sights below from a safe distance out my window. For me it was the best show in town. I was not brave enough to join the partying. I traveled alone and the fellows seemed to be running in packs. That was not a safe situation for a single young lady from the Bush.

From Fairbanks I flew to Whitehorse, Yukon Territory. Whitehorse, now the capitol of the Yukon, at the end of the nineteenth century was a stop for gold miners coming overland from Skagway, Alaska en route to the gold fields in Dawson, Yukon Territory. They hiked or accompanied pack horses from Skagway to Lake Bennett, then travelled in hastily built open boats, through the dangerous Miles Canyon rapids south of White-horse. From Whitehorse the miners boarded sternwheelers that travelled the Yukon River the final stretch to the gold fields. During World War II, the Alaska Highway was constructed connecting Alaska and the Yukon to mainland Canada and the United States. The highway ensured the continued growth of Whitehorse, and now it is a major hub to the rest of the Yukon.

From Whitehorse I traveled the narrow-gauge White Pass and Yukon railway to Skagway to board the Alaska State Ferry for a three-day sail to Prince Rupert, British Columbia. The train line was built to connect the Alaskan port to the Interior. It ran from Whitehorse to the summit of the White Pass then snaked down the White Pass to the gold rush town of Skagway, carrying both passengers and vehicles. In 1970, there was no road connecting Skagway to Whitehorse. Vehicles were driven onto flatbed rail cars for the journey. Midway, the train stopped at Lake Bennett near the BC border where passengers were treated to a delicious homemade meal of beef stew, biscuits and pie served family style in a large dining room at the Bennett station. The route continued to Skagway carrying passengers past waterfalls spilling down mountainsides and on trestle bridges over deep gullies. As it swung around the curves, I could look out the window and see cars and campers resting on a flatbed, heading into the curve behind me. The building of the train route to the Interior began in 1897 with the line beginning at and running the full length of Broadway, Skagway's main street. The remainder of the line to Whitehorse was not completed till 1900. Until then, miners travelled over the Chilkoot and

White Pass, hauling their supplies with them.

Ferry travel was a new experience for me and this trip was my maiden voyage on Alaska's Marine Highway which began service to Southeast Alaska in January of 1963. It was three days of leisure with a private cabin, a cafeteria and a dining room serving delicious meals while we sailed through lush forest greenery, docking at small towns to allow people and vehicles to board or disembark. It was a wonderful trip ending in Prince Rupert, British Columbia where my family met me. We then drove through the scenic Rocky Mountains of Jasper and Banff National Parks to my home to Calgary.

I took a small jar of seal oil with me for friends and family to taste. In Kotzebue it was used as a condiment for meat, and I enjoyed its flavor. By the time I got home, the oil had turned rancid. Disappointed, I quickly put the lid back on and threw it out. When I returned to Kotzebue, I related my tale of the seal oil to a coworker from town. She was shocked that I had thrown the oil out, saying that it was best when it was rancid. Again, I was failing miserably in understanding Native cuisine.

I spent a wonderful ten days relaxing with family and visiting friends and relatives, all who wanted to know about life in the Arctic and how I was fairing in such a cold barren place. I soon had them envious of my adventures and experiences. At the Calgary airport on my return trip, I noticed how sharply people were dressed. The atmosphere was subdued, and people hugged gingerly so as to not mess hair or outfits. Even luggage was in subdued colors. At Seattle's much larger airport people dressed more casually wearing slacks and pant suits, carrying bright colored luggage and there was definitely more activity in that airport. Not only did people move faster, the noise level was higher. It was an international airport and if you paid attention, you could pick up snatches of foreign languages spoken in quiet voices. I loved sitting in a busy area of the terminal watching people while waiting for my flight. And if I sat long enough, there was always an interesting conversation to listen in on, while pretending not to. After spending any length of time in a large airport, I was always happy to be heading back to Alaska and the solitude of my new home.

At the Anchorage airport, it became apparent I was back in the last frontier. Although dress was a mixture of city and casual bluejeans and work clothes were the norm. Anchorage clothing was practical, based on the weather and not necessarily put together from a sense of fashion. At the airport excited hunters and fishermen waited to begin wilderness adventures. Rural village residents gathered in jeans and parkas or kupuks. Their luggage often consisted of boxes tied with rope, and sometimes there were questionable smells coming from them. The Anchorage airport was one of the best places for seeing a wide variety of people. It was easy to spot those from the city and those from the villages, and fun to watch them all scurrying about. At my departure gate, there were always people I knew. Chatter and laughter filled those areas as people caught up with each other's travels and the latest news. And the languages heard at that airport, other than English, included those of the state's Native populations along with those of international travelers.

People seemed friendlier in Alaska airports, and it was common to meet interesting new people. Conversations started easily. Everyone seemed interested in what other people were doing in Alaska. The most common conversation starter being, "Where are you from?" quickly leading to "What brought you to Alaska?" then on to, "So what are you doing now?"

My return trip from vacation was most eventful. I decided to visit Sitka in Southeast Alaska to see Mt. Edgecumbe High School and Sheldon Jackson College, the two boarding schools where, over the years, students from Kotzebue and Barrow attended school. Since Sitka was in Southeast Alaska, it was an opportunity for me to see another part of the state. I flew to Anchorage before flying south to Sitka. Because I was not traveling on official business, I assumed (wrongly), that quarters at the hospital in Anchorage would not be available to me and booked into the Red Ram Motor Inn located between the PHS hospital and the city center, then spent the rest of the day shopping.

Early the next morning, as I was waiting in the hotel lobby for the airport limo, a tall, nice looking gentleman came whistling down the stairs to the checkout desk.

"Good morning," he said as he swept past me, a big smile on his face. It was six a.m. I am not a morning person and my reaction to him was a somewhat negative thought about how much I disliked cheerful people so early in the morning.

After checking out, he came back to me.

"Are you going to the airport?" he asked.

"Yes."

"Great, me too. How are you getting there?"

"Airport limo."

"Think I could ride along with you?" he asked.

"I'm sure if you pay the driver he would be happy to take you too," I quipped, showing no mercy or interest. I was not in the mood for chit chat.

"So where are you headed today?"

When I replied that I was going to Sitka, he again lit up with a big smile.

"Hey, I'm going to Juneau," he said. "That's the stop before Sitka. We'll probably be on the same plane."

"Great," I replied with a decisive lack of enthusiasm. But he was not deterred by my monosyllabic responses, and seemed determined to have a conversation with me. A quick check of our tickets on the way to the airport determined we were, indeed, on the same flight. At the airport, we checked in together.

"Any chance you could seat me with this young lady," he asked the agent as he checked in. "If that's OK with you," he said, as he turned and flashed me another charming smile. I managed a smile back, and shortly we settled into the departure lounge to await our flight.

"By the way," he said, my name is Bob. I'm from Juneau."

"I'm Sue, pleased to meet you."

"So where are you from, Sue? Sitka?"

And so I broke down and told him I was from Canada, but living in Kotzebue, and going to see the boarding schools in Sitka. The conversation was off to an informative start. In spite of my earlier grumpy mood, I was just starting to enjoy our conversation, when it was announced our plane had a mechanical problem and would be at least two hours late. Back then mechanical delays were not an uncommon occurrence. This one was exceptionally long, and at such an early hour. I groaned thinking how I could have had at least another hour of sleep. Bob invited me to breakfast. After a cup or two of coffee and more delightful conversation,

I was beginning to feel human again. By the end of breakfast, I too, was feeling cheerful, and very much enjoying his company. He was a bridge engineer for the state and had been doing annual bridge inspections out of Anchorage. We sat together during the flight, chatting the whole time before saying our goodbyes when he got off in Juneau. I flew on to Sitka and had a delightful day of sightseeing.

Sitka has a rich history of Russian occupation and is the site where Russia transferred Alaska to the United States in 1867. In Sitka I was pleased to see another PHS hospital, and surprised at how large it was. It was a lovely day, and I did a lot of walking and window shopping in the small downtown area. In the center of the little fishing town sat a very impressive large Russian Orthodox church.

The next morning while waiting at the Sitka airport for my flight to Anchorage and on to Kotzebue, I was paged. It was Bob from Juneau. He was a scuba diver and after arriving in Juneau, he had packed up his diving gear and flown to Sitka to dive with friends. He was calling the airport to ask me to wait for the next flight so we could fly to Juneau together.

On personal trips out of Kotzebue I always came back a day early in case weather prevented me from getting back in time for my next shift. I called it my "weathered in" day. It stemmed from my first trip to Kotzebue that was cancelled due to a blizzard. Bob asked if I would consider using my weathered in day to visit Juneau, and offered to be my tour guide. I surprised myself by accepting. Not something I would normally do with a fellow I barely knew, but I rationalized it would be a way to see yet another Alaskan town. As our plane left Sitka, I began to wonder a little more about this fellow. I wondered why such a nice guy was single, or if he was, in fact, single. We were sitting on the ground at a stop in Gustavus when curiosity got the best of me, and I asked him his status. He started to answer just as the plane began its wind up. It was a prop jet and the noise of takeoff drowned out his answer. Once in the air, I was too embarrassed to ask again. Oh well, I thought, I would probably not see him again after today, and so I let it slide. Bob showed me a wonderful day in Juneau, pie a la mode at the Visitor's center while viewing Alaska's spectacular Mendenhall Glacier, a drive out the road north of Juneau following Lynn Canal, where I had cruised a couple of weeks earlier on the state ferry. That had happened at night, so it was nice to see a little part of where I had been, all the while with a running commentary from Bob on shipwrecks in the canal. The day ended with a before dinner drink at the famous Red Dog Saloon in downtown Juneau, then watching a Canadian Princess cruise ship sail out of town as we ate dinner at Mike's Place Restaurant across the channel from Juneau in the small town of Douglas.

Next morning, I flew back to Kotzebue. I sent Bob a thank-you note and invited him to come visit Kotzebue if he were ever inspecting bridges in the North again. We had exchanged addresses and phone numbers and promised to let each other know if we were going to be in Anchorage any time in the future. We lived at opposite ends of the state, and I didn't get to Anchorage often, although I was open to meeting with him again in the future, but in reality I doubted our paths would cross again. My story with Bob was typical of many Alaskan stories about meeting people in the most unlikely places. The population of the whole state of Alaska in 1970 was a little over 300,000, the size of a large city down south. People were open and eager to strike up conversations. Friendships started easily with that common question, "Where are you from?" Because we were all from somewhere else, and felt a bond with others who had travelled so far from home for new experiences and adventures. I never complained again about mechanicals holding up flights as I had learned those mechanicals allow time for new friendships to flourish.

Chapter 22

Problems with Alcohol

Return trips from Anchorage always found a quart or two of real milk in my luggage. When Kotzebue was dry, there were those who preferred bottles of alcohol over milk to bring back in their luggage. Once, when one of the hospital officers was returning from a trip outside, his luggage had apparently been handled rough enough for the bottles in his luggage to smack together and break. Everyone at the Kotzebue airport that afternoon knew what the officer was bringing home from the smell emanating from his luggage. State Trooper Ben was not there and no one else seemed to care, except perhaps for a few fellow travelers who were silently thankful their stash had remained intact. For me, a bottle of wine now and then from a friendly Air Force officer from the base cache was enough to satisfy my desire for the occasional glass or two.

My first year in Kotzebue, the town was wet. It was my understanding it had always been wet, but the second year, 1970, the town, for the first time, voted to go dry and it remained dry until I left in January of 1971. It was during this time that many of the Native villages around the state were beginning to address the problems caused by the abuse of alcohol by village residents. Voting to become a dry village was the first attempt to show unity against the problems caused by overindulgence.

The bootleggers in town had very profitable businesses. Overinflated prices charged for alcohol would have been better spent on food, but for those on a liquid diet, their needs were met by illegal means. I knew who one of the bootleggers was, and if I knew, it was safe to assume Trooper Ben also knew, but I was never aware of any arrests. Perhaps they served a purpose, if only to allow the inebriates to stay at home when they drank. I do know that when the town was dry there were fewer fights in public and no one stumbled and froze to death going home from the bars in town.

Whenever there was a suspicious death in any of the villages, the trooper was called to investigate. He was often accompanied by the town magistrate and frequently requested a medical person to join them. I had the privilege of being that person on one such occasion as I was the first off duty nurse contacted, and I was always willing to try something new. A man in one of the surrounding villages had apparently died while drinking home brew with a friend. Since home brew was illegal, both the trooper and the magistrate were called to investigate the death and hold an inquest. The magistrate was a respected Native elder in Kotzebue. This was going to be a new experience for me both medically and legally. I was asked to bring my camera as the trooper's camera was broken. I had visions of snapping crime scene photos just like in the movies. While flying to the village, Trooper Ben, who was from a large city environment somewhere down south, mentioned how stressed he was feeling as he had two unsolved murders on the books, with no leads in either case. Both were alcohol related and now this death was also rumored to be due to drinking. Three deaths in such a small population base were challenging. Ben was the only trooper in the service unit and seemed to always be on duty. I don't think I ever saw him without his uniform. He was a mild mannered, pleasant man liked by everyone, but he was wearing thin from his heavy workload. In the village, the man who had been drinking with the deceased was being held in the town jail. I was excited to be a part of the inquiry but nervous about the circumstances and what would be required of me. I did feel it was a privilege to have the opportunity to see how the justice system worked in this part of rural Alaska although we didn't have much information as to what had happened.

It was February, one of the darkest and coldest months of the year. Our plane landed on a cleared stretch of frozen river that ran alongside the town. I had enjoyed flying into the villages in summer months when the sun was shining. Women and children came to the landing strip to welcome anyone who was coming to town and to follow the mail bags to the post office. Today there were no smiles, just the somber faces of the local policeman and a few other men with sleds hooked to their snow machines to transport us into town. They were unusually quiet. Trooper Ben, in his friendly manner, attempted to strike up a conversation after the initial greetings, but the town men, especially the policeman, were very businesslike and did not say much even though one of their own townsmen had just died under unusual circumstances. I was hustled to one of the sleds lined with furs and once settled in, was covered with other furs for the trip to the home of the deceased. The two men I was accompanying followed behind in similar fashion. Approaching the home, which was a long single-story dwelling with a residence on each side, the curtains on one side were pulled back and worried faces peeked out at us before the curtains quickly closed again.

When we arrived and climbed out of the sleds, the trooper began asking questions, but the village policeman kept his head down as he unlocked the door and stepped aside. No one seemed to want to talk to us. The policeman mumbled something about letting us examine the scene for ourselves, and to look him up when we were done. This was not shaping up to my movie going expectations of crime scene investigations. The frost on the windows was my first clue that the heat had been turned off. It was freezing. I could see every breath I exhaled. When the lamp was lit, we were able to see the victim. He was lying on top of a single bed in the one room residence. His tiny home had been turned into a morgue. I walked to the side of the bed to view the deceased, put my camera and gloves on top of the cold stove and concentrated on what I should be looking for to determine a cause of death. I felt my presence there was a privilege I had been given, but didn't feel qualified to perform it. A coroner would be the one to do that.

The trooper asked for the bottle the two men had been drinking from. There was some alcohol left and he thought it should be taken back for analysis. There seemed to be an assumption on the part of Trooper Ben that alcohol was the cause of death. I knew I wouldn't be able to back that up and was feeling like there wasn't much I could do as I didn't have the knowledge. The trooper and magistrate began a conversation about the problem of alcohol in the villages, and how best to address it. There were no social service programs in the villages nor any treatment programs for those affected.

I began viewing the deceased in earnest. Feeling inadequate and a little unsettled about the place we were working in, I took a deep breath and began my examination. The body had been placed on the bed and the man looked as though he were sleeping. He was wearing a clean shirt and pants and his arms were folded across his chest. I tried to move his arms but they were frozen in that position. I wondered if he had fallen and hit his head but there were no signs of blood. I began to focus on his face. If he had choked would the face coloring be different, perhaps a bluish tinge? Had something come out his nose as it often does when someone chokes? But it was apparent he had been cleaned. His face had been washed. In trying to see the facial color better in the dim light and check the back of the head for injuries, I raised his head up off the pillow. In doing so my hand bumped a heavy object that slid to the edge of the bed and dropped to my feet on the floor. I was shocked when I looked down and saw it was a pistol. I released the head, jumped back and gave a little gasp of horror.

"Oh gosh," I said, "there's a gun here."

"Everyone has guns in the villages," replied the trooper waving a hand towards me as he continued his conversation with the magistrate.

"But it's a pistol and it was under the pillow," I said in a slightly higher octave.

"Yep," he replied, not even turning to look. I shuffled over closer to him, reached out and tugged at his coat. When he turned, I pointed to the gun lying on the floor.

"Look at that," I said. "A pistol, and it fell from under his head that was lying on the pillow."

"Hmm," he said absently.

"Do you suppose it has anything to do with his death?" I suggested. At that he turned to me with a loud sigh and said in a very patient voice, "I can see the gun is upsetting to you, Sue, but it's really not that unusual out here."

Well, it was for me. The guns I was used to seeing in Kotzebue were rifles and kept in the arctic entries. But being a young city-bred girl, I wasn't going to argue with an Alaska State Trooper. I was also not going to pick up the gun. No one would find my fingerprints on a possible murder weapon, but then, maybe I had watched too many murder mystery movies. It was all very unsettling to me.

That particular weekend many of the townspeople had travelled to another village for a church quarterly meeting, but the trooper wanted to hold an inquest. The magistrate put out the call for 12 people who were not related to the victim to form the body of the inquest into the cause of this sudden and unexplained death. With many of the villagers gone, getting twelve adults together became a near impossibility. It was the "not related" part that slowed things down. I was taken to the home of the current missionary, a single middle-aged lady from Colorado. She had been there for a couple of years and had become a good hunter. She served a wonderful lunch of caribou stew. I enjoyed visiting with her and hearing her hunting tales while I waited until there were finally twelve unrelated people brought together to start the inquest.

We soon learned that the man in jail was a distant relative of the deceased and was from another village. I wondered why he was being held in the jail. No one offered any other information, which seemed strange to me as there was a family living on the other side of the wall between the two dwellings. And it was a very thin wall, as I heard them trying to be quiet the whole time we were on the other side. The trooper then gave a very impassioned lecture on the evils of home brew. Since this village had a long history of making their own alcohol, it seemed appropriate to remind them it was not only illegal, but bad for all concerned, but to me something didn't seem to fit. If the cause of death was home brew, why wasn't the man he was drinking with also affected? And knowing how much everyone knew about everyone else in small villages (and this was a very small village), people had very little to say, good or bad, about either of the two men.

After the inquest, during which nothing was learned to help determine the cause of death, we all headed to the planes for the trip back to Kotzebue. A second plane was brought in to bring the body back where it would be transported to Anchorage for an autopsy. On the way to the plane, we stopped at the jail to pick up the other man involved in the incident. He sat next to me on our way back to Kotzebue. We conversed about the weather and other mundane topics, but nothing was said about what had happened in that tiny home the night before. It was not my place to ask questions.

Two days later the coroner called from Anchorage to tell our doctor what they had found when the victim thawed and they laid his arms at his side. As they were removing his clean shirt, they discovered a bullet hole in his chest. I am convinced that everyone in that town knew exactly what had happened, and the people next door, who I'm sure had heard everything going on through the thin walls, probably knew why. They certainly would have heard the gunshot, and I suspected they had also heard the pre-shot argument. Since the other fellow was put in the jail, it was probably the townsfolk who had cleaned the victim and set the scene we found the next morning. I felt sorry for Trooper Ben for this his third murder, but at least the suspect was in custody and eventually all questions would be answered. I decided I enjoyed taking care of the sick more than trying to solve causes of death. As far as I know, that is the closest I have been to a murderer. Oh, and my camera froze while we were in the victim's house, so no pictures were taken.

There was a rumor that someone, it was never divulged who, was interested in purchasing the abandoned jet liner that had experienced a wheelless landing at the airport sometime before my arrival. It was further rumored that the buyer was interested in turning the plane into a bar since it was outside the city limits and the town was often dry. Although I'm sure they would have made a lot of money, those of us in the health care field shuddered at the idea. Fortunately, the plane becoming a bar did not happen. Perhaps it was never more than just a rumor.

When the town was voted dry, the amount of alcohol-related Emergency Room visits declined. As far as I knew, the bootleggers were never shut down, but I assumed they were closely watched. Many villages throughout Alaska were going dry, giving a message to those who abused alcohol that it was not acceptable behavior. One of our doctors went a little further. If someone was drunk and needed suturing, this doctor did not use local anesthetic when sewing them up. Surprisingly, it didn't seem to bother the patients too much although word got around, and often we would get calls to see which doctor was on duty. If it was that particular doctor, the injured party came in much later. I suspect it was to give them time to do more "self-medicating" before getting treated. It appears that alcohol numbs as well as lidocaine. Back home, I had had little experience with alcohol problems. It was not in my immediate family nor within my group of friends. It was easy for me to disassociate with anyone with a drinking problem. Here in Kotzebue, with everyone either related or closely associated with each other, the negative effects of alcohol touched everyone and, in one way or another, it became everyone's problem.

Settling In At Barrow

Barrow from the Air

In August a request came to Kotzebue asking for a nurse to work TDY (temporary duty) in Barrow, Alaska (now called (Utqiagvik), to cover a staffing shortage at their twelve-bed hospital. Barrow (the name I knew it by) is situated northeast of Kotzebue on the shores of the Arctic Ocean. I immediately expressed my desire to go and was fortunate to be the one chosen. And so, at the end of August 1969, I boarded a jet to Barrow via Fairbanks. On the plane from Fairbanks to Barrow, I met Glen, the first of many Barrow residents I would come to know. He was a recent high school graduate who had been working the summer on the North Slope. He was on his way home for a short visit before flying south to attend college.

After seating myself, I watched this young fellow elbow his way through the group of tourists dressed in multi-colored airline-issued parkas until he arrived at my row.

"Hi," he said as he slid into the seat beside me.

"Hi," I said rather timidly.

"So where are you from?" he asked with a big grin as he settled in.

For a moment I debated what to answer. Was I from Calgary or Kotzebue? I determined that by this time Calgary was in the past, and I was now from Kotzebue, and so I replied with my own big smile, "I'm from Kotzebue."

"Aha," he answered, "I knew you weren't a tourist."

"How would you know that?" I queried.

"You aren't wearing one of those bright colored parkas that all the tourists wear and that's a pretty nifty fur parka you have on your lap. It is definitely not from the Sears catalog."

Of course! He had seen me carrying my muskrat fur coat. Although it was late summer, winter would soon be approaching and I wanted to be prepared for colder weather.

"How very observant. It's from the village of Shungnak," I informed him, thankful that I had not said I was from Calgary, "But, what's wrong with the tourists?"

"Oh nothing," he replied. "They just ask so many questions and you know, you get tired of answering the same ones over and over again."

"Oh good," I said, "'cause I have some questions they probably wouldn't know to ask."

"Oh yeah, like what?" he challenged with a sparkle in his eye.

"Like how often and where are the Native dances held in Barrow?"

"That's a good question," he said. "I have an aunt who is in a dance group. Maybe I could introduce you, and she'll keep you in the loop."

He laughed and leaned over and said, "That's a much better question than, "Do Eskimos really kiss by rubbing noses?"

"Well, that was going to be my next question," I said.

And that was the beginning of a lively conversation on our way to his home and my new temporary home.

"So, I assume you are from Barrow," I said. "Where have you been?"

"I just graduated from high school and spent the summer working for an oil company on the North Slope. I'm going home for a few weeks before going south to college."

As it turned out I knew friends of his family in Kotzebue. It gave us something in common for conversation and elevated me another step above the tourists. That fact was to hold true for the rest of my time in Barrow. When introduced to someone as coming from Kotzebue, I would be asked if I knew a relative or friend living there. If I did, it gave us a common link that enabled me to make a number of personal attachments in a very short period of time. The fact that I wasn't new to the culture also gave me an advantage. As the plane landed, I leaned over and said to him… "So do you?"

"Do I what?" he said looking puzzled.

"Rub noses?" I asked with a straight face.

"Maybe you'll get the answer before you go back to Kotzebue," he said with a grin.

He then told me about one of his brothers who he said was probably about my age.

"I could introduce you to him. You could check out the rubbing noses theory yourself with him." I politely declined his generous offer.

Umiak and Whale Arch on the Shore of the Arctic Ocean

Barrow is the most northern community in the United States and is over three hundred miles north of the Arctic Circle. In 1969 the population was slightly larger than Kotzebue at 1,800. There is a history of settlements in the area dating back over a century. The people of Barrow have deep ancestral roots to the land and sea in this part of Alaska. Their livelihood is primarily oriented to hunting sea mammals, with the whale being a chief source of food. In Kotzebue the smaller white beluga whale was hunted, in Barrow it was the larger black bowhead whale. Traditionally Barrow people had an active trade with the inland people of Anaktuvuk Pass whose livelihoods were oriented toward the land, hunting caribou and other land animals for their main food staples. Both places benefitted from trading. Seal and whale oil from the coast were used for heat and light and was traded for caribou skins which are significantly warmer than sea mammal skins for clothing and blankets.

The land around Barrow is flat and treeless. Although the temperatures quoted in the Public Health Service information sheets didn't look extreme, showing summer temperatures that hovered around 40 degrees and winter averages quoted as minus seventeen Fahrenheit, the wind chill in winter made temperatures feel much colder, were deeply penetrating, and could be life threatening. By this time there were no mosquitoes in Barrow, a fact not lost on me, since that summer the mosquitoes in Kotzebue had caused me much suffering. The season had passed and the weather and freezing ponds were contributing to their demise. A few evenings after arriving, I was wandering the town to get my bearings when a familiar voice called out.

"Hey nurse, whatcha doing?" It was Glen, my young airline companion.

"Being a tourist," I quipped.

He laughed and offered to be my tour guide. And a wonderful guide he was. We covered the streets of town where he pointed out stores and other businesses. There were three churches in town, Presbyterian, Catholic and Church of God.

"That's the Polar Bear Theater," he said. "And on weekends after the movie, there are modern dances with a band from town, and they are really good. Maybe you'd find someone to rub noses with if you go," he said with a smirk on his face. Later in my stay, I would experience those dances. The movies in Barrow were much more recent. It was in Barrow, Alaska that I saw the movie "2001 Space Odyssey," ironically, in a place that still lived by subsistence hunting.

My new friend took me to Browerville, a group of homes to the east of town separated by a lake and connected to the main town by a road running along the shore of the Arctic Ocean. Brower's Cafe, next to a large whalebone arch on the shore, was full of interesting old whaling items and served good food. There were three White whaling captains who came to Barrow around the turn of the century, married into the community, and stayed. Their names were Brower, Leavitt and Hopson, names that are still prominent in the community.

And true to Glen's word, I was taken to meet his Aunt Bonnie She promised to call me whenever there was a dance as the tourist season was winding down and times and location would be by word of mouth. Walking back to Barrow from Browerville, Glen again mentioned his older brother and offered to introduce me to him. Again, I declined his offer. I was not interested in a blind date.

The store in Barrow was larger than the one in Kotzebue and carried more food and clothing choices. It also had wonderful Native made items. I bought some gifts and items for my own collection. I also had a pair of sealskin mukluks made to order for myself. Prices for food and other goods were high and much shopping was done by mail order. I sometimes wondered if it were the Bush villages that kept stores like J.C. Penny's and Sears alive and well in Alaska. The Sear's catalogue was anxiously awaited each year and pages were soon frayed from family members thumbing through. But for handmade Native items, the local stores and souvenir shops were places for quality and authenticity, and items were well worth the price.

As in Kotzebue, the hospital and the school were government run with professional jobs filled by outsiders. Most other jobs went to towns-people. The Licensed Practical Nurses and aides in both Kotzebue and Barrow were from town. Not only were they excellent workers, they were part of the town and knew the patients and their histories, which can be meaningful in helping along the healing process. The homes in Barrow seemed larger and in better condition than those in Kotzebue. I was told that many of them were built from the wood of old shipwrecked whaling ships. The town was also supplied with natural gas by lines supported by square arches over the main street. Gas was discovered along with oil in the North Slope region in 1968, but an earlier large deposit found close to Barrow in 1965 provided the town's heat and light. The gas comes from the National Petroleum Reserve operated by the Federal Government.

There were other government facilities near Barrow, the largest being the Naval Arctic Research Lab (NARL) owned and operated by the U.S. Navy. The University of Alaska had run arctic research projects out of this lab since 1954. It had also maintained floating research stations on ice floes north of Barrow in the Arctic Ocean. The lab had large numbers of native plants and animals for ongoing research.

The military also had a presence close to Barrow. The DEW line system was a line of radar defense installations that were built in the 1950s during the Cold War. They stretched from Alaska to Greenland and were built in cooperation with both the Canadian and American governments to monitor aircraft activity in the far north. The base in Kotzebue was connected to the DEW line installations.

Although the Public Health Service complex was spread over a large area, the hospital itself was small with only 12 patient beds. The entire complex was built on pilings above ground level. This was, I was told, to counteract the frozen tundra. This concept had been pioneered in Inuvik in the Canadian north. In fact, even the utility lines in Inuvik were above ground. Permafrost, the frozen layer of soil just below the surface, remains stable unlike the surface soil that thaws as the temperature warms in summer months and refreezes when winter sets in. This constant surface thaw and freeze along with the heat from buildings set on the ground can cause shifting foundations. Buildings on pilings anchored in the permafrost were more stable.

The pace at the Barrow hospital was slower than what I was used to, and I was happy to have more time at work to visit with patients and staff. The Emergency Department, however, was very active. A large sign on the front door of the hospital read:

Emergencies Only on Weekends
This does not include colds or VD

Barrow Hospital

VD referred to venereal disease, nowadays referred to as STD's. I was shocked at the bluntness. In place of an ambulance, the hospital emergency vehicle was a flat-bed truck which was dispatched if there was a need for a stretcher case. People also brought patients to hospital on sleds pulled by snow machines.

The quarters were cozy, comfortable and connected to the hospital by enclosed indoor walkways as were officers' quarters and other residences and out buildings. These even extended to a large hall where social events were held. A person need never leave the hospital complex, as all one's physical needs could be met within the conjoined buildings radiating from the hospital proper. It was possible, but how sad that would be, to not experience the town, its people, and all the town activities.

It was a quick adjustment for me to my new work place as the policies and paperwork were the same as Kotzebue. The bulk of my orienting time was spent finding where the supplies and other items were kept. The staff were friendly and great fun to work with. People made me feel welcome from my first day. As I began to put people from town together into family units, I discovered that people in Barrow were much more connected to the whole of the population than they were in Kotzebue. Not only were there siblings and their immediate families, but aunts and uncles and cousins. Many cousins, and in laws and their families and pretty soon, it seemed, everyone was interconnected. One better not make a negative comment about anyone, as the person you were talking to just might be related to the one about whom you were making the comment.

"Emma sure is funny. Is she always doing crazy things?"

To which Dora replies. "Oh yah. Sort of. She's my cousin."

"Oh, well I mean funny in a good way. Just different from what I would ever think of."

"Yah, different from what any of us would dare do. It's what makes her so fun."

"Right, fun, that's what I meant."

And I would make a mental note that Dora and Emma were cousins and be careful what I said about anyone with their two last names. After a while, it finally registered with me that I should keep any negative thoughts to myself, which is what one ought to do anyway.

The people of Barrow also had a great sense of humor and there was a lot of teasing and joking. It made me feel accepted when people were comfortable enough to joke with me and about me. And all teasing ended with the words "I jokes," just to make sure I didn't take their banter the wrong way.

The biggest surprise at the hospital was television in all the patient rooms. I was delighted. It had been a very long time since I had seen a TV program. Unfortunately, there was no TV in the living quarters. I must have been quite visibly enjoying this new treat as one day, one of my patients who had a very interesting program on in his room, said to an LPN who wandered in:

"Don't watch the TV, watch nurse. More fun to watch her expressions while she's watching the program. And she keeps bringing me coffee and cleaning up my room." And they howled with laughter until I chastised them:

"Shh, quiet, I can't hear what they're saying."

That set off another round of laughter. But my patient was right. I found myself frequently offering to bring patients coffee and juice and doing a lot of tidying up in the rooms when something good came on. Anything to see the program.

The dining room at the Barrow Hospital was very small; in fact, there were two separate rooms. Much to my disappointment, they were divided into Native employees in one and non-Native employees in the other. There definitely wasn't room for all of us in one room, and I was told the town employees liked it that way as they spoke in their own language when together, but to me it was segregation, and I didn't like it. After being there for a month, I decided to have my after lunch coffee in the other room, much to the surprise and amusement of my coworkers. The folks in the other room also seemed surprised to see me but smiled and continued on with their conversation in their language.

That was another difference between the two villages. In Kotzebue if there were two White people and four Natives gathered anywhere, the conversation was in English. There was not much Native language spoken at work unless it was to a patient who did not understand English. In Barrow the Inupiaq language was spoken by not only the elders, but by my peers. This younger age group was bilingual. If there were two Natives and four White people anywhere together, the two Native people conversed with each other in Inupiaq. Barrow people were attempting to carry on the traditions, language and culture of their ancestors. Not an easy task when another culture, very different from their own, had been thrust upon them.

At first, I was a little uncomfortable in that dining room as clearly I did not understand what they were talking about, but when it was something I was privy to, someone would repeat it to me in English. I certainly didn't feel they were saying anything about me, and I enjoyed listening to the language being spoken in conversation. The language of a people is their essence and I was glad it was being spoken so freely here. In Kotzebue there were two dialects spoken, Yup'ik and Inupiaq. That was probably a factor in undermining the town's cohesiveness. I had learned a few Inupiaq words and so I was straining to figure out what was being said. As luck would have it, at one point I actually did have an inkling. I'm not sure how, except that I heard a name and knew that person was going to Anchorage that evening. I also heard the words Alaska Airlines and then someone else responded with the word sounding "achoo," and I knew from a recent experience that meant "I don't know." I felt the person was asking what time the evening flight left for Anchorage. I knew, and so I answered:

"The evening flight to Anchorage leaves at 6:45 this evening," I said shyly.

The room got very quiet and everyone turned to look at me. A few quick questions were directed in the Native tongue to the LPN I worked with on the ward and her response was:

"Achoo. She's from Kotzebue."

Finally, someone asked me if I understood what they were saying and I realized that they were wondering, since I had been in Kotzebue for a while, what the chances were that I really could understand what they were saying. They were also probably thinking back to their last conversation to make sure they hadn't said anything that might upset me or embarrass them. And I realized it was my turn to have some fun. Tease me, huh?

"Oh," I said, with a sly little smile as I started to get up. "Maybe." And then I left.

It remained quiet in the room, at least until I was out of earshot. By the end of the shift, I'm sure every Native employee in the hospital had been alerted to be careful what they said around the Kotzebue nurse as she might understand them. For the next couple of days, I had different people ask me if it was true that I might understand the language, and it was all I could do to keep a straight face as I said "maybe," over and over. Finally, one of the maintenance men leaned on our nurse's station desk and began asking me questions in Inupiaq. He made a point of phrasing them slowly and distinctly and of course I couldn't answer. Finally, he smiled, turned and announced to all those around:

"She don't know." Then he turned to me saying, "Right?" And when I answered "Right!" there were noticeable sighs of relief and much laughter.

"You got us good" someone said. To which I replied:

"I jokes too."

But trying to communicate using words of different languages can also lead to confusion as one conversation proved. This was a conversation I had with a hospital employee when I first arrived in Barrow and was eager to attend one of their dances. It went something like this.

(Me) "When will the next dance be at the Polar Bear Theater?"

(Iva) "Achoo!"

(Me) "Gesundheit!"

(Iva) "What?"

(Me) "The dances, when is the next one?"

(Iva) "Achoo!"

(Me) "Gesundheit."

(Iva) "What are you saying? I don't know that word."

(Me) "I'm blessing your sneeze."

(Iva) "What sneeze? What makes you think I'm sneezing?"

(Me) "You said Achoo. You know, the sound you make when you sneeze. I was saying what we say when someone does actually sneeze."

(Iva) "But I'm not sneezing. Achoo means 'I don't know.' What was the word you said? I don't know what that means!"

I explained the meaning of Gesundheit, and we both had a good laugh.

The spoken language is accompanied by gestures and facial expressions that also speak volumes. And it always amazed me how quickly folks in Barrow could go from Inupiaq to English without missing a beat. I wondered how I would have fared if I had come here and been forced to understand and speak their language, as they had experienced just one generation before I arrived. I'm afraid I would not have been able to communicate for a very long time. There were, however, one or two Inupiaq words that I picked up and used frequently. One word was "alapah," which means "it's cold." That is the translation, but it seemed to be used for a specific degree of cold and was generally accompanied by facial and body gestures. For instance, instead of saying, "It's freezing out," or, "It's really cold today," one would say alapah. I noticed that I would use the term long before my Inupiaq friends used it. It appeared the term "really cold" varied from their viewpoint to mine. The other word was "ahdee." It meant "ouch" or was used to convey something painful or hurtful or sad. Some non-Native staff were uncomfortable when around townspeople speaking their own language. They wondered what was being said and if it was anything about them. Being around a conversation I didn't understand could leave me feeling a little left out when it happened, but that did not bother me. I enjoyed hearing the language spoken in conversation.

Thanks to Glen's personal tour of the town and the friendliness of the hospital staff, I was quickly settling in and feeling at home in my new surroundings. I was surprised at the differences between Barrow and Kotzebue, differences in the homes, the interrelatedness of the town's people, and the use of traditional language. I was also impressed with the people I was meeting and the feel of the town. I was looking forward to experiencing Barrow and all it had to offer, and to learning more about the culture in this part of Alaska.

CHAPTER 24

Big Ships: The *North Star* and the *Manhattan*

I arrived in Barrow towards the end of August to fill a temporary vacancy in the nursing staff and was there until the middle of November when a new nurse was hired permanently.

Arctic summers are brief and busy. It was a joy to experience daylight for what seemed to be one very long glorious day. But winter, with its cold dark bluster, is always just around the corner. In September daylight lasted from 9 a.m. to 6 p.m. followed by a long period of dusk. By October the sun set at 4 p.m., by November 3 p.m. and in December we had twenty -four hours of darkness.

In Barrow snow fell on the first of October and snow machines, popular with the Barrow PHS male employees, were cleaned and oiled to make them ready for winter use. I went on one or two snow machine trips during my stay there. The one I remember most was twelve miles out of town to the site of the Will Rogers and Wiley Post Monument.

Will Rogers and Wiley Post Monument

It marked the place where actor, entertainer, and humorist Will Rogers and aviator Wiley Post died in 1935 when their plane crashed after taking off from Barrow. On our way, we passed an old movie set replicating a Native village site. I was told, but no longer recall, the name of the movie. I had not been aware of any movies depicting Inupiat people, only cowboys and Indians and a lot of John Wayne Westerns. A monument had been erected at the crash site. Arriving, we stretched our legs and broke into two teams for a hard and fast snowball fight, leaving all of us plastered with snow, sweaty and very hungry. Blankets were unfolded in the sleds and a picnic ensued before heading back to town. There seemed to be just as many picnics held in winter as in summer in the Arctic.

Shortly after arriving in Barrow, the yearly supply ship *North Star* came. That year, 1969, the pack ice was impassable in many areas. The ship made it to Wainwright (about 85 miles southwest of Barrow), and had continued on to Barrow until the ice was too thick for the ship to break through. Dynamite charges were set on the ice and, although the ship didn't get as close to shore as it had other years, the blasting brought it close enough for barges to bridge the gap. The town shut down when it was announced offloading of supplies would begin. There was an agreement with employers that allowed townsfolk to have time off to participate in this yearly event without fear of losing their jobs. Employers had come to the realization that the whole town focused on the arrival of yearly goods, and all able-bodied men were assisting in the transfer of supplies from ship to shore. The ship unloaded everything from yearly food orders of our own doctors and commissioned officers, to non-perishable store goods, building material that could be easily assembled, and even vehicles. The most precious cargo was the yearly supply of fuel oil. Men assembled on the beach where cranes and equipment used for offloading had been left from the previous year. It took groups of men working around the clock to get the equipment up and running after sitting on the beach for a year, and to keep it running during off-loading. Other men were part of the off-loaders. Various shifts ran 24 hours a day until the last load was transported from the ship. This varied from year to year but always lasted a number of days to up to a week.

The *North Star*

Every year the ship's captain invited the nurses aboard for coffee, and so I too became caught up in the frenzy of its arrival. I travelled out to the ship on a large empty landing craft with two other off duty nurses plus five barge crew members. Just getting to the ship was exciting. Being empty, the front end of the landing craft rode higher than the back. The driver, a man from the ship, stationed in the back, could not see the condition nor gauge the thickness of the ice directly in front of him. Two Native guides climbed to the top of the front end to help the driver navigate. They would visually survey the ice directly ahead of the craft, point with exaggerated flinging of arms in whatever direction looked most promising for the barge to ram forward through the ice to make progress.

No one knows snow and ice as well as the Inupiaq. As they spend a great deal of the year living in a variety of winter conditions, they have, by necessity, developed a large number of descriptive words for both ice and snow. The notion that their language has more than one hundred words for snow is somewhat exaggerated, but their livelihood and safety rely on knowledge of a variety of snow and sea ice conditions.

The driver of our landing craft depended on the men stationed on the front. He would back up, power forward in the direction they pointed out, going full speed until we hit the resistance of the ice. The whole craft shuddered and tilted to one side or the other. When it righted, the procedure would begin again. Point, back into the channel made on the last ram, and plow ahead through the ice until, after many successes and failures, the vessel finally made it to open water and the ship.

From first standing in the middle of the vessel, I began dashing from one side to the other in order to see what was happening. I was in utter disbelief as our vessel moaned and grated through ice pans of varying size and thickness until we came to a grinding stop. The first time this happened, I was holding on to the side rail of the barge to steady myself. When the barge hit the ice on the bow and started to tilt, I pulled my hand off the edge just in time to hear the very spot I had been holding crunch against the ice. It hit so hard I almost lost my footing. I am sure, had I not moved my hand when I did, I most certainly would have lost some fingers.

Barge in Pack Ice

Finally, we reached the ship. For a young woman from the prairies, this was the largest ship I had ever seen. The landing craft pulled alongside it and was secured to the side of the vessel, after which, a huge box like container was lowered onto the landing craft. We nurses stepped inside and were hoisted up the side of the ship and swung over onto the deck. As soon as our box cleared the craft, the barge crew untied it from the ship and began moving to where the unloading was taking place. As it left, I prayed there would be no cables breaking as we would have dropped directly into the icy water below. When we were safely on deck and helped out of the box, we were led upstairs and down hallways to the captain's cabin. I don't know what I had expected, but was amazed at how spacious and elegant this living space was in comparison to the outside of this massive working boat. It was a delight to be in such lovely surroundings. But the biggest surprise was the large baby grand piano that sat in the middle of the cabin. Not only did we have coffee and sweets, but we were serenaded by music the captain played on this beautiful piano. Not at all what I had expected of a supply ship in the Arctic Ocean.

An annual tradition of the *North Star* involved the ship's first mate who had a long-standing date with the children of Barrow. He came to the school yard each year throwing out handfuls of candy. I don't know if he did this in other villages, but it was definitely a favorite tradition in Barrow. The following year, back in Kotzebue, word came that the ice was so thick north of Barrow, that the *North Star* was unable to make it through close enough to offload. Essential supplies such as food and fuel were airlifted into Barrow from a point close to Kotzebue at enormous cost, that would be passed on to the Barrow townspeople.

After my memorable trip to the *North Star*, I found myself on another trip. This time in the hospital truck, driving out the road to Point Barrow north of the town. The road led past the duck hunting area marked by a number of small shacks. When we made it to the Point, there were large blue tinged icebergs floating in the ocean. The light blue color indicated the icebergs had recently broken off from the solid ice pack. At the Point there were many whale bones scattered around, including large vertebrae that people retrieved to make into footstools. Unfortunately, the cost of shipping them was prohibitive, and so, as unique as they would have been to own, I just admired them. I also dipped my toes into the Arctic Ocean at the top of the world, just to say I had been there and done that.

Now that all the necessary supplies had made it through the ice and been unloaded for another year, we were able to celebrate the coming of winter and the many things the *North Star* had delivered with a mini picnic. And celebrate we did, at the most northern point of the United

States, with thermoses of hot coffee, any leftovers from our fridges, including sandwiches made by the gals, chips and store-bought sweets from the guys, all while dressed in long johns, scarves and warm hats, coats, and gloves. Winter was definitely on its way. As we headed back to town, I realized that so many of the things that made life comfortable and enjoyable here in the high Arctic had arrived on the yearly supply boat, and how critical that ship was for the town. Little did we know, an even larger ship was on its way.

One very foggy evening, myself and a few other nurses, were making our way back through one of the long indoor corridors from a storage room to the main hospital, when one of us happened to look out one of the windows facing the ocean. The fog had lifted for a few minutes and exposed the outline of a huge ship out in open water offshore. At first, I thought it was just thicker fog, but it was definitely darker than what we had been seeing and was the outline of a ship. As quick as it had appeared, it disappeared in a swirl of fog, and we wondered if we had imagined it. I worked the night shift and by morning I was very tired and happy to finally be going to bed. I had just crawled under the covers and was slipping into dreamland, when I was awakened by loud banging on my door. It was Brenda, one of the older widowed nurses, hollering at me to get up, get dressed, and go outside. The town, she announced, was full of White men.

That very huge ship whose outline we had seen the night before was the American icebreaker and oil tanker, the *Manhattan*. It had successfully completed a maiden voyage through the ice choked Northwest Passage. It was a test run to see if oil could be successfully shipped through a northern route. It was many times larger than the *North Star* and it did appear that a large number of its crew were indeed roaming the streets of Barrow. There was a helicopter, I was told, bringing crew to and from the ship. Some of the nurses had gone onboard. Brenda was sure I too could get on board if I smiled sweetly at the nice young men. I stood watching all those "nice young men" and realized they probably had not seen any girls for quite some time and decided I just wasn't up for all that that entailed. After a long night shift, I was very tired. I went back to bed.

For a few days after this momentous occasion, the staff, especially the men, were boasting of their American accomplishment making sure I, a Canadian, realized it was an American vessel that had conquered the Canadian Arctic. Then, while listening to the news on the television at work, I learned that the *Manhattan* had only made it through the ice with the backup help of the Canadian ice breaker the *Sir John A. McDonald*. It took two icebreakers to make a path through the arctic ice. Today, they are talking about cruise ships touring those same waters and yet still there are people who do not believe in global warming. The next day I made sure all those boastful Americans knew their ship would not have made it to Barrow without the help of the Canadian ship and put an end to the boasting. I later regretted that I had given up the opportunity to go aboard the massive tanker to see and explore a piece of history in the making. Sometimes we are fortunate to be at the right place at the right time to expand our knowledge and witness an important event. For me, this time, sleep was more important than meeting nice young men or experiencing another big ship.

CHAPTER 25

Dancing

Sometimes a chance for a fun time is offered when you least expect it. It happened for me while I was working an evening shift at the Barrow hospital during the unloading of the *North Star*. I was called to the Emergency Room for an accident victim from the beach. Two young men from town were helping a third who had experienced the unfortunate landing of a full oil drum on one of his big toes. At first the foot was numb, but in the middle of being x-rayed, the pain set in. Amazingly, neither the toe nor the foot were broken and all the patient needed was some pain control. I went back to his friends to tell them to stick around as he would need help going home, when one of them exclaimed:

"You must be the nurse from Kotzebue." Surprised, I turned to look at him and knew immediately who he was.

"And you must be Glen's brother," I said.

"How did you know?" he asked.

"Well, I said, "I have a feeling that nose is a family trait." It was a big nose. My comment set off peals of laughter from the other fellows.

"Boy she got that right," one said. And, to my relief, Glen's brother laughed too. His name was Loren and he told me Glen had mentioned me. Before their injured friend returned for discharge, Loren had invited me to a dance that weekend sponsored by the Junior Chamber of Commerce. I accepted. A few days later, the hospital social worker announced the dance to everyone at the lunch table. I was surprised that others didn't seem too interested. I couldn't understand why young single nurses weren't excited about a dance.

"Is anyone going?" I asked. No one answered.

"Well, I am," I said.

A silence followed, the kind that makes you wonder what you said to cause it to set in, and all eyes in the dining room turned toward me.

"That's probably not an event you should go to alone," said the social worker.

"I'm not," I replied.

Then, not only was every eye on me, but every mouth dropped open as well. I wondered why they were so shocked. Maybe they were a little jealous that I had a date to a dance so soon after arriving.

"Who are you going with?" the social worker asked with a frown of trepidation on his face. And so I told him.

"Someone I met in the emergency room earlier this week. I met his brother on the plane from Fairbanks coming here. They both seem very nice." The room remained quiet as all eyes then turned to the social worker who proceeded to give me the "big brother" talk. The conversation that ensued made me wonder if folks were showing the same kind of concern they would for any young girl new in a town anywhere, or if there was an underlying message that perhaps I should not be fraternizing with young men from town. Like Kotzebue, the nursing staff did not appear to interact much with the town. I hoped that, in this case, the concern was that I didn't know him very well versus any negative incident in the past between nurses and Native men. I did not want to think there was any subtext of racism in their concern for me dating someone from town. There was no Air Force base in Barrow offering imported men from down South as a social outlet, yet the nurses showed no interest in the dance.

"Doesn't sound like you know him too well," the social worker said, helping allay thoughts of any racially motivated reasons for his concern. "You can never be too safe. I would definitely arrange for a chaperone. You know, just to be sure." I began to wonder what he thought might be unsafe, the dance or my date. And a chaperone? It was 1969 and I was 24 years old. I didn't need a chaperone! I had been dealing with, and surviving, those men at the base in Kotzebue for heaven's sake! When he saw the puzzled look on my face, he said he and his wife would also be there, and he would keep an eye out for me and for me to not hesitate to come to him if I had any problem. I agreed, and everyone present, who I knew thought this new girl in town was jumping into things too fast, seemed to be appeased.

I had a great time at the dance. The live band from town was fabulous and played all the latest hits along with some oldies. And I danced with not just Loren but a large number of other fellows that stopped by for him to introduce to me. Most were somehow related to Loren. Finally, when I began to feel I would be dancing with almost every male there, I jokingly said he surely couldn't be related to that many people. Turns out he was, and it was the beginning of a very wonderful friendship. We got together frequently, often in my quarters for cards and conversation. Although we were peers, we had grown up in different worlds. Often our conversations explored those differences well into the night.

Through work I also met and became friends with two of Loren's sisters and a brother-in-law who worked in maintenance. This guy really did have relatives everywhere. Throughout my years living in Alaska, I continue to have contact with Loren's family. A high school reunion at the boarding school in Sitka brought two sisters, nieces and a nephew to spend an afternoon at my home in Juneau between ferries on their way to the reunion. Another sister stayed with me when she was in town for a conference. She accompanied my son as he delivered newspapers to the neighborhood.

"I want to go with you," she said, "We don't do this in Barrow!"

It was before boxes were in place to hold the local papers. My son announced she was a good thrower with perfect aim. Another sister, a Presbyterian minister, became the associate pastor of Native Ministries in my church in the 1980s.

True to her word, Glen and Lorens's Aunt Brenda called me whenever there was a dance in town. She came by the hospital quarters in her Pug, the summertime version of transportation in the villages. Her Pug was a 4-wheel two-seater. In Kotzebue most people used three wheelers.

The Native dances in Barrow were as fun as they were in Kotzebue; however, the beat and consequent movement of the dancers was slightly different from what I was used to. Somehow, I felt a little off beat when I danced. I felt very honored when someone at the dance I attended with Brenda came to me as we were leaving and said I danced like Kotzebue people. Feeling very proud, I replied with a big smile, "I am Kotzebue people."

I also went to the modern dances at the Polar Bear Theater with Loren. The town had a very swinging local band and the dances in Barrow were as good as any I had attended down south. At our first dance we jumped up to the first song played, a favorite for us both. Very quickly it was apparent we were the only couple on a very large dance floor. It also appeared I was the only White girl in the theater. I began to blush and felt as if I was making a spectacle of myself. Ah, life's embarrassing moments! We kept dancing, but I could feel my face turning beet red. Keeping my head down, I waited and prayed for other couples to join us. They did not. I was convinced the band, all local young people, played that song longer than usual just to keep us in that awkward place. When no one joined us on the dance floor, I began to think it was on purpose, and when everyone clapped when the music ended, I knew I had been right. They were having fun with us at our expense. Poor Loren was as embarrassed as I was, and probably suffered teasing long after the dance from his "many relatives."

We attended the Polar Bear Theater dances often. I enjoyed dancing with him but I thought it would be nice for us to go to one of the Native dances. One night on our way back to the nurses' quarters after a dance at the Polar Bear Theater, I decided to broach the topic.

"So Loren, I have been going to town dances with your Aunt Brenda. Glen set me up with her and I am enjoying it a lot as I go to the town dances in Kotzebue too. I've been thinking It would be fun if you took me to a town dance sometime."

But you're going with Aunt Brenda," he said.

"Yes, but I'd like to see you dance," I replied.

That's more for the elders, he said. "People our age prefer the band dances to the drum dances. Besides, I haven't been to a town dance in a long time. I'm pretty rusty." That's when I declared, "No more Polar Bear dances until we go together to a town dance." He laughed, then relented and soon after we went together to a town dance.

The drums are the beat of the dance. Made from intestines and membranes of animal organs stretched over oval wooden frames, they are played by the men. A drum is held in one hand while a stick in the other hand beats the rhythm, striking the drum from the underside. They can be very loud as they mark the beat of each song. Both men and women sing which, to me, sound like chants. If it was a story dance, the story was often self-evident from the dancing. Men and women dance differently. Women keep their feet rooted to the ground and bob and sway from the knees. They use their hands to show the motions for the song. Men move their feet and do more bending, twisting and moving about than the women.

Men are very theatrical in their dance moves as they imitate animals with exaggerated motions and cries. When dancing begins in Eskimo dances, it is soft and gentle through the first round then, BAM! with a single loud beat on the drum, the pace quickens and the actions of the dance become more pronounced. It is exciting to watch and always thrilling to be a part of the dance. Story dances are owned by specific dance groups and are not to be performed by others without permission. For me, the beat of the drum always roused my desire to be a part of the dance and to move in rhythm to its beat.

Eskimo Dances

Another custom, still followed by Inupiaq dancers, is to wear gloves when dancing. I asked many people about the significance of the gloves and no one, either in Kotzebue or Barrow, could tell me the reason behind them. Even if the gloves weren't worn, they were clutched in the dancer's hands. I was told only that it was the polite thing to do. Whatever the reason was, it was lost in time long ago, but the practice has been carried forward. I bought a pair of calf skin gloves with fringes that became my prized dance gloves. At a town dance, there was always a common or invitational dance announced where everyone present was

Dancing Couple

invited to dance with the group. The summer tourists loved it and it was fun watching them imitating the Native dancers.

The dance group Loren took me to was not the same one I had been going to with his Aunt Brenda. We watched for a long time before Loren said, "OK, watch close, as I'm only going to dance a couple of dances, then we'll leave and go to the Polar Bear dance." I grinned and nodded my head as he got up and headed to the dance floor. It was an invitational dance but I stayed in the bleachers, intent on watching Loren dance. I had also been watching the drummers and chanters, and I saw that one of the elder drummers was very white skinned, abnormally white skinned, as if his skin had been bleached. He looked like me after a winter in the Arctic.

"Who is that white man doing the drums?" I asked Loren when he returned to his seat.

"That's my dad." The statement wasn't followed by "I jokes," the common phrase used to signify one is pulling your leg, and so I was a little confused.

"Quit fooling," I replied, "He's white. You're not." Loren had proudly announced to me early on that he was 100% Inupiaq. If that were true, how could this extremely white-skinned man be his dad?

"He can't be your dad," I said as I summed up my limited knowledge of genetics.

"I think I know who my dad is," he replied grinning.

No, he wasn't kidding. Then I took a closer look at the fair skinned man. Sure enough, this man with white skin had Eskimo features. "But he's white," I exclaimed, voicing the obvious. And this is the story I was told about Loren's dad, who was also full blood Inupiat.

Many years ago, while his dad was hunting alone, he had just shot and killed a polar bear when a severe winter storm blew in, stranding him. In order to keep his hands warm, he slit open the fresh kill and put his bare hands inside. He eventually made it home but quickly began to lose the pigment in his skin. Polar bear liver is toxic to humans and it was felt he had rested his hands on the liver, then afterward had somehow ingested some of the organ secretions left on his hands. It was the only thing that had happened to explain the drastic change in skin color. Thyroid conditions can also cause the loss of skin pigment but that generally occurs over a longer period of time and that type of pigment loss can start out blotchy before it affects the total skin surface. His medical record was vague, only listing what had happened and not attempting to explain why. The case of the changed skin color will forever be a mystery, but my guess, being a rational nurse, is that the loss of pigment was pretty much tied to a malfunctioning thyroid gland.

The other type of dancing I experienced in Barrow took place in the night skies. One evening, coworkers alerted me to the spectacle outside our quarters and a group of us went out in our warmest outerwear to lie in the snow and watch the show. I had not seen northern lights until that cold clear November night. A kaleidoscope of color in the northern sky made the display so unforgettably special. They literally danced and sang. I would not have believed it if I had not seen it with my own eyes and heard it with my own ears. Waves of green and red and yellow moved not only across the sky, but swirled in ever increasing long and wide undulating wavelike bands, until it seemed they would touch us on the ground. And then they hummed. Not as any human would hum, but a high-pitched sound that made me think that maybe they were announcing the coming of an alien space ship. It was both beautiful and eerie at the same time. There are scientists that say the aurora does not emit sound, but I was there and heard it with my own ears. There were continuous ohs and ahs as we lay enthralled under this divine spectacle. After a time, it slowly faded into green waves sweeping across the sky. And as the quiet of the night again settled around us, we became aware of how cold we were. Reluctantly, we brushed ourselves off and went in for hot chocolate. It wasn't until I was climbing into bed that I realized I hadn't taken my camera. I wondered though if my little camera would have been able to capture the dazzling display God had put before us that winter night. In doing some research on the northern lights, I discovered that these beautiful multi-color displays of light, also called the Aurora Borealis and mainly visible in the dark winter months, are caused by collisions of electrically charged particles from the sun that collide with gas particles from the Earth's atmosphere. The colors that are displayed depend on which gas particles are colliding. For all the descriptive words we used that night for the spectacle we saw, the Inupiaq term, "ahzaa" summed it up for me. The word ahzaa is an expression of amazement and is voiced in such a way that there is no doubt an exclamation point should follow.

CHAPTER 26

Understanding Cultural Differences

In Kotzebue, I asked questions about Inupiaq ways and customs and tried to immerse myself as much as possible into the town and culture. Although the living conditions I saw in town sometimes depressed me, the people never failed to lift my spirits. I was greeted with smiles in passing. Perhaps that was a cultural adaptation for people who lived in harsh conditions where it was dark and cold for much of the year. These people worked hard to survive and, in traditional times, lived in close proximity to one another in semi-subterranean sod dwellings. Perhaps the best and most positive way of coping with such a harsh environment is to present with smiles and a good sense of humor. At least that's what my anthropology book suggested.

In my first year in Kotzebue, I enrolled in an anthropology correspondence course from the University of Alaska in a desperate attempt to understand the things I was seeing and experiencing. One thing I learned from this course was that in cross-cultural situations we look at things from our own cultural point of view. This puts blinders on how we interpret situations, as we don't consider other interpretations. This, I learned, was known as having an ethnocentric, or one-sided point of view. For instance, in Kotzebue I would hear grumblings from non-Native supervisors about male workers from town who frequently did not show up for work. These observations became generalized to include most Native men, referring to "those people" as lazy or irresponsible. These generalizations bothered me. I knew from spending time visiting in town, "those people" were definitely not lazy, but I also could not explain their frequency for not showing up for work. I worked with their wives and the women were very reliable. Perhaps the correspondence course could have helped me to understand, but, unfortunately, I dropped it. All the fun I was having on my time off work didn't leave much time for studying.

Questions I had about the Inupiaq culture were addressed to people of my own culture who had only been living in Kotzebue a year or two longer than myself. Their opinions were based on their limited perspective and not from a Native point of view. Meeting Loren gave me insight from his cultural perspective. We spent many hours talking as young adult peers from two very different worlds. True to my culture, I asked many questions. Finally, he said:

"Let me tell you about my life and my experiences."

In response to my questions, Loren proceeded to tell me stories about his experiences growing up that gave me a different point of view. I asked why so many Inupiaq people had English names.

"Well," said Loren, "missionaries had trouble saying Inupiaq names and so gave us English names that were easier for them to pronounce and write. We still had our Inupiaq names but we became known only by our English names. To this day, children are given both Inupiaq and English names at birth, but in public they are still known by their English names." I was shocked that the names parents gave their children were disregarded. It felt like identity theft to me.

"I was six years old when my family moved to Barrow from a village on Alaska's North Slope close to the Canadian border. I, along with my older siblings, had to enroll in school. I did not speak English but someone translated the teacher's questions to me. When I answered in Inupiaq, I saw nods of approval from my classmates. But unless I gave the answer in English, the teacher said it was wrong. We had to use English to be right. This was done to all students to encourage them to speak English, but to me it was equivalent to being told that his language was meaningless."

Education is a powerful tool, but what my culture prized as knowledge needed for success and what the Inupiaq prized were very different. For high school, teens in the Arctic were sent to a boarding school in Sitka, in Southeast Alaska run by the Presbyterian church and although they received a high school education, they lost precious time for learning their own cultural skills, such as hunting for the boys and, for the girls, how to process what the men brought home. Cultures are intricately woven together and when one or two threads are cut, much more unravels. After high school, the teens had to decide whether to stay in a village and settle into a changing way of life at home or go to Fairbanks or further south to attend a university. It was a difficult choice.

This was before the Alaska Native Land Claims Settlement Act and, although people were living a subsistence lifestyle, they also needed jobs to purchase snowmobiles, gas, oil and other necessities.

"After graduating from high school," Loren explained, "I went down south for more education, but I soon realized that what I was studying would not land me a job at home. I would have to live in a larger city to put my new knowledge to work." Loren did not want to give up his roots or subsistence lifestyle. He returned home and got a job driving a truck, one of the few jobs in town before corporations and government agencies became part of the new landscape. He knew he had more to offer than being a truck driver, but was thankful to have a paying job. Many men in town did not.

And then Loren gave me the answer to the question that had plagued me in Kotzebue about not showing up to work.

"Caribou," Loren informed me, "do not run just on weekends and holidays. One must hunt them when they present themselves. Knowing this, would you rather miss a day or two of work to go hunting, or would you rather go to work and risk going hungry later? I phrase it in a question, but for a Native man there is no question, just the need to provide for family, and the extended family, and those in the community no longer able to hunt."

Years later, I took anthropology and cross-cultural communication courses while working on a Liberal Arts degree. It echoed much of what I had learned from Loren. I wish I had been given some of those explanations as part of my orientation before being sent into the bush. I was basically a "mail order" nurse from Canada with little or no understanding of the culture I was being dropped into. It led to many communication misunderstandings.

For example, I often felt I was doing most of the talking when I was with people from town. As I later discovered, I probably was. In my anthropology classes, I learned that every culture has a different verbal response time. If you ask me a question, I often answer you before you have said the last word, but in other cultures the response time can be longer. Before the person starts to answer, the person asking the question is often talking again, usually rephrasing what they've just said, or expanding on it with an assumption that if you didn't answer immediately, you did not understand the question or what was said.

Communication by facial expressions, body gestures and movements is also cultural as I learned at work one day when I was assigned to a four bed pediatric ward. I was ready to start the day's work, but didn't know if the children had eaten breakfast yet. And so, as I entered the ward, I smiled and introduced myself.

"Good morning. My name is Sue and I'm going to be your nurse today. Have you had breakfast yet?" I asked. I was scrutinized with much curiosity, but when I asked about breakfast, I got no answer. They were all looking at me but not a word came out of any of their mouths. I thought I detected a quizzical look on their faces and wondered if they spoke English. I returned to the nurse's station and asked the charge nurse if my little fellows would have trouble understanding me. "No," I was told, they all understand and speak English." Back I went and repeated my question again in a much slower and somewhat louder tone of voice. Nothing. Just those quizzical looks. Was I that strange? What was it about me that made them so quiet? Maybe they were just shy? I certainly hoped they weren't afraid of me. Back out to the nurses station once more.

"They are not responding to me," I said with much angst. "Why won't they talk to me?" Seeing my distress, an LPN from town accompanied me back to the room.

"You had breakfast?" she asked. Again silence. She turned to me and said, "Yes they have," and turned to go back to the desk.

"Wait," I cried running after her. "What do you mean? I didn't hear any answer." By then we were back at the desk and the others, hearing my plight, began to laugh.

"She doesn't know our face talk," said the LPN. And they laughed louder. It turns out the children had been raising their eyebrows, which meant "yes." "No" was signified by a scrunching up of the nose.

After working more with children, I adopted similar expressions myself without apparently being aware of it. When I was home during one of my vacations, my mother and I were having a nice conversation until she blurted out:

"Will you please answer me!" I was taken aback as I thought I was answering her.

"What do you mean?" I asked. Her response, "When I ask you a question you don't answer, you just make a funny face." Sure enough, I was doing "face talk."

Another non-verbal form of communication that unfortunately can cause serious problems is use of eye contact. In American culture, eye contact is a sign of politeness, of being engaged with the other person. It also signals self-assurance. That does not apply, however, to Native culture. In fact, it is the opposite. In Native culture, in deference to others, the eyes remain averted, sometimes even downcast. This sends people of my culture mixed signals. We would interpret downcast eyes as someone being evasive or inattentive. In a job interview, the applicant, from a dominant culture, talks up his assets, commonly known as putting one's best foot forward. In Native culture, this is looked upon as bragging and is considered impolite. A Native applicant who presents to a personnel manager for an interview with downcast eyes and a reluctance to speak of their accomplishments, might find themselves at a disadvantage in seeking employment.

Long talks with Loren certainly broadened my horizons. It gave me another perspective to analyze things I didn't understand, made me realize that perhaps at those times, I needed to ask for explanations. Personal friendships allow us to be more open to differences and new experiences, which leads to better understanding. I wasn't experiencing the "town life" Loren was living as I was living in "down south" comfort, and understanding does not necessarily mean adapting. To this day, I am uncomfortable with silence but knowing how silence functions in another culture, I can power through it. It helps if a radio or TV is playing in the background, anything but silence.

Although my culture holds sharing as a value, the culture I was living in actually lived by sharing. That sharing added a new depth to my Christian values. Those values were tested once when a friend from town asked to borrow my snow machine to go hunting. He had not been hunting for a very long time and only once in the Kotzebue area. He also had a drinking problem. I wasn't comfortable with the request. What if my machine broke down? Could he do the needed repairs? Was he reliable?

Would he be sober? I had become good friends with his wife and daughter and decided to trust him and hope for the best. I was relieved when he returned my machine with only a minor repair needed. Unfortunately, his hunt was unsuccessful.

When we judge behavior that is different from ours or not perceived as correct from our cultural perspective, as did the boss when his employees didn't always show up for work, the next step is to declare it as either wrong or bad which can lead to negative generalizations and stereotyping. When the misunderstanding is on a personal level, often we feel slighted, threatened or hurt, and we may lash out in anger.

I experienced this when I left Barrow to return to Kotzebue. My stay in Barrow had always been temporary duty until a permanent nurse was hired to fill the position. I was sad when it came time to return to Kotzebue because I had made many new friends. Word of my departure spread quickly through the hospital. I was sure Loren had heard of my leaving from one of his sisters, but I did not hear from him. I thought maybe he would be at the airport to say goodbye; instead, someone said they thought he had gone hunting. If I was unhappy about leaving, I was devastated at not being able to say goodbye to someone to whom I had become close.

I did not realize how important saying goodbye was to me. Much of what we do or don't do and say, is learned at an early age, and we may not be aware, on a conscious level, why we do or say what we do. By the time I was changing planes in Fairbanks, my hurt had morphed into anger, and I began to make negative assumptions. Perhaps he just didn't care. Maybe he was relieved to see me go. Maybe he was just satisfying a curiosity by getting to know me. How embarrassing! How could I have been so naive? But deep inside I had a feeling my assumptions were wrong. This was something I didn't understand and couldn't explain. That was in November.

In February, back in Kotzebue, on one of my days off, I got a call from the hospital.

"Hey Sue, you got a visitor here," Rose said in a sing song voice. "It's a guy," she said, with emphasis on guy. "From town. Well, from some town. I've never seen him before." Rose had lived in Kotzebue for a long time, so my curiosity was piqued.

"What's his name?" I asked. There was a pause. "Loren," she said. I was stunned. The only Loren I knew was my friend from Barrow, and I had worked hard to bury the hurt I had felt when I left there. My spirits soared.

"Send him over to the quarters," I said. I'll meet him at the door."

"So who is this guy?" Rose said in a muffled voice. You sure you know him. He doesn't look like anyone from here."

"NOW, Rose! Send him over right now. No questions asked!"

And over he came. After we settled in with a cup of coffee, he handed me a large paper bag he had been carrying. It contained a beautiful caribou skin mask made by his mother. I realized then that my gut feelings had been right last November. We were friends. I still did not understand what had (or had not) happened but it didn't matter. What mattered was that we were still friends. I later learned there is no word for goodbye in Inupiaq. Instead, perhaps adapting to our way of parting, people would say, "See you." This is a hopeful sign that perhaps we will see each other again, not like goodbye which signals closure, finality or ending.

Clues that perhaps there is a miscommunication occurring is a sudden stop in the flow of conversation or a feeling of "what just happened," a quizzical look on the other person's face. In 1969, people were not aware of, or concerned about the reasons communications broke down between people of different cultural backgrounds, or as I called it, different worlds. Today cross-cultural communications is big business. Our world has shrunk and our awareness has grown with hope for greater understanding and tolerance for difference.

Chapter 27

Back to Kotzebue

In early November, after spending three and a half months in Barrow, I arrived back in Kotzebue. It was winter and time to break out my snow machine. I looked forward to more trips and hoped to venture further afield this winter. The fish racks were empty, dried fish stored away for the long winter. Boats bobbing in the water off Front Street had been replaced by small planes on the ice ready for polar bear hunters. Young adults, as in all arctic towns, had left to attend high school in Southeast Alaska.

Boarding schools caused many problems for the young people. Not only did it separate them from their families, it introduced them to the benefits of modern-day cities. For many it was their first encounter living with electric lights, flush toilets, washing machines and phones. Adjusting to a different diet and ways of doing things must have been difficult. When returning home after adjusting and enjoying all the modern conveniences, it was just as hard adjusting to life without them. It appeared adjusting to any change in status was difficult as I learned from friends in town. They were a family of five who had been living in a one room house. They received a new home from the housing authority. Their new home had three small bedrooms and a main room with a stove in the middle for heat. I was delighted for them but when I visited, the mother told me:

"The kids are afraid to sleep alone in separate rooms. They want to be close to mom and dad like they always have been. The heat from the stove in the main room doesn't always keep the bedrooms warm, so we are all sleeping together in the main room around the stove." Sometimes bigger does not mean better.

There was had been an ongoing turnover of personnel at the Air Force base while I was away, including a new major. With this major came a more positive and professional standard of behavior in the men than there had been under the previous commanding officer. We nurses greatly appreciated the change in attitude. Amazing what good leadership can achieve. And among the new arrivals was Jim, a lieutenant from Florida. Not long after I returned from Barrow, we started dating. Another nurse was dating the second in command at the base and another was engaged to an officer she had followed north so they could be close. So much for remote postings. So, because of who we were dating, we three nurses held some rank at the base. We also, because of who we were seeing, spent a lot of time in the officer's club. We enjoyed private movie showings in the comfort of their lounge, not inundated with drinks we did not want. I could even get a pop on request. Jim was also a singer and played bass guitar. He and a few others started a band that played in the non-commissioned officers' (NCO) club on weekends. Those dances were great fun. They were a good way to get to know a lot of fellows, and, because they knew I was with Jim, I was not monopolized and was able to move from one dance partner to another while my lieutenant provided the music. His band also put on concerts at the school which I think every young person in town attended.

The only problem with dating Jim was my fear of driving with him. You never knew what the road to the base would be like in winter. Ice forming on the lakes was new to Jim. To me that, and coming from Florida, were good signs he was not familiar with winter driving. And this was Arctic winter. The five miles from town to base could be an eternity as we were soon to find out. I always sighed with relief upon arriving at the base safely. Up we would go to the officer's lounge and always, after he had taken off his layer of outer wear and was getting ready to settle in with a drink, the major would ask him, with a straight face and twinkle in his eye:

"Jim, did you plug in the truck?" Jim would sputter and hang his head and say:

"No, whoever heard of plugging in a truck?" to which the rest of us would answer:

"We have." Poor fellow would pull on his coat and boots and head back down to plug in the truck. I most always made sure I had my survival gear with me in winter conditions, especially if I was driving with Jim. But one fateful night I was lazy and didn't bring it with me. That was the one night I should have had it very close at hand.

The nurse recruiter in Anchorage asked some of us to write a story about one of our experiences living in the bush and I decided to write

about my very unusual date with the lieutenant that winter night. This is
what I wrote.

```
Kotzebue, Alaska
November 26, 1970

Dear Diana:
        As I write this, the winds are howling around
our residence, lashing clouds of snow against the window,
winds gusting up to 60 knots, chill factor -50, almost a
total whiteout and the drifts are up to the rooftops of
many of the buildings. FAA says it won't let up till late
tomorrow night and we here in the residence had planned
a whopper of a party for tomorrow evening…ah well, that's
life in the Arctic!
        You had mentioned you would like to hear about
our life in the bush, so thought I'd write and tell you
how one could end up on a Saturday evening in Kotzebue.
I've been on some pretty different dates, but this one
takes the cake.
        As you know, the Air Force base just outside
of town is a social outlet for the nurses in the form of
movies, bowling, dancing and male companionship. Last
weekend, I was blessed with four days off and had plans
for a wonderful Saturday evening with one of the fellows
from the base whose crew was also off that weekend. We
had decided to "paint the town red" starting at the base
then hitting the local spots in town. Earlier that week
we had a storm which lasted from Monday till Wednesday…
ahza! (Eskimo exclamation). It was the worst blizzard I
had seen in my time here. But Friday and Saturday the
weather was good and thoughts of a night out were
foremost in my mind.
        Jim, a lieutenant, was to pick me up on the
7 p.m. rec run to the base and we would take a later
run back to town. It became windy and cold in the late
afternoon, nothing unusual for Kotzebue, and so,
```

oblivious to the elements, we started out. It wasn't until
we were well on our way that someone mentioned that a storm
was forecast to blow in later that night. I began to worry.
After two winters in the Arctic, I knew one should always
be prepared for bad weather, but tonight my clothes were
no match for arctic weather such as a skimpy pair of ankle
boots, nylons and bellbottom slacks. After all, wool pants
and heavy socks aren't very fashionable or attractive when
a gal is trying to impress a handsome Air Force lieutenant,
and definitely too hot for dancing. My date assured me that
at worst, it would mean I would have to take the earlier
rec run back to town and the storm wasn't due to hit till
midnight. Did I mention my lieutenant was from Florida?
The first time he had seen ice was a month ago! I took
solace in HIS words! As we were shedding our coats at
the base, an announcement boomed over the P.A. system:
"Due to an impending storm, this will be the last rec run
to town. All civilians should prepare to leave." Worry
turned to anxiety, but again Jim reassured me saying the
major would allow him to take me home after the movie in
one of the officer's trucks. Did I mention the lieutenant
was very handsome and that I liked him a lot? I stayed!

        The pizza was hot, the beer was cold and the movie
was great. It was after 10 p.m. when the drapes were pulled
back to peek outside for a check on the weather. THEN I
panicked! Outside the howling wind was all but blowing
down buildings and swirling snow had created whiteout
conditions. I knew a truck would be too dangerous to drive,
but after a conference with the major it was decided we
would make the five-mile trek into town in a tracmaster.
This "cat" is an all-terrain vehicle with huge elliptical
metal treads that would at least keep us upright on the
road, IF we could even see the road. I had previously
ridden a "cat" on the tail end of another storm and had
enough faith in their ability to agree to attempt the trip.
All my lieutenant could say was, "This is unbelievable!"
a phrase he would repeat many times that night. As we

lumbered along the five miles to town, my spirits lifted.
This was going to be a cinch. Of course, we were on flat
wind-swept tundra where the snow could follow the wind into
eternity. The driver, who was from Tennessee, couldn't see
the margins of the road, so the nice fellow from some other
southern state who was riding shotgun kept swinging the
large front-mounted search light continuously back and
forth to spot the sides of the road. At one point, we
lurched downward before the driver realized he was heading
off the road. At that point, I realized our safety depended
on our supply of gas. If we were to get stuck in a
snowbank, or lost, or start going around in circles,
we would eventually run out of gas. No gas meant no heat
which could lead to all of us freezing to death before
anyone missed us. We had lost all communication with the
base. An hour later, we made it to the FAA station on
the outskirts of town, and that's when our troubles
really began. Visibility was zero and the blowing snow
was drifting against any object in its whirling path,
like houses and vehicles. At one point we got the
sensation we were sinking. I looked out the window and
directly down into the window of one of the FAA houses.
We were heading up the side of the house and sinking into
the soft snow that had drifted up against it. A quick
reverse put us on level ground again. The hospital and my
residence were on the far side of town and a gallant effort
was made to get me there. The road, at least I think we
were on the road, had become large waves of endless packed
snowdrifts which we would climb, teeter on top, then lumber
down the other side only to encounter another drift. About
three blocks from the hospital (at least I think that's
where we were), we encountered an abandoned truck that
appeared to have stalled sideways in the middle of the
road. Since we couldn't go over it, and there was no
place to go around, it was decided to go back to the base.
My date suggested maybe we could get to the hospital by
walking. When the driver eyed our apparel, he brought us

back to reality by reminding us that, "this white stuff
weren't no Florida beach sand." And so we began our slow
and perilous journey back to the base arriving at 3:30
a.m. We had been driving blind for four hours. It certainly
wasn't the glorious night we had planned, but that's life
in the Arctic!

The next day the storm subsided and by that afternoon the snowplows had the road cleared enough for a truck
to get me back to the hospital. I learned my lesson.
Future dates found me toting my survival gear any time I
ventured out. And my lieutenant? Needless to say, he gained
a healthy respect for Arctic climate and stocked up on his
own supply of long johns and woolens for the remainder of
his tour of duty.

Sue Robinson

It certainly was a date to remember. At one point the driver thought
it might be better to go back to the base on the ice off Front Street. The
shoreline followed all the way to the base. I frantically put a stop to that.
During a storm, I had been told, the swells under the ice keep going until
they hit a barrier, which in our case, would be Front Street in town. I was
warned never to ride my snow machine on the ice during or shortly after a
storm as the ice became weakened by wave action. A number of machines
had fallen through the ice due to overflow, so I knew to be very careful. If
a snow machine was in danger, a large tracmaster would be an accident
waiting to happen. Thankfully, the southern boys listened to me, and we
made it back to the safety of the base on the road.

I was happy to be back home in Kotzebue but promised myself from
then on that I would be careful what situations I put myself in for the rest
of my stay. Fortunately, I did not have to refuse any adventures with my
friends in town, and a Native family I had become very close to, continued
to provided me with opportunities I couldn't resist.

Chapter 28

Fishing and Hunting

Ice fishing was an important winter activity for feeding both humans and dogs. Even though the huskies were not working dogs, they still had big appetites and their owners jigged for sheefish to feed them. The place of choice to fish was on the ice just off Front Street. On my trips to town, I would see women huddled over holes in the ice, pulling fish, stacking them in bundles beside them as the fish quickly froze. Sheefish is a silvery whitefish that closely compares to walleye in taste. Coming from the prairies, I had never fished in open water, let alone through ice. The more I watched the women hovering over the holes, the more I wanted to try ice fishing for myself.

I had become close with the Kentons, especially to Leila the mother. There were two children, an older boy who was away at school during the winter months, and a nine-year-old daughter affectionately known as Bunny. Leila's husband gave me good advice about my snow machine and did minor fixes and adjustments for me now and then. Their house was on Front Street, and I often stopped in for tea when going to and from town. I referred to Leila as my Eskimo mama. She kept me informed of all the goings on in town even though I didn't know half the people she mentioned. Leila had a positive, cheerful personality, and I always felt better after having a cup of tea with her. So it was Leila I went to when the fishing desire hit me because I knew she fished. She agreed to take me with her the next time.

"You never fish ever? she said in amazement. "What they teach you in those big cities? Everyone knows how to fish."

"Well, I don't Leila, so I would like you to teach me."

"Even Bunny can fish," she said looking at me with disbelief.

"Think you're up to it, city girl?" she asked laughing. "Think you're strong enough to pull up the fish when they bite?" she asked, grinning at me.

"How big are these fish?" I asked.

"OK, I'm teasing you now," she said, "but be sure you dress warm. It gets real cold just sitting so long."

"I will," I promised.

"And bring coffee to keep warm."

"OK. What else do I need? What kind of fishing pole? Do I need bait?"

"Just come with warm clothes and hot coffee. I'll bring everything else. You could bring some good luck with you. Not sure if a White girl is good or bad luck," she said, looking me up and down. Then she broke into laughter. "I jokes," she said. We arranged to go on my next day off.

I dressed in my fur parka and warmest wool gloves (my wolf head mittens didn't have fingers in them) and my newly acquired sealskin mukluks from Barrow. I was excited and felt I was off to a new adventure that would teach me a new skill. It was a clear day, at least when we started, and we drove our snow machines out onto the ice a little further from the shoreline than I had seen others fishing. I wondered if people had their own spots as Leila proceeded to remove slush and ice chunks from a small round hole in the ice.

"Walter," she said. Walter was her husband. "He spend hours chopping ice making this hole. Ice is thick here but a good spot to catch fish," she explained. "Some years he gets lucky and borrows someone's auger, you know, electric drill. Makes a hole fast that way. I come often to fish and have to chip through new ice forming to keep the hole open." She then strung me a line with a weighted hook on the end onto a piece of antler and we settled in to do some serious fishing.

We were fishing for a whitefish called sheefish. Jigging involved a piece of wood (usually coveted driftwood offered up from the sea) or a piece of antler with a hole drilled into the end. The fishing line is threaded through it and attached to a weighted hook. The hook is dropped into the hole in the ice to the bottom then gently raised some and "jigged" a few times by rapidly moving the wrist up and down. The line is then allowed to rest. This process is repeated now and then, and if one detects movement, the line is jerked upward to embed the hook into the fish before drawing it to the surface.

We used the seats of our snow machines to sit on and made sure our thermoses of coffee were close by. We sat for a long time with nothing happening. Since I wasn't familiar with any kind of fishing, I asked if this was normal.

"Be patient," she said. "Sometimes it takes a while to get fish to come. Keep jigging!"

And so, I did. And then she caught one, and I caught one. I became very excited clapping my cold hands and again asking questions.

"Do you think we've hit a school of them? Will they keep coming? How many do the dogs eat each meal? How much longer will it take to get enough?" Leila had let me know we were jigging for her neighbor's dogs. She and Walter did not have dogs, and she had plenty of fish for her family.

"No more questions young one," she hissed. "Be patient and you will see. Now keep jigging. We have many more to catch." And so it was back to sitting, jigging and waiting. By this time, I was getting cold. Especially my fingers. Wool mittens were not as warm as my wolf head gloves, and I was beginning to wish I had brought them to use during all this sitting. My legs were next to feel the cold. From below my three-quarter length fur parka to the tops of my long-legged mukluks I was definitely starting to get numb. And still we sat. And then it started to snow. Again, we were successful in pulling in a number of fish, after which there would be another long period of nothing. I could envision a group of fish happily traveling together under the ice looking up and seeing our shadows and doing a sharp turn to avoid us. Smart fish! There was no talking to help pass the time. Every attempt at conversation was met with a "shush." I assumed that was so as to not scare the fish, but it was becoming boring as well as freezing cold. And the snow kept falling. I began to feel like the dogs chained in the yards and that soon we too would be buried in the snow. Still, not wanting to give up, I sat.

The final straw came when Mother Nature began to call. Finally, I told Leila my predicament and said I had to get back to the residence. She laughed and said I wasn't wearing the right coat. I wondered what she meant but would discover the meaning of that pronouncement later. At the moment, my need for modern plumbing outweighed my need for new experiences. She felt we should have stayed longer to get more fish, but I felt we had waited long enough for the ones we had and the dogs would never know how much cold dead time had gone into their dinner that night. I'm sad to say that the thrill of jigging had faded, and I never went out again. I've seen many whimsical pictures since my time up north depicting ways of Native women berry picking, carrying their babies on their backs or smiling as they congregate by the post office waiting for the mail plane, but when I see a picture or photo of women jigging for fish I automatically shiver. I can still feel that deep penetrating cold as we sat waiting for the fish to bite.

In early spring, I was invited to accompany Leila, Walter and their daughter Bunny on a hunting trip to Leila's home village of Noatak. Snow machine trips were always great adventures, but this one promised so much more. Walter was going hunting for caribou and said I would be welcome to come along with them if I did everything asked of me, which I soon discovered meant mostly what I should not do. I would agree to anything to be a part of a caribou hunt. Noatak was a small village thirty some miles up the Noatak River east of Kotzebue. We would have two snow machines and two sleds. One of the sleds would be hooked to my snow machine to transport some of the catch back to Kotzebue. I began asking questions.

"How far from the village would we be going to hunt? How many caribou would we maybe encounter? How many did they want to shoot? What were our chances of getting them?" Walter was reluctant to talk much about the hunt.

"You ask too many questions," he told me. "Be patient." Asking questions, I later learned in my anthropology classes, forced a hunter to predict an outcome which, it was believed, could diminish his luck at the hunt. The animals are believed to give themselves to the hunters, which is not a concept familiar to European hunters who like to boast about their skills.

I carefully packed warm sweaters, socks and gloves. We would only be gone three days. I had to be back to work for an evening shift on the third day. We left in the late morning and had a leisurely trip to our destination arriving in the late afternoon. I was very excited to be making such a long-distance trip.

Our route was occasionally lined with wooden markers stuck into the snow to mark the trail that appeared to have been well travelled. It was easy to follow as there were no trees or falling snow to block our view. In my excitement and eagerness to get ahead, I kept increasing my speed until, in a spurt of his own speed, I was overtaken by Walter's snow machine and sled, forcing me to stop.

"Where you going in such a hurry?" he asked. "This is not a freeway."

"But the trail is easy to follow," I said. "And it's fun to go fast. It's thrilling."

"Yes," he said, "until you hit a bump or big dip which is hard to see. Then your machine and sled will go off in different directions, and something is bound to break. You don't want that to happen so far from town. You follow behind my sled. Then I know where you are."

Leila laughed and waved back at me as we started out again. I had been properly put in my place.

After a couple of hours, we stopped for tea and some lunch. I stretched my legs as Leila got water boiling on the camp stove and made Tundra Tea from plants she had collected from the land in the summer months. It was hot and strong and along with the sandwiches I had prepared. I began to feel refreshed. It was a lovely day, with clear skies and comfortable temperatures. There was also much laughing at me, the "hurry up girl," as we drank tea and ate lunch.

I had been told by some of the hospital staff that town people didn't like being on the trail at night and left early to avoid having to camp overnight. They said that in the old days they had been attacked by the "Inyukens," also called the "little people," who would shoot fire arrows down the smoke holes of their semi-subterranean dwellings in the villages or temporary snow huts when they were travelling. The term "Inyuken" sounded like Indian to me. Inyuken/Indian. Evidently, the Athabaskan Indians of the Interior had historically been enemies of the Inupiat people. I wonder if the folks who planned the ward populations at the TB hospitals knew there had been tensions between the two groups of Natives? I thought the men just wanted to be close to their own kind on the ward I worked on, as there had definitely been a noticeable separation in the placement of beds of the two groups. It was the nurses that traversed the artificial tribal barrier on the wards.

I was offered sunglasses to wear. It was a clear day, but I didn't think I needed sunglasses and started to waved them away. I was thankful that most of the time I had spent on my machine had not been in direct sunshine. But this was spring and the sun was much higher in the sky for longer periods. I accepted the glasses she offered me.

Not long after our tea break, my body reminded me that what goes in must come out. It was then I learned what Leila had meant when she had told me I had been wearing the wrong kind of coat when we were fishing. Now we were much further from town in the middle of the vast arctic wilderness with not a bush, tree or large rock in sight. That's when I discovered how very practical those long winter women's coats were. All they had to do was squat and they were covered. Instant privacy. My parka was above the knees and didn't cover anything, and it hadn't kept my legs warm from the bottom of the short coat to the tops of the fur mukluks when jigging for fish. After a good laugh, once again at my dumb tunic expense, Leila and Bunny took pity on me and gave me cover assuring me Walter would not turn around. Needless to say, I felt very exposed. And very chilled. Time to look for a more practical traveling coat.

When we arrived in Noatak, we unloaded our gear at Leila's family home which appeared to have no one currently living in it. This was where we stayed. Leila was eager to visit friends and invited me along with her. I sat through a few conversations in Inupiaq with hearty laughter and occasionally all eyes on me. Then came a particularly raucous outburst. I presumed they were laughing at my eagerness to go fast on the trail and my impractical short coat, but I wondered what else I may have done worth chuckling over. In each home we were offered food. I was quietly enjoying the camaraderie and tasty tidbits of whatever was offered until we reached the last home. The meat was chewy and oily and I was enjoying it. I asked what we were eating and was told it was called quaq, which sounded a little ominous to me. Then I asked how it was cooked.

"Oh, no," I was told with hearty laughter, "not cooked." I could not take another bite. It was dried seal meat dipped in seal oil. It was the term "not cooked" that ended my desire for any more.

"But you already ate some," Leila rationalized. "You said it was good."

Try as I might, my mind would not let me eat another bite. We returned to Leila's place for a cooked meal. English explorers in the Arctic a century earlier had starved to death when their ships became locked in the Arctic ice and they ran out of their supply of food. There was food all around them, food that sustained the Native people that lived in that climate. But it was not English food. They did not equate what had sustained the Native population for centuries as edible food, and died of starvation. I fit squarely into this category. Fortunately, I had my processed store-bought food available to eat.

When evening approached, Walter pulled down a lantern to light the wick. I had never seen a wick like this and reached for the wick to feel it. The look of shock on Walter's face should have warned me to stop, but I was moving too fast. When I touched the wick, it crumbled in my fingers. Another dumb tunic moment. I felt like I had stepped back in time in this small village in the Arctic, without any of the amenities that I had enjoyed all my life. There was a lantern for light, a honey bucket for the toilet and water from melted ice from the river in a large metal tank outside the small home. This was not a campsite. This was the home my Inupiaq mama was raised in, and it was only a year ago that a man had landed on the moon! The irony of the situation did not escape me.

The next morning, we were up early getting ready for the hunt. My stomach was doing flip flops and I could hardly keep still. Walter made a last-minute replacement of something on my snow machine and Leila made a lunch for us, including a peanut butter and jam sandwich for this tunic girl who could not eat "real food." I tried to make myself helpful hauling supplies out to Walter. Apparently more than he needed, as I was frequently told:

"No, not that, take it back" or "What is this? What you gonna do with that! Take it back." When I tried to help Leila, she finally sat me down with another cup of coffee saying:

"You got too much energy. Save it for later. Sit down and calm down." She was right. I was wound tighter than a drum and eager to be off after the caribou. Another man from the village was going with us. He would be traveling with Walter, and Leila would be with me on my machine. As we left, it felt like the whole village knew of our quest. People smiled and waved as we drove by. I followed in the rear as we roared out across the flat white tundra. We seemed to cover a lot of miles, though one direction looked the same to me as the next. The landscape offered nothing that might give me bearings as to where we were in relation to the village. Finally, as we topped a small hill, we saw caribou in the distance. A group of them that seemed to be feeding as they pawed the snow and slowly moved from place to place. We stopped, turned off our machines and watched them for a while. I was warned to be very quiet so as to not spook the herd. After sometime, rifles were readied as the men prepared for the chase. Walter nodded to Leila then turned to me giving me very stern instructions.

"You must stay with Leila at all times, do not come closer until signaled, and do not turn on your machine until then. And no hollering, OK?" I solemnly agreed. Leila stayed with me as the men fired up their machines and headed towards the animals at a very fast pace.

"They go fast," she said. "Want to get real close before the caribou hear the machines. The noise spooks them and they start running. If they run too far before the kill it makes the meat tough." The chase was on and it was thrilling to watch. The men got reasonably close before the caribou heads rose up and, in a flash, they began bolting away. But the men had come close enough to shoot and two large caribou fell before the others escaped.

Leila and I were signaled to come. That's when the work began. The animals were gutted and butchered where they had fallen. I sat wide eyed on my machine and watched. No amount of coaxing could get me to join in. It looked like a large massacre as the snow turned red in ever increasing patches. Everything, it seemed, was salvaged. I was told even the bones made delicious bone marrow soup. I appreciated my peanut butter and jam sandwich for lunch and decided that in the future I could go to a store and buy my meat clean and packaged. I would not have made a good Eskimo wife.

The caribou were loaded into the two sleds. My sled carried the legs and other unknown parts. I felt pretty proud to be returning to the village with successful hunters. Some of the meat was given to their friends in town, the rest covered for the night before our trip home. Spirits were high, and I was thrilled to have been a part of the hunt even though I had done none of the work. Fortunately, it did not affect my love of caribou steaks

Caribou Hunt

The Hunt

and roasts. Sometimes I wonder if that hunting trip was the basis of my always cooking beef well done. No red "juice" coming off my meat.

The next day we headed back to Kotzebue. It was the beginning of spring and the weather had warmed in the last two days. There had been much talk about the condition of the ice on the Noatak River in front of the village. We would have to cross the river on our return. And this time we both had loaded sleds. The longer people talked about it, the more nervous I became. Finally, we were packed up, and I was given instructions. Since I now knew the route and how to look for any trail markers, I was allowed to drive in front for short periods. Sometimes we would ride side by side but with some space between us.

But first, we needed to get across that wide river. It looked wider to me than it had when we first crossed it. I was aware of the warm weather and the possibility of a decrease in thickness of the ice. Walter said he and Leila would go first and make tracks for me to follow. He would then signal Bunny and me from the other side to follow in their path. I watched as he and the heavily laden sled slowly made it safely to the other side. He turned and waved for me to come, but I froze. I began to think that if the ice was thin, he had weakened it with his machine and load. It was me whose load would break through the ice. He and Leila were wildly waving their arms to get me moving as I sat envisioning the worst. I prayed that they knew better than me and would not put me in harm's way. Besides, they wouldn't want to lose half their catch and their daughter. I made the leap of faith against my fears, revved my engine and followed the tracks before me. Much to my relief, I made it safely across the river.

"What took you so long?" they asked, followed by hearty laughs. With that, we departed for our long trek home.

The trip was plagued with some snags. The snow was not as crisp as when we had come. The trail was not as visible as it had snowed the day before, making it harder to spot the markers. Because of the snow conditions and the heavy load I carried, the return took a little more effort. Nevertheless, I was the lead machine a few times and it was a thrill to break trail. Fortunately, I was not in the lead when we hit our first stream. I wondered why Walter had stopped as I pulled up beside him. Then I saw the melting ice, enough to have caused us a problem if we had crossed at that spot. Walter pointed out the difference in the color of the ice and said if I saw that again to not cross but to wait for him to find a safer spot. Sure enough, the place he found to cross was solid and the ice had a very different clear and solid look. From then on, I proceeded cautiously so I had enough time to stop. Unfortunately, snow machines don't go in reverse and both the sled and the machine had to be manually pulled back far enough for me to aim at the new spot Walter had found, cross, then wait for him to catch up. This did not happen often, and I was proud of myself when I was able to spot some unsafe places in the small rivers.

We stopped for tea and a snack, but I was anxious to keep moving as I had to be at work for an evening shift. We were just a few miles from Kotzebue when Walter's machine broke down. I was told to go on ahead and send a friend of the family out with the piece he needed to fix his machine. Walter unhooked my sled with the caribou parts from my snow machine. He told me his friend would bring it back with his machine. Off I went on Little Red down the home stretch, slowing down when I reached the outskirts of town.

I still had plenty of time to notify the friend, shower and be at work on time. As I approached a main road on the outskirts of town, I saw a large fuel truck coming down the road. I slammed on my brakes only to go into a slide on a patch of ice, straight into the path of the truck. The truck had three sets of double wheels and as I saw the first set flash past me, I was sure I was going to go under the truck between the next two sets of wheels. But the skis of my snow machine hit square in the middle of the second set of tires. The impact flipped me backwards off my machine. The machine followed suit, tipping over and landing on top of my legs. I wasn't hurt but didn't have enough strength to shift my machine off my legs. The truck came to a sliding stop, and I waited for the driver to come so he could lift my machine back onto its tracks and off my legs.

"Hello," I hollered when the truck stopped. No response, so I waited for him to come round the front of the truck where he could see my predicament. I waited, and waited some more.

"Are you there," I called. Still no answer. I was beginning to get angry. I was on a time line here and nothing was happening until I got this machine off my legs. Since I was pinned down, I had no option but to wait.

Finally, I heard the truck door slam and the driver appeared around the front of the truck. Impatiently, I hollered at him for some help.

"What took you so long?" I asked impatiently, as he rolled the snow machine off my legs. I looked up to see as pale a face as any Native face could get.

"I was preparing myself for a body under my tires," he said in a quavering voice. I just didn't have any strength in my legs to come out and see." I felt bad for the poor man. I told him I had slid on ice while breaking and lost control. I assured him I was fine and asked how his legs were doing.

"Better," he said. "I'm gonna have a cup of tea from my thermos before I go any further."

Unfortunately, I was in a hurry to get to work and needed to find Walter's friend. I did make it to work and Leila and Walter made it back home before dark. Hopefully, the poor truck driver fully recovered.

My foray into the heart of a Native culture, that has survived from living off the land hunting and fishing, was always interesting and informative. I have since fished in open water off a comfortable boat but, ice fishing is not something I would ever again pursue. Hunting on the wild arctic tundra was a very exciting adventure that gave me a true insight into the meaning of living off the land. I became again a city girl but will always cherish these Arctic experiences.

Chapter 29

To Drink or Not to Drink

When I had been in Barrow, the director of nurses and her husband started an Alcoholics Anonymous chapter. Peter, one of our young maintenance men was a member. He was trying very hard to become alcohol free. For a man in his twenties, interconnected by both friendship and blood to other indulging youth in such a small town, it was a hard goal to achieve. Peter was fortunate to have a job but felt he would do better in his quest for sobriety by moving to a smaller village. He was not the only person in town who became disillusioned with life in Barrow. In 1940 the residents of the small village of Nuiqsut moved to Barrow looking for a better life, but after three decades, there were many that wanted to return to a more traditional lifestyle. In the 1970s, Peter, and others originally from Nuiqsut, relocated from Barrow to their old village site. Another town, Atqasuk, had a similar history of being reestablished in 1980. In larger centers like Kotzebue and Barrow, Inupiat and European lifestyles were colliding, causing high levels of stress for Native people trying to adapt to new ways.

Occasionally, cultural clashes played out in small, isolated villages as well as the larger centers like Kotzebue and Barrow. Problems had a habit of occurring at night, and emergencies frequently happened during blizzards or other weather situations that grounded planes. I was to experience all these situations one sad and stormy winter night shift when I received a frantic call from a teacher in one of our smaller villages. The radio call began at about one in the morning with, "This is an emergency, this is an emergency. Is anyone there?" I was confused. This was not the health aid calling. It was a man, and he sounded very stressed.

"This is KIK 735 Kotzebue Hospital. This is the night nurse. What is the emergency?"

"I'm the teacher here, and my wife and I are barricaded in the school. We are locked in the radio room and are requesting a state trooper and plane to come and rescue us."

"Rescue from what?" I asked.

"My wife and I are new teachers here in the village. We have a janitor at the school who often shows up to work hung over from too much drinking the night before. It happened again today, and I fired him. This evening he showed up outside our door, drunk and shouting obscenities at us. That's when we came here and locked the school doors. My wife is pregnant, and now he is wandering around town carrying a rifle and muttering about how unfair we are. We feel threatened and want out of here now."

He sounded hysterical, and I tried to alleviate his fear. If he was in the school, he was safe. I also knew, from similar experiences, the townspeople would not let the aggrieved man do anything rash.

"I know you are scared," I said, "but you are safe in the school. The janitor is just venting his anger at being fired, but the people in town won't let him harm you."

"You don't know that; you're not here," he said with escalating panic.

"No," I said, "but I know how these things go, and I'm pretty sure the townsfolk won't let him hurt you." I was used to dealing with drunks in the emergency room and in town, and never did I feel threatened even when a drunk was sounding off to me. I felt that was partly because of my position in the community and that the same protection would be there for he and his wife in their position as teachers in the village.

"But he has a gun and is waving it around a lot during his rants. And none of the townspeople are even trying to stop him."

"Then that tells me they realize he isn't a threat. If you were in danger, they would do something. He'll soon wear out and fall asleep." But the teacher remained agitated. Feeling the husband might need to be medicated to calm him down, I called the doctor. I was relieved when he came and took over the call. The doctor spent a lot of time talking the man down and reassuring him that if they were barricaded in the school, they were safe. We called for a plane to pick them up and bring them to Kotzebue, but the pilot informed us the weather was not conducive to flying. He would fly out in the morning if the weather didn't worsen. The doctor reassured the teacher someone would come for them as soon as possible.

It was a long night, but the doctor kept talking with the teacher till morning. By then, the storm had abated, and the pilot said he was on his way to the village with the trooper. The doctor went home to bed.

Later, we heard the rest of the story from one of the Kotzebue teachers. It seems the janitor did indeed have a drinking problem, but he had had it for years and it had never really caused any one else any problems. He had also been the school janitor for many years and had weathered many teachers. The man had a large family and in that very small town he held the prize job. Previous teachers had recognized his long-term commitment, even if he was a little under the weather once in a while when he came to work. Over the years, there had been a good working relationship and much tolerance until this year. And the teacher was right about the rest of the town. They were definitely on the side of the janitor. The trooper freed the teachers from the school. They went straight to their home, packed their bags and flew back to Kotzebue with the trooper. Once in Kotzebue, they went to the school office, handed in their resignation and caught the next jet out of town, never to return. And the janitor? He had passed out and was home sound asleep. He was reinstated to his job the next week. Most everyone, except the poor teacher, realized that he would run out of steam, never make good on his threats, and that all would be over by morning. That is no excuse for his behavior, but unfortunately the teachers were in a much smaller town and a very different culture than they were used to. It would have been wiser to check with their bosses in Kotzebue before doing something as rash as firing a long-term employee.

On another occasion, alcohol was used for medicinal purposes. One of our pregnant LPNs from town went into early labor at eight months. Hoping to give her more time before she delivered, the doctor started her on an intravenous alcohol drip to slow down the contractions. This was not an unusual treatment for early labor at the time. When it became apparent this wasn't having the desired effect, it was arranged for her to be sent to Anchorage on a commercial flight. Her alcohol drip was discontinued for the trip south, but the doctor instructed the nurse escorting her to have the stewardess bring the patient alcoholic beverages of her choice throughout the flight. He even gave money to the flight attendant for the drinks. Well, our poor gal was beside herself. She was, of course, very worried about the baby but she also was not a drinker and wasn't too eager to be consuming so much alcohol. She made it to Anchorage in time to deliver a small but healthy baby, for which we were all thankful. We tried to convince ourselves, and her, that the drinks on the plane held off the delivery until she arrived in Anchorage. When she returned, she was quick to inform us she didn't like how those drinks made her feel, but on the other hand she said:

"The more I drank the less I cared. They had to use a wheelchair to get me off the plane, not just because I was pregnant, but because I couldn't have walked a straight line by the time we got to Anchorage." And she was not at all happy with the hangover headache she had the next day. I wonder how the baby felt?

In Kotzebue there was only one emergency surgery performed while I was there. That surgery was on a gentleman who seemed to want to end it all, but was too inebriated to make a good choice as to where and how to do it. In fact, we took his actions to be a serious call for help. The poor man had come into the hospital entryway in the middle of the night during a bad storm. In order to get assistance after hours, patients had to push a buzzer which rang at the nurses' station in the center of the building. He rang the bell, then promptly shot himself in the abdomen with a rifle. Two of our doctors operated on him to remove the shot and sew up the multiple little holes that damaged his bowel. When he woke up the next morning, he had not only a very painful abdomen, but a number of IVs and tubes stuck into him. He swore he didn't remember shooting himself. After the storm blew over, he was medivaced to Anchorage for recovery. Perhaps all the IVs and tubes we put in him would be a deterrent from drinking again. One could only hope.

Of the many incidents involving alcohol during my time up north, one was of my own doing, and I suppose I was lucky to not have been found out by my bosses. It could have caused me some trouble, maybe even cost me my job. One of the social workers that lived in town was telling a group of us at lunch one cold winter day about how he had made his own batch of home brew. He had been collecting bottles for some time and now had some very good beer stashed away at his house in town. The weather had been miserable, not good for visiting or snowmobiling. Making my own brew sounded like something fun to try, and the end result would be good to serve at a pizza party. Pizza and beer were very popular at the 20 unit. I must also say that the town had gone wet, and so it was not illegal to have alcohol in one's residence, but making it in government quarters would have been frowned upon. Being young and reckless, I decided to take the chance that no one would know that I was making home brew in my apartment. I can no longer remember the step-by-step process. I do remember the finished product had a layer of sludge at the bottom of the bottles. I warned my guests to avoid the sludge by pouring the clear brew into a glass leaving the sludge in the bottles. All went well the first time we tried it. My beer making was a success and everyone seemed to enjoy my brew with no ill effects. When it was gone, feeling smug with my success, I decided to make another batch.

When I was done, I put all the bottles in a crate on the floor hidden away under my clothes and uniforms in the open closet next to the bathroom. But this batch was not like the first. In the middle of the night, I was awakened by a loud bang, then another, and another. I leapt out of bed thinking I was hearing gunshots before I realized the sound was caps popping off the bottles of my new batch of home brew. Beer was shooting up from the bottles. I grabbed the box of bottles, dragged them into the bathroom while the lids kept popping and placed them in the bathtub. I collapsed on the floor for a minute waiting for the rest of the unit residents to come banging on my door, but no one stirred, and I began the process of mopping up. Spilled water is messy but spilled beer is smelly and sticky. I spent the next day scrubbing walls, floors and washing all my clothes. But some people never learn. I was determined to do it right again. I didn't want the last disaster to be the one I would remember.

Fortunately, the third time was a charm, and, though I stored the bottles in the bathtub for a couple of days with a cover over the top, there was no popping, and they were readily consumed at the next pizza party. That was the end of my brewing days.

CHAPTER 30

Nalukatuq (Whale Feast)

In June I chartered local pilot Don Ferguson and his new twin-engine plane to fly to Barrow to attend the whale feast (Nalukatuq) held after the spring whale hunt. There were six of us on the charter, myself and five others from town who were eager to visit relatives and take part in the festivities celebrating the hunting and successful landing of the large bowhead whale. We flew a direct route from Kotzebue northeast to Barrow, giving me a look at an area of the Arctic I had not previously seen. I took leave from work to allow time while there to visit old friends. Arriving back in Barrow felt like coming home, as I had good memories of Barrow and still knew most of the hospital staff, but there were a few new faces that had arrived in the seven months since I had been there. With such constant turnover, I wondered if the long-term staff from town handled an ever-changing shift of coworkers any better than our long-term staff in Kotzebue.

In Barrow the bowhead whale is hunted for both its meat, which provides the bulk of their dietary needs, and oil rendered from the blubber or fat. The whales are hunted twice a year, in the spring as they head north for summer months in the Arctic, and again in the fall as they migrate south to warmer climates to mate. There had been a successful whale hunt in Barrow that spring. Each captain has a crew of nine or ten men to man the boat, plus helpers to set up camp on the ice to watch patiently for whales to appear. Whaling was an expensive activity requiring boats, harpoons, lines, explosives and a crew. The bowhead whale is hunted in Barrow in wood frame skin boats called umiaks. When one is spotted, the crew paddles their umiak to within ten feet of the whale before firing a harpoon head fitted with a bomb into the whale that explodes within ten seconds of the strike. The dead whale is towed to the ice flow or shore, if that is where they launched from, and the butchering begins. When a whale is killed, a runner is sent into town bearing their crew flag. The flag is planted in the town center so everyone knows to which crew the whale offered itself. Townsfolk then go to the kill site to help land and butcher the whale. Landing the whale means hauling a 50- to 100-ton animal from water to ice or land for processing. Ropes are attached to the whale and using block and tackle and a long line of strong men, the whale is dragged ashore to begin the butchering. During this time everyone in town exudes excitement and pure joy. Whale meat, muktuk and whale oil will be available for another year. Then the hard work of butchering begins. First the skin and blubber (muktuk) and then the meat. There is a strict protocol about dividing all parts of the whale, with the captain and crew getting first and special cuts and parts. Then those who helped land and carve the whale get shares of meat and blubber.

Butchering the Whale

Muktuk Pieces

Eventually, everyone who joins in the festivities will receive a piece or two of their favorite food. Some of the whale even travels to relatives in the Lower-48 states. There is also some meat and pickings left on the bones for polar bears to snack on, another example of the Native way of sharing.

During the whale festival, everyone gathers around the flags of the successful crews. There is much laughter, visiting and celebrating. I was told to bring a large plastic garbage bag as everyone there would get some of the whale. And I did. I opened my bag when crew members and their relatives came around distributing some of the catch. Much to my delight, good size pieces of muktuk and whale meat were thrown inside my bag. I took these precious pieces home, giving most of it away to friends in Kotzebue, but I did keep some fat and meat for myself. The whale meat was very good. To my surprise it tasted like beef, not fish. Not Alberta beef good, but quite delicious fried in bacon grease. The muktuk I was happy to give to friends, but I cut off a good portion of the whale fat for myself to make agutaq which is called Eskimo ice cream. I developed a taste for it when made from seal oil, but wanted to try it made from whale oil. Here is the recipe:

> Put the fat in a bowl and allow the oil to seep out for a day
> or two, stirring it a number of times. Then mix together:
>> 1/2 cup seal or whale oil
>> 1 cup melted reindeer fat (or Crisco)
>> Dash of sugar and milk
> Beat this together until you think your arms will fall off, or it
> doubles in size and becomes light and creamy, add berries or
> meat and there you have it, Eskimo ice cream!

I preferred it made with seal oil and I also kept a small jar of seal oil in my freezer as a condiment. Instead of dipping meat in ketchup or smothering it in A.1. Sauce, I preferred to dip my caribou steaks into seal oil. Seal oil was milder tasting than whale oil.

For all the fat and oil consumed in the Native diet, our doctors in Kotzebue said there had been no recorded cases of MI's (heart attacks) or heart disease in the people of our service unit in the two years I had been there. Unfortunately, the high sugar diet introduced by Europeans had caused many problems. Type two diabetes was becoming prevalent and the dentist was kept very busy with tooth decay.

After the celebration, I spent time with my friends in town. Loren and I took many walks on the tundra where he pointed out much of the flora and fauna along with their many uses in the local diet. I especially enjoyed the bird's nests hidden on the ground, but was cautioned to keep back from them so the mother bird would not abandon the eggs.

On one outing with Loren, his friend and another nurse, the men brought along guns and were doing some target practice. Not a typical dating activity for me. I had never held a gun, let alone shoot one, so, of course my interest was piqued.

"Can I have a try," I asked with a smile.

"Have you ever shot this type of gun before?" asked Loren.

"No, none like that one," I said with a straight face.

So he handed me the gun, showed me how to use it, then stepped back as I took aim. Of course, I had neglected to mention I had never shot ANY gun. I have no idea what kind it was, but I gripped hard, took aim and fired. Well! The kick jerked my hand up and the noise deafened me. In an instant, Loren was standing next to me with his hand outstretched saying very quietly:

"Give me the gun," which I was only too happy to do. The color was drained from his face, and I didn't think he had been near a polar bear recently.

"What's wrong?" I asked.

"You came very close to shooting out one of the airport runway lights, and I'm pretty sure I can't afford to replace any of them." That is the only time I have shot a gun. I did not admit to my lie or error of omission about my inexperience with guns, and Loren did not ask any more questions. I think, by the stern look he gave me when he retrieved the gun, he understood exactly where I stood on gun knowledge.

As usual, when two townspeople were together, they conversed in their own language. After my disastrous "single shot," there was a lot of talking between the two men with much accompanying laughter. The other nurse and I felt their laughter was at my expense, but of course we couldn't understand them.

"That annoys me when they do that," she said. "Sue, do you speak any German?"

"Unfortunately not. Just the Queen's English," I told her.

"Well," she said, "Fake it. Let's see how they like it when they can't understand what is being said." And so, with a slow rising voice, she launched into a long dissertation in German, to which, every now and then, I said the only word I knew, "Ja" or, for emphasis, "Ja Ja." The conversation in Inupiaq abruptly ended, and the fellows looked at us in such a quizzical manner that I couldn't help laughing. She had made her point and the conversation continued in English for the rest of the evening. We gave up the "shooting" for an evening of cards in the residence, leaving the airport lights intact.

Again, leaving Barrow was sad. This time I got a "see you" from my friend and, although I still didn't understand the lack of a need to say good-bye, I knew our friendship was secure. On the trip back, one of the engines in the new plane cut out. One wing tipped and the plane start to drop. The pilot, who had turned to chat with one of the passengers, jerked around and whipped into action. His fingers glanced across the instrument panel and in a minute the quick flick of a switch righted the plane and the pilot visibly relaxed. I did not, and when he turned and looked at my face, he quickly explained that he had turned on the back up fuel tank to the wing and all was well.

"You're sure?" I asked. How much further is there to go? This is not the first time you have scared me to death in your planes. I still remember our Cape Lisburne trip. I think you enjoyed my reaction a little too much."

"Ah, that's where I remember you from. Yep, same look on your face this time too."

I gave him a sly smirk and said:

"If you happen to be admitted to the hospital in the near future, you better hope I won't be your nurse. I could give you a scare or two," I warned.

"No, no," he said, laughing. "Everything is fine now, and I didn't plan it to scare anyone. Just getting used to my new plane." My survival kit was with me, but the thought of having to use it was unnerving. Fortunately, I and my share of the whale, along with the other passengers made it back to Kotzebue unscathed. It gave me great pleasure to take pieces of muktuk to my closest friends. I couldn't understand why the other nurses weren't anxious to try the Eskimo ice cream I had made with the whale oil. But when I had the gals from town come to taste it, I received rave reviews. Perhaps my appreciation of Native food was improving. And since learning how much work went into it getting my share of the whale into my kitchen, I had a greater appreciation for it. Well, except for muktuk.

The trip to Barrow capped off a lot of traveling and visiting that year, but I also had visitors come to Kotzebue. And the wedding of the year for one of our nurses was to take place right here in town.

Chapter 31

Visitors

The annual summer influx of tourists into Kotzebue was the summer's best entertainment. Practically a full plane every day from both Alaska Airlines and Wien Air. I met interesting people from all over the world during those months. The tourists would always stop us on the street to ask questions.

"Do you live here?" they'd ask hesitantly.

"I do this year," I'd reply.

"You aren't Eskimo, are you?" they'd ask with sheepish grins on their faces.

"No," I'd say with my own grin. "What gave it away?"

"Well, do the Eskimo people here speak English?" they'd want to know.

"Most do." I'd explain, "and they speak Eskimo too, which is better than me. I can only speak one language."

They wanted to know, among other things, what it was like living in such an isolated place. Then: "Why are you here?" and "How long will you stay?"

The second most popular topic they asked about was the weather.

"What is the weather like in winter?" and "How cold does it get?" I felt they should ask the townspeople who had lived here all their lives, but I suppose it is more comfortable to approach those who look more like one's self. Perhaps they thought there would be a language barrier.

We would ask the tourists where they were from. We nurses had a little competition among ourselves. At the end of the summer, the nurse whose tourist had travelled the farthest won a prize of something sweet and home baked.

Visitors to the hospital complex were always a treat. We often had temporary duty doctors who filled in when our regular doctors were on vacation, or if there was a time gap between hiring a new one. That second summer we had a famous visitor. Caroline Kennedy, the daughter of

President John F. Kennedy, came to Kotzebue. She was part of a group of young people, perhaps a school trip. Everyone was excited that she was coming, but no one seemed to know the purpose of the visit. Being Canadian, I wasn't as enthralled as the other nurses and didn't pay much attention or listen to all the excited chatter. I was, however, having lunch at the hospital dining room with some of the other nurses, when she and a friend came in to eat.

"There she is! There she is!" they squealed.

"Oh my gosh, she looks just like the pictures."

"Are you sure that's really her?" I asked. "I mean, what is she doing here?"

"Oh my gosh, doubting Thomas. Of course, it's her. You may have kings and queens, but we have royalty too. Right now, it's the Kennedys. As we watched her every move during lunch, I thought that in the future I could always boast I had dined with a president's daughter, without ever mentioning we were not actually sitting together.

We were also visited by a medical student from UCLA who shadowed the doctors for a short while. Unfortunately, the big city boy wasn't very impressed with the surroundings.

"How could you spend two years of your life in this godforsaken place?" he asked me after being there just two weeks. You must go crazy in the winter. Are you stuck inside all the time?"

"Well," I replied, "I know you want to be a doctor, not a world explorer, but aren't you just a little curious about the place and the people?"

In his favor, he was very intent on learning all things medical and some of us helped him along. One day he was sitting in the nurses' station with a needle on the end of IV tubing in one hand and an orange in the other.

"What on earth are you doing?" I asked. "Well, this orange is for practicing starting IVs but I'm ready for the real thing," he replied.

"No one on the ward needs an IV start just now, but I'll keep you in mind," I told him.

"But I've been poking this darned orange for an hour, and I really want to try it for real. If you could just let me try it on you..."

"Are you serious? No, you can't go poking a needle into my veins."

"Awe, come on Sue, just once. Let me see your arm, bet you have nice veins. There was a first time for you on some patient. It's payback time now for an eager, sincere med student. Please!"

"Alright, just take a look. Make sure you can see the vein. I don't want you to go digging around in my arm to find one." And the next thing I knew I had a pretend IV in my arm. The needle was real, and it had slipped in neat as could be. I wasn't the only nurse he cornered, and soon we all had one or two little bruises where his attempt had not been successful. Then he began feeling for the buried veins, the ones not visible. Again, he practiced on us until he felt confident, or until some of us said, "enough!" and wore long sleeves until the bruises faded from his failed attempts.

One day, in the nursery, while preparing to do a circumcision on a newborn baby boy, the doctor was called away to the emergency room and asked the med student to do the procedure. This was not the student's first circumcision. He had done one or two with the doctor supervising, but still, he appeared to be nervous. I mentioned how simple the procedure was, that even I could do it. I couldn't of course, legally or otherwise, but he was not going to let this nurse upstage him. His back straightened and he began gloving for the procedure. Yes, he was going to make a good doctor, and all the nurses were going to know it. I believe the division of power between nurse and doctor began in that nursery for that future doctor that day.

The circumcision went fine. I asked him to explain what he was going to do before he did anything. That seemed to focus his thoughts and also let me know if he was doing the right thing before he did it. He very definitely knew what he was doing, and did a fabulous job. The other nurses and I also worked hard to impress on him how important nurses were in the medical chain of events and how beneficial it would be for him, as a doctor, to keep on our good side. We were aware this was a great opportunity to influence a new doctor, aligning him to the side of nurses, no matter where his future career took him. Nurses can use all the help they can get.

In July I received a note from Bob, the cheerful-at-six-a.m. engineer from Juneau I had met in the hotel lobby in Anchorage a few months earlier. He was going to be doing bridge inspections out of

Fairbanks for a week and wondered if I was serious about my invitation for him to come to Kotzebue for a visit. I wrote back assuring him I would be happy to be his Arctic tour guide.

His weekend visit to Kotzebue was delightful. I walked him over every square inch of town giving running commentary on the people, the lifestyle and the geography. While we were walking the beach, one of the hospital maintenance men offered to take us out in his boat to pick salmon from his nets. Bob said he'd love to help, and we climbed aboard the large open boat. It was another new experience for me. The two men quickly had the nets up and many salmon on board. I sat at the front of the boat, watching them pull the net from the depths of the water and pluck salmon from it onto the bottom of the boat. Back on shore, after Bob helped him untangle and fold the net ready for his next trip, we were given one of the salmon, which Bob cleaned and cooked for dinner that evening.

The town was wet at that time. After dinner, I took Bob to one of the bars in town. Things in those bars could get quite loud, and occasionally, a little wild. At one point, as Bob was standing against the back wall taking it all in, one of the men from town took a swing at him. Fortunately, the fellow was too drunk to connect and apologized profusely when he realized Bob was with me and wasn't an airman from the base looking to steal the attention of a girl from town.

When Bob left Kotzebue, he asked me to be sure and let him know anytime I would be going to Anchorage, as he would come meet me there. Unfortunately, I never did.

Kotzebue visitors gave us glimpses of what was going on in other parts of the country. For instance, I heard someone mention the music at Woodstock, but it wasn't until I returned south that I realized what a cultural event I had missed. I knew about hippies, but I did not understand their movement until much later and then through documentaries seen on television. These visitors gave us a little insight into things we were not experiencing in the Arctic.

But life here was not dull. We had our own special events. Weddings were at the top of the "special" list.

Chapter 32

Weddings

Romance thrived in the Arctic. The first summer, one of our nurses married a pilot who regularly came to town to work the tourist traffic. We threw a bridal shower for her at the residence, then bid them both farewell when they flew south for their wedding. During my second winter in Kotzebue, we all became involved in another wedding. One of our nurses was marrying the second in command at the base. The wedding would be at a church in town, the reception at the base. The planning involved most of the nurses and other females in the quarters. For us, the preparations were as fun as the wedding itself. Material for our outfits, which were made in the nurses' quarters, was ordered from down south well in advance, as were gifts, candles, special goblets, cake cutting knives and all the little incidentals that make a wedding elegant. Even though this wedding was taking place in winter in a remote village and the reception at a very remote radar site, it was special and personal for all involved at both the hospital and the base. Those of us in the wedding party made our own outfits: long red velvet skirts with black band borders that we wore with white blouses. The maid of honor wore a black skirt and a white blouse and the bride wore a beautiful traditional long white wedding dress, again ordered from down south. We kept busy with sewing parties making our special outfits. There were other sessions to plan food and beverage lists. The boys from the base arranged the logistics for transporting the wedding party and guests to and from the base for the reception, with many prayers for good weather.

Finally, the big day arrived. The outfits were ready, the cake had been baked at the base kitchen, and cooks there had been busy preparing dishes for the reception. The flowers arrived a few days before the wedding and were chilling in the fridges in the basement of the nurses' quarters. The hall at the base was decorated, tables set up and extra wine kept on hand. We were as ready as we could ever be.

The morning of the big day, we awoke to blizzard conditions. Snow was swirling everywhere and appeared to have been falling all night.

We tried not let it dampen our spirits. After quiet individual reflection, standing in front of our own room windows, wondering how the conditions we were seeing would affect the big day, we gathered in the bride's room to prepare for this very special occasion. We fussed and helped each other with our hairdos, applied our makeup with helpful suggestions from each other on the application, then helped the bride with her hair and makeup and into her dress. Finally, we were all ready. We had done it. It was time for the wedding to take place.

The bride was beautiful and radiated her happiness. Spirits were high despite the weather, but as we made our way to the church, the reality of the weather hit us. Driving in town was not a problem, and although the snow was swirling, visibility was good enough to see the road and where we were going. Snow was still falling, but the storm had subsided considerably. Still, the maid of honor became distraught.

"Oh my goodness," she cried, "this is not good. The roads might be bad from the base. What if they can't see, or the snow is too deep. They might not make it to the church."

"Of course, they'll make it," the bride said. "I have no doubts."

"But it was really stormy during the night," I said. "Did you hear the wind?" I was remembering my fateful trip from the base in their tracmaster not so long ago.

"They WILL make it!" she said again, in a tone meant for no one to doubt, and we all agreed.

There had been some frantic calls to the base but, due to the weather, the radio reception was poor, and we had no idea how things were going at the base or about road conditions. Just as we began to think maybe the wedding might not happen, the base's large tracmaster with the rest of the wedding party came lumbering through the swirling snow. Cheers and huge sighs of relief. The wedding was on. They had made it!

And a beautiful wedding it was. The major escorted the bride down the aisle. All the men were dressed in suits. It was the only time I saw folks formally dressed in my two years in the Arctic.

But would we be able to make it back to the base for the reception? The storm had subsided, but the condition of the road to the base was any-one's guess. At least the bride and groom would be together. The major was

Arriving in a Tracmaster

anxious to get back to the base because he was, after all, the commander and his second in command, the groom, obviously wasn't available, and so those of us in the wedding party piled into the large-base Tracmaster and started the long five-mile trek to the base. By then, the worst of the storm was over, and the road was clearly visible through the gently falling snow. Although we were a little late, the wedding party arrived at the base in high spirits and eager for the wonderful buffet that awaited us. There were lots of speeches and even more wine. Those radar-watching boys sure could put it away although we nurses weren't too far behind. We danced the night away to the wee hours of the morning when we headed back to town in those lumbering prehistoric-looking vehicles that were the reason all had gone as planned. The Tracmaster had saved the day.

These special events kept us all connected and gave us reasons to celebrate life, even if we were far from our homes and families. We continued to celebrate the special occasions of life, Christmas, birthdays and weddings with those around us. We became each other's support system.

The Happy Couple

CHAPTER 33

The Last Days

~

My contract with Public Health Service would end in January 1971. It was time to make a decision as to my next move. Nineteen seventy had been a busy year. Lots of travel, including experiences with large jets and small planes, boats and ferries and trains in Alaska, visiting new places in other areas of the state, and meeting people outside the great cloak of the Public Health Service.

Winter came hard and fast the fall of 1970 and was harsher and colder than the year before. There were definitely longer lasting storms and more of them. It was always exciting to check the mailbox after such severe weather, as we would sometimes receive a week or more mail all at once. I enjoyed the mounting anticipation of heading back from the mailroom at the hospital to my apartment, making a cup of hot coffee, and settling into a comfortable chair to read the latest news from home and friends. The Internet gives daily news and instantaneous communications but does not hold the intimacy I felt from a hand-written personal letter. I miss that exciting feeling of receiving letters through the mail.

There seemed to be a heavier snowfall that winter that piled up and over the buildings in town. Sometimes you could not see out patient room windows as snow totally covered them. I also had more snow sifting in through my living room window that winter. Perhaps it was that the winds were stronger. It was not uncommon to have gusts up to 60 to 70 miles per hour and wind chill temperatures of minus 60 to minus 80 degrees. It was entertaining to watch the weather out my residence windows, especially since I was warm and safe inside. I felt sorry for the nursing aides in town who had to come to work in those storms. Occasionally, they were forced to stay overnight when the storms worsened as it was not safe for them to go home in such inclement weather. This was the Arctic I had imagined, and I was certainly experiencing weather beyond the limits of any winters I had ever encountered back home.

I considered extending my time in the Arctic and requesting a transfer to Barrow, but I wanted to see someplace different and to experience some warm sun to thaw my bones before returning home to Canada. My American coworkers suggested sunny California. Others pushed for me to go to the East Coast. Both sounded like interesting places I might want to see.

Reluctantly, I decided that I had accomplished what I had set out to do by coming north, and the thoughts of sun and warm weather won out over extending my stay in the Arctic. I had spent two years immersing myself as much as possible in another culture and another way of life and seeing a very different landscape and human adaptation to it. Although I was leaving the Arctic and life in a small Eskimo village, these two years had changed my world view. I was now aware of other realities and different ways of interpreting and interacting with the world. Because of my many cross-cultural miscommunications, I now question and seek clarification for what I don't understand when communicating. From my experience seeing a lifestyle different from my own, I am careful not to judge difference in a negative way. I learned the fundamental basics of my profession could be applied in different ways in different environments. I came to respect the force of nature and to be patiently respectful and mindful of her power. But the best takeaway from my two years in Kotzebue was the people I met. The Inupiat people who invited me into their lives, treated me with kindness and tolerated my ignorance and never-ending questions. By observing their way of life, I learned that there are many different realities in the world. I now strive to understand cultural differences instead of judging them. Under our outward differences, we are all human beings with the same needs and desires. My two years in the Arctic brought me to the belief that there are ways to connect with others through our similarities while respecting our differences.

But now there were other places calling my name. I decided on California. It would keep me on the West Coast and somehow sounded more exciting. Perhaps because it housed Hollywood and movie stars. My nurse mates placed a large map of the state in front of me, sat me down, blind folded me, and told me to pick a place with my finger. With a little coaching, my finger landed on Santa Barbara on the southern coast of California. I felt I had picked a great place with sunshine and ocean beaches. I sent an application to Cottage Hospital hoping to be hired.

I kept busy both at work and off duty so as to not overthink my decision, or feel too sad about leaving. As my departure date approached, I spent time in town visiting friends to say my goodbyes. My coworkers held a farewell party for me at the quarters, but the best farewell was at the hospital cafeteria where, in keeping with the California theme, I was given a rabbit skin bikini. They told me they had a lady from town sew it, but before she could start, they had to show her a picture of a bikini from a Sears catalog. She was quite shocked at the brevity of the item, and frankly, so was I. I was definitely not a bikini kind of girl, and after two years in the Arctic, the thought of having so much skin exposed was unnerving. It would be enough to shed coats, long johns and heavy wool sweaters. It didn't take long in the California sunshine to change my mind and change to shorts and light summer tops, but I never did wear a bikini, let alone a rabbit skin one.

The Rabbit Skin Bikini

And so, I left the Arctic. I went home to Calgary for a few weeks waiting to hear from the hospital in Santa Barbara. In March I was hired and made the move to sun and surf in southern California. The director of nurses at Cottage Hospital told me there was a freeze on hiring but one of the hospital administrators told her to hire me when she showed him my application from Kotzebue. That administrator was Mr. Gaines, the one who met me in a tracmaster at the plane in Kotzebue the day I arrived. I knew he and his wife had gone to California when they left Kotzebue, but I didn't know it was to Santa Barbara. It's a small world. I bought my first car in California and quickly learned to drive on freeways. I drove to Los Angeles to visit the med student that had spent time with us in Kotzebue. I went through the next winter without snow and wasn't as excited about it as I had thought I would be. In fact, I missed it. I did, however, enjoy California. I spent days off driving to places with exciting attractions, many in the Los Angeles area including Disneyland and Long Beach to see Howard Hughes' Spruce Goose. I spent many hours relaxing and suntanning on the beach, tasting seafood, some for the first time, at excellent restaurants in Santa Barbara, and even dating an intern or two from work. In September, as I was driving to the beach, news came on the car radio about an Alaska Airlines crash just outside Juneau that killed all 111 people onboard. My knees went to jelly, and I had to pull over and park. I thought about Bob, the engineer I had met from Juneau. We had not spoken or written for over a year. I wondered if he was still traveling doing bridge inspections, and if he had been on that plane. Two weeks later my mother called to say she was sending on a letter to me.

"Who is it from mom?" I asked.

"Well, it doesn't say, but it has been rerouted from Kotzebue."

"Doesn't it say who it is from?"

"No, just says the Nordale Hotel."

Relief flooded over me as I was sure it was from Bob. We had talked about our experiences staying at the infamous Nordale Hotel. The letter was indeed from him, and I replied giving him my new location. The following month, while he was visiting family in Oregon, we met in San Francisco for a weekend and caught up on our lives. A week later, before going back to Juneau, he came to see me in Santa Barbara and our conversations took a serious turn.

In the spring of 1972, after spending a total of just nine days together over a two-year period, Bob and I met in Honolulu and were married. I returned to Alaska, this time to Juneau where Bob lived and worked. That cheerful-at-6-a.m. guy I met in a hotel lobby in Anchorage two years earlier, woke up cheerfully beside me for thirty-four wonderful years before his passing in 2006. But that's another story. Alaska became my forever home, and all because I had wanted to experience something different.

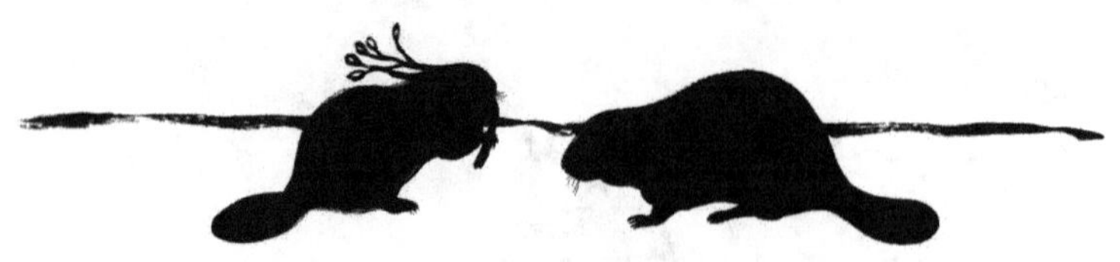

Author's Note

From the time of contact with the New Bedford whalers in the mid-1800s forward, Native peoples had experienced the painful process of acculturation, forced through contact with our industrialized European culture to live in two worlds with two very different basic ways of being. This included Western views and interactions with our surroundings, our use of time, the way we communicated, our language, our value systems, and even what we did and didn't eat. I wondered how well I would do if I had to live under the conditions townspeople in Kotzebue lived and if I would be able to adapt to such different ways of life and diet. I hadn't done too well with the diet I had tried. The Europeans that came before me may have had good intentions but caused disruption of a very old and very functional society, eroding Native self-worth in the wake of Western actions.

Alcohol is often the medicine of choice to diminish pain and stress and an excellent method of escape from the harsh realities of life. My time in the villages occurred prior to the Alaska Native Claims Settlement Act, after which the pace of change increased and traditional ways of relating to something as basic as the land lived and subsisted on would change as never before. With these changes, the Natives of Alaska would fight their biggest battle of the twentieth century.

The late 1960s early 1970s saw the beginning of a cultural revival in rural Alaska. It was preceded by a political battle which began much earlier. The struggle between development and conservation came to a head in the early 1960s when the Atomic Energy Commission (AEC) proposed a chain nuclear explosion the equivalent of five atomic bombs to be set off on the northwestern Alaska shoreline. It was called Project Chariot and its claimed purpose was to create a deep-water port at Cape Thompson, Alaska, an area between the villages of Kivalina and Point Hope north of Kotzebue. Native people relied on these places for marine mammals for the bulk of their food and hunted extensively over a wide area of land surrounding each village. The land animals they hunted fed on lichen and other vegetation which obtained nutrients from the air. The major areas of Inupiat subsistence would be greatly affected by radiation from such a blast.

Alaskans who had previously supported development in the state began to look closer at its possible negative effects. To continue subsistence practices after such a blast would expose Native people to unknown levels of radiation and health hazards. Subsistence hunting and gathering would have to be suspended for at least a year. For the first time in Alaska Native relationships, the different Alaska Native cultures began to band together in protest and to voice their concerns for the land on which their livelihood depended. Finally, in 1962, the project was abandoned. A positive result of the proposed project was to unite Native people from all parts of Alaska to come together as one voice. As a result of their public objections, the Association of American Indians sponsored a meeting in 1961 where representatives of both the Inupiat and Yup'ik Eskimos came together to discuss Native rights. In 1966, a group of four hundred Natives representing seventeen Native organizations from around the state came together for a three-day conference to discuss aboriginal land rights. This was the beginning of the Alaska Federation of Natives (AFN).

The mission of AFN was, and still is, to enhance and promote the cultural, economic and political voice of the entire Alaska Native community. In 1968, the discovery of oil on the North Slope gave rise to a sense of urgency to settle Native land claims. The AFN worked hard towards that end. In December 1971, just one year after I left the Arctic, the Alaska Native Claims Settlement Act (ANCSA), was passed. The AFN has continued to be the vehicle for Native rights regarding social, economic and tribal issues, helping to preserve Native cultures and fighting for programs and systems that will instill pride and confidence in Alaska Natives. The AFN continues to hold yearly meetings.

The Alaska Native Claims Settlement Act or ANCSA was, at the time (1971), the largest land claims settlement in United States' history. The purpose of the act was to settle Native claims to their traditional lands. It allowed clear rights to lands they had always used and paid them for surrendering potential claims to other lands. That monetary amount was 962.5 million dollars. The land settlement was 44 million acres for twelve Regional Native Corporations and later one more was created for Natives living outside Alaska. Within the regions, village corporations were formed for places with 25 or more residents. Village corporations held surface rights to their land but the Regional Corporations owned sub-surface rights to both Regional and Village lands. This land settlement cleared the way for oil companies on the North Slope to drill for oil and build the Trans-Alaska Pipeline to transfer oil to Valdez for shipment south. Native people did not understand the concept of owning land. Land had always been something all the people shared. The settlement put them into a corporate mode with huge cash flows and a type of management totally foreign to Native culture. I was in the American Arctic at a very specific time in history. Land claims forever changed the way business was done in rural Alaska. I am grateful that I was there to have had a glimpse of life before those changes occurred.

Photo Credits

~

All photos are from the author's collection except the following:

Page 4   *Aerial View of Kotzebue*, Alaska, Wien Collection, Frank H. Whaley photo, AMRC-b85-27-1403, Anchorage Museum at Rasmuson Center

Page 47   *Front Street Fish Racks and Boats*, Ruth A.M. Schmidt papers, 1912-2014, UAA-HMC-0792-b10-f7-sheet01-04, Archives and Special Collections, Consortium Library, University of Alaska Anchorage

Page 112   *Kotzebue National Forest*, Wien Collection, Frank H. Whaley photo, AMRC-b85-27-1401, Anchorage Museum at Rasmuson Center

Page 169   *Barrow from the Air*, Ruth A.M. Schmidt papers, 1912-2014, UAA-HMC-0792-b9-f15-sheet01-17, Archives and Special Collections, Consortium Library, University of Alaska Anchorage

Acknowledgments

~ 251 ~

I would like to thank those who helped me bring this book to completion: Carol Price who sent back all my letters to her from Kotzebue those many long years ago and has enthusiastically supported me over this long journey; John Kinnear who gave me my first taste of the joy of publishing and encouraged me with positive feedback after reading the very first rendition of this many times revised edition; and Lorry Juteau-Davis and Marie Olsen who also read and critiqued early editions. Special thanks to the writers of the Burn Thompson writer's group in Juneau who patiently read and critiqued each chapter more than once and encouraged me to submit the manuscript to a publisher, and finally to Mike Burwell and Sandy Klevin of Cirque Press and designer Dale Champlin who turned my memoir into a book.

About the Author

~

Sue Lium (nee Robinson) was born and raised in Calgary, Alberta, Canada. She moved to Alaska after graduating nursing school from the Misericordia Hospital in Edmonton, Alberta and worked for the U.S. Public Health Service in hospitals in Kotzebue and Barrow. After leaving the Arctic, she worked at Cottage Hospital in Santa Barbara, California before marrying and returning to Alaska. She retired after working thirty years at Bartlett Regional Hospital in Juneau, Alaska. Now widowed, she is the mother of two boys and grandmother to five grandchildren. She can be reached at suelium@hotmail.com.

About Cirque Press

~

Cirque Press grew out of *Cirque*, a literary journal that publishes the works of writers and artists from the North Pacific Rim, a region that reaches north from Oregon to the Yukon Territory, south through Alaska to Hawaii, and west to the Russian Far East.

Cirque Press is a partnership of Sandra Kleven, publisher, and Michael Burwell, editor. Ten years ago, we recognized that works of talented writers in the region were going unpublished, and the Press was launched to bring those works to fruition. We publish fiction, nonfiction, and poetry, and we seek to produce art that provides a deeper understanding about the region and its cultures. The writing of our authors is significant, personal, and strong.

Sandra Kleven — Michael Burwell, publishers and editors
www.cirquejournal.com

Books From Cirque Press

Apportioning the Light by Karen Tschannen (2018)

The Lure of Impermanence by Carey Taylor (2018)

Echolocation by Kristin Berger (2018)

Like Painted Kites & Collected Works by Clifton Bates (2019)

Athabaskan Fractal: Poems of the Far North by Karla Linn Merrifield (2019)

Holy Ghost Town by Tim Sherry (2019)

Drunk on Love: Twelve Stories to Savor Responsibly by Kerry Dean Feldman (2019)

Wide Open Eyes: Surfacing from Vietnam by Paul Kirk Haeder (2020)

Silty Water People by Vivian Faith Prescott (2020)

Life Revised by Leah Stenson (2020)

Oasis Earth: Planet in Peril by Rick Steiner (2020)

The Way to Gaamaak Cove by Doug Pope (2020)

Loggers Don't Make Love by Dave Rowan (2020)

The Dream That Is Childhood by Sandra Wassilie (2020)

Seward Soundboard by Sean Ulman (2020)

The Fox Boy by Gretchen Brinck (2021)

Lily Is Leaving: Poems by Leslie Ann Fried (2021)

One Headlight by Matt Caprioli (2021)

November Reconsidered by Marc Janssen (2021)

Callie Comes of Age by Dale Champlin (2021)

Someday I'll Miss This Place Too by Dan Branch (2021)

Out There In The Out There by Jerry McDonnell (2021)

Fish the Dead Water Hard by Eric Heyne (2021)

Salt & Roses by Buffy McKay (2022)

Growing Older In This Place: A Life in Alaska's Rainforest
    by Margo Wasserman Waring (2022)

Kettle Dance: A Big Sky Murder by Kerry Dean Feldman (2022)

Nothing Got Broke by Larry F. Slonaker (2022)

On the Beach: Poems 2016-2021 by Alan Weltzien (2022)

Sky Changes on the Kuskokwim by Clifton Bates (2022)

Transplanted by Birgit Lennertz Sarrimanolis (2022)

Between Promise and Sadness by Joanne Townsend (2022)

Yosemite Dawning by Shauna Potocky (2022)

The Woman Within by Tami Phelps and Kerry Dean Feldman (2023)

In the Winter of the Orange Snow by Diane S. Carpenter (2023)

Mail Order Nurse by Sue Lium (2023)

Infinite Meditations For Inspiration and Daily Practice
    by Scott Hanson (2023)

All in Due Time by Kate Troll (2023)

Getting Home from Here by Anne Ward-Masterson (2023)

Circles
Illustrated books from Cirque Press

Baby Abe: A Lullaby for Lincoln by Ann Chandonnet (2021)

Miss Tami, Is Today Tomorrow? by Tami Phelps (2021)

Miss Bebe Goes to America by Lynda Humphrey (2022)

More Praise for *Mail Order Nurse*

~ 258 ~

As a young man reading Sue's letters from Kotzebue to our family in Southern Alberta, I was transported into a world of intrigue and adventure. Her writing made me feel a part of the adventure. Her shared experiences were exhilarating. This book is a must read whether you have experienced being immersed into another way of life or are simply an armchair adventurer.

> —Greg Robinson MSW, RSW, RCSW,
> Registered clinical social worker (retired)

Fifty years ago, fresh from nursing school, Sue Lium started her career by joining the United States Public Health Service in Northern Alaska. Open to experience and ready for adventure, Sue spent two years absorbing a rapidly changing culture in communities beginning momentous transitions. Her engagement with colleagues and residents and the challenge of living in the Arctic mark this delightful memoir.

> —Margo Wasserman Waring, author of *Sheltering,*
> *A Covid Journal* and *Growing Older in This Place*